K

Between Anthropology and Literature

In this original volume, literature becomes both a creation and creator of culture with anthropology as the observer/reader/interpreter. The dual role of literature and the repositioning of anthropology allow for a multiplicity of possibilities in reading, writing about, and interpreting people, places and perspectives, real or imagined. Crossing the traditional boundaries of the canon, the authors consider fiction, poetry, and drama and cover an array of literary and anthropological concerns from the more palpable ethnographic studies to the liminal discussions of ritual. In an exciting new approach, they bring together in a common space those elements of both disciplines that remained disparate only because they remained separate.

The collection suggests that these two core disciplines are not static, bounded entities but instead fluid sites of shifting cultural currents and academic interests; that neither literature nor anthropology is a unified, self-contained discipline; that critical discussions in each field do not emanate from a single center but originate from a variety of sources and intersect at various, sometimes non-contiguous, points. Most importantly, the essays conclude that the origins, sources, and intersections of the two disciplines are constantly revised, reconceived, or replaced, breaching boundaries that lead not to chaos but rather to creativity and new possibilities of understanding and explicating texts, both literary and anthropological.

The authors of this volume all address the ways in which the language of social science fuses with that of the literary imagination and contributes to the ongoing debate on the merits of interdisciplinarity. The essays fit excellently with the current interest in cultural studies and challenge students, both undergraduate and graduate, to see texts not as isolated artifacts, but as parts of a larger global and cultural matrix.

Rose De Angelis is Associate Professor of English at Marist College and was editor of the book series *Anthropology and Literature* from 1996–2001.

Between Anthropology and Literature

Interdisciplinary discourse

Edited by Rose De Angelis

Routledge
Taylor & Francis Group

London and New York

First published 2002
by Routledge
11 New Fetter Lane, London EC4P 4EE

Simultaneously published in the USA and Canada
by Routledge
29 West 35th Street, New York, NY 10001

Transferred to Digital Printing 2003

Routledge is an imprint of the Taylor & Francis Group

© 2002 Taylor & Francis Books Ltd

Typeset in Bembo by
HWA Text and Data Management, Tunbridge Wells
Printed and bound in Great Britain by
Hobbs the Printers Ltd, Totton, Hants

British Library Cataloguing in Publication Data
A catalogue record for this book is available from the British Library

Library of Congress Cataloging in Publication Data
A catalog record for this book has been requested

ISBN 0-415-28714-6

In memory of Fortuna De Angelis (1931–1997)

Contents

Contributors

Susan P. Berardini is Assistant Professor of Spanish at Pace University. Her research currently focuses on contemporary Spanish theatre, Spanish cultural studies, metatheatre, and the function of ritual in theatre. She has recently published "El toreo como via de la identidad en *Invierno de luna alegre*" for Iberoamericana in Madrid, "Huellas mitológicas en el teatro de Paloma Pedrero" in *Gestos*, and "*La isla amarilla*: (Re)vision and Subversion of the Discovery" in a collection entitled *A Twice-Told Tale*.

Mario Cesareo is Associate Professor of Hispanic Studies at Vassar College. His published work includes theatre semiotics, Argentine novelistic production under militarized neoliberalism, Latin American cinema under globalization, Black Liberation Theology, and nineteenth-century slave narratives of the English Caribbean. His book, *Cruzados, mártires, y beatos: emplazamientos del cuerpo colonial*, on colonial cultural studies was published by Purdue University Press in 1995. He is currently co-editing a book on the poetics of social movements.

Rose De Angelis is Associate Professor of English at Marist College and was editor of the book series *Anthropology and Literature*. Her interests include Ethnic and American Literature and Gender Studies. Her work on the cultural construction of the Italian female in fiction has appeared in *Forum Italicum* and *Italian Americana*. A recent article on the sociocultural impact of names, "'What's in a name?': Conflicted Identities in Black and White," was published in *Shades of Black and White*.

Richard W. Grinnell is Assistant Professor of English at Marist College. His recent work on the relationship between drama and the witchcraft persecutions of the late Sixteenth and early Seventeenth centuries in England has been published in *Essays in Theatre, Studies in the Humanities*, and *The Upstart Crow*. He is currently finishing a book entitled *English Demonology and Renaissance Drama: The Politics of Fear*.

Jan Berkowitz Gross is Seth Richards Professor in Modern Languages at Grinnell College where she teaches courses in French language and literature, contemporary francophone cultures, and theatre. Recent work includes a study on the depiction of violence and trauma by French women playwrights and multiple entries in the *Feminist Encyclopedia of French Literature*. Her article on Algerian playwright Fatima Gallaire's theatre is part of a collection on contemporary Algerian writing, and her recent interview with Gallaire will appear in *Le Maghreb littéraire*. She is currently working on a book that examines the intercultural act of translating and staging French-language plays by authors of the Maghreb for Western audiences.

Janet Ruth Heller is Assistant Professor of English at Albion College. She is the founder of *Primavera*, an award-wining literary magazine based in Chicago. She has published literary criticism in *Poetics, Theatre Journal, Women's Studies, Language and Style, Twentieth Century Literature* and authored *Coleridge, Lamb, Hazlitt, and the Reader of Drama* (1990). Her most recent scholarship deals with the work of Native American writer Judith Minty.

Roseanne L. Hoefel is Associate Professor of English and Women's Studies at Alma College. She combines her interests in American Indian, African-American, and Interdisciplinary Studies in her teaching. Her articles have appeared in *Studies in American Indian Literature, Studies in Short Fiction, Feminisms*, and *Women's Studies Review* (In Memoriam 1962–2001).

Lisabeth Paravisini-Gebert is Professor of Hispanic and Africana Studies at Vassar College. She is author of *Caribbean Women Novelists: A Critical Bibliography* (1993), *Phyllis Shand Allfrey: A Caribbean Life* (1996), and *Jamaica Kincaid: A Critical Companion* (1999). Her edited volumes include *Green Cane and Juicy Flotsam* (1991), *Pleasure and the Word: Erotic Writings by Latin America Women* (1993), and *Sacred Possessions: Vodoun, Santería, Obeah, and the Caribbean* (1997). She is working currently on a study of geological exploration and cultural history at the turn-of-the-century Caribbean.

Ivette Romero-Cesareo is Associate Professor of Modern Languages at Marist College, where she has taught courses in Spanish, English, Foreign Cultures, and Women's Studies. Her research focuses on women's testimonial narrative and women travelers in the Caribbean and Latin America. She has published a variety of essays in *Cultural Conflicts in Contemporary Literature, Sacred Possessions: Santería, Vodoun, and Obeah in Caribbean Literature, Letras Femeninas, Journal of Caribbean Studies, Callaloo*, and *Anales del Caribe*. She recently co-edited *Women at Sea: Travel Writing and the Margins of the Caribbean Discourse* with Lisa Paravisini-Gebert.

Janet Tallman holds a Ph.D. in Anthropology from the University of California at Berkeley. She has taught at John F. Kennedy University, the University of Victoria, and Malaspina University. She has carried out ethnolinguistic fieldwork in the former Yugoslavia and continues researching language styles and language shifting in North America, along with non-traditional research in anthropology and anthropology and literature. She is currently living on an island off the coast of British Columbia studying British Columbia culture through literature. She is also writing a novel.

Acknowledgments

I would like to thank Anthony L. LaRuffa and Carol Hollander for their encouragement and guidance at the initial stages of the project and Julene Barnes and her assistant Polly Osborn for helping me bring it to fruition. I am grateful to Dean Reginetta Haboucha at Marist College for her efforts in getting me some release time to complete it; to the Dean's secretary and my dear friend Maria Belmonte who puts everything, including me, on the right track; to my student Benjamin Fischelman for his help in collating and cataloguing incoming material; to my colleague and friend Mark Morreale for being the wizard of tech. Special thanks to Ivette Romero, the sister I always wanted, for her unwavering loyalty and her endless cheer in the midst of chaos; to my husband Donald Anderson, who did the indexing, for his unflagging editorial commentary and for the love and support that brings me peace; to my son Andrea, my best friend, for making the sun shine even on the darkest of days.

Introduction

Meyer Fortes, in defining classic ethnography, wrote,

> Writing an anthropological monograph is itself an instrument of research, and perhaps the most significant instrument of research in the anthropologist's armoury. It involves breaking up the vivid, kaleidoscopic reality of human action, thought, and emotion which lives in the anthropologist's note-books and memory, and creating out of the pieces a coherent representation of a society.
>
> (qtd. in Jacobson, 1991, p. 3–4)

Fortes' definition could easily characterize many of the works of literature written by men and women who use society and culture as a backdrop for their writing. Bringing together two bodies of knowledge, one scientific and the other literary, they, too, enjoy "breaking up the ... reality of human action, thought, and emotion" with utmost accuracy to depict the characters in the society about which they are writing. The problem, however, as Nathan Tarn notes, is not in documenting the obvious links between the two disciplines but rather in "trying to house, and perhaps mate, 'recording' and 'creative angels' in the same physical body" (1991, p. x). Social scientists and anthropologists "borrow" from the analogies and imagery often used in literary analysis; literary people cull ideas from anthropologists (the fashionable ones like Geertz and Turner, both of whom have backgrounds in literature) and transmogrify models, methods, and terminology in the social sciences. That anthropological writing should be subjected to literary analysis and that the relationship works just as well in the other direction not only underscores the linkage between the two disciplines that culminates in interpretive essays uncovering and saying something new, but also recognizes an intimate relationship worth examining more closely. This penchant for "crossing over" by practitioners in both disciplines and the ongoing desire to redefine literature as a cultural "artifact" or social "discourse" continue to fuel the debate on the merits of interdisciplinarity. Therefore, it is not surprising that there be a lasting relationship between literature and anthropology and a proliferation of books and journals exploring the situating of literature within a social and cultural milieu.

Addressing the ways in which the language of social science fuses with that of the literary imagination, something that was clearly established early on with the works of Sir James Frazer and Ruth Benedict, *Between Anthropology and Literature: Interdisciplinary Discourse* takes its place among other works published in the last two decades as a result of the polemics surrounding cultural and interdisciplinary studies: John Leavitt's *Poetry and Prophecy: The Anthropology of Inspiration* (1997) links the relationship of prophecy, folk poetry, and literature with the cultural phenomenology of inspiration, while Nathan Tarn's *Views from the Weaving Mountain* (1991) deals with what is called ethnopoetics. *Anthropology and Literature* (1993), edited by Paul Benson and published as a special issue of the *Journal of the Steward Anthropological Society*, focuses on ethnographic writing, while *Literature and Anthropology* (1989), edited by Philip Dennis and Wendell Aycock, and *Literary Anthropology* (1988), edited by Fernando Poyatos, discourse on the inter-relationship between literary texts and anthropology. Cultural critic Kathleen A. Ashley analyzes Victor Turner's chief theoretical concepts and their application to literature in *Victor Turner and the Construction of Cultural Criticism: Between Literature and Anthropology* (1990).

Following a tradition that has been clearly well established, this present collection also fits in nicely with the current interest in cultural studies, especially if we accept the notion that cultural studies represents the "weakening of the traditional boundaries among the disciplines and of the growth of forms of interdisciplinary research that doesn't fit ... within the confines of existing divisions of knowledge" (Hall, 1992, p. 11). The essays challenge what some critics call "particularism," the exaltation of particular values, borders, and qualities that force and reinforce definition (Graff and Robbins, 1992, p. 435), and if we acknowledge Antonio Gramsci's concept of hegemony, the authority of a consensus to shape the meaning of reality, their challenge to the ways in which people become prisoners of their "particular values" allows present and future readers the possibility of breaking free from prevailing assumptions and forming a new consensus.

A commentary on this interdisciplinary moment in time when schools, big and small, are hiring faculty with cross-over appeal and establishing courses that speak to two or more disciplines, *Between Anthropology and Literature: Interdisciplinary Discourse* acknowledges the need for teachers to challenge their students to look at reading material within social, political, and historical contexts and to see texts not as isolated artifacts, but rather as parts of a larger global and cultural matrix. Documenting the eclecticism of scholarly research in the two fields, emphasizing the different modes of analysis, and underscoring the plurality of thought advanced by the interconnectedness of these disciplines, the essays included in this collection cross the traditional boundaries of the established canon, or, rather, they suggest flexible and refashionable boundaries. They bring together in a communal space those elements of both disciplines that had remained disparate only because they had remained separate. In so doing, the disciplines become no longer static, bounded entities but fluid sites of shifting cultural currents and academic interests. Literature becomes both a creation and creator of culture, with anthropology as observer/reader/interpreter. The dual role for literature and the repositioning of anthropology allows for a multiplicity of possibilities in reading, writing about, and interpreting people, places, and perspectives, real or imagined.

Underscoring the fact that anthropology and literature share similar intellectual concerns not so dissimilar and that they have something to offer to each other, the essays will appeal to undergraduate and graduate students alike who are interested in discourse analysis and taking courses in ethnic studies, cultural studies, and women's studies; they may attract the attention of literary scholars and anthropologists working in traditional and non-traditional areas as they address the intersection of literature and anthropological theory in courses such as Ethnography and Literature, Ethnographic Theory, and Ethnographic Methods. Collectively, the contributors in this collection cover a wide range of literary texts and anthropological perspectives, from the more palpable ethnographic studies to the liminal discussions of ritual in literary texts. The essays stress that neither literature nor anthropology is a unified, self-contained discipline; that critical discussions in each field do not emanate from a single center but originate from a variety of sources and intersect at various, sometimes non-contiguous, points. More importantly, the origins, sources, and intersections of the two disciplines are constantly revised, reconceived, or replaced, breaching boundaries that lead not to chaos, but rather to creativity and new possibilities of understanding and explicating texts, literary and anthropological.

Reading a text becomes more than identifying themes, ideas, and patterns; it becomes a way of relating the written word, whether scientific or humanistic, to the prevailing ideologies in which the work was produced. Whether it is an investigative analysis or a rhetorical dissection of a text, the process is literary because it allows the awakened imagination to reconsider and reconfigure the literary text, and it is scientific because the literary text establishes links between the work itself and values, institutions, and practices elsewhere in the culture. The text as cultural artifact becomes a symbol for analysis and a tool for exploration. The collection, therefore, emphasizes the resistance against inherited associations with any text, literary or anthropological, and encourages diverse perspectives and innovative paradigms by reconfiguring the relationship between what were once established borders: it obfuscates the rigid distinctions between what is inside and outside the text. For the most part, the essays themselves are dedicated to the traditional values of clear writing and reasoning in critical writing. In recent years, scholarly essays have become more and more esoteric and inaccessible, except to the specialist. In addressing the jargonization of the arts and sciences, I have chosen essays that are more accessible, that address a wider audience, and that cover an array of literary texts and anthropological concerns within a broader cultural spectrum. Hopefully, they will continue fueling the fires of scholarly debate on and about the relationship between anthropology and literature.

The collection begins with an essay that highlights the relationship between the ethnographer and the writer of fiction. Literary writers are ethnographers by virtue of the fact that they write stories about people and their sentiments, about places and happenings, and about contexts. Characteristically, the ethnographer participates, either overtly or covertly, in the daily lives of a group of people, watching, listening, and collecting data that will shed light on the observed subject or subjects. In literature, the writer/observer shares a piece of the other, and the overlapping pieces provide a window through which the reader may gain insights—social and cultural data—into particular cultures and societies. Reading the text as a cultural artifact becomes a way of participating in social research. The writer/ethnographer presents information to the reader/participant who acts as both subject and object as he or she reads the information presented and make his or her own observations. Historians, classicists, folklorists, mythologists, archaeologists, and ethnographers have all cited literary works for purposes of creating and interpreting the past or for identifying cultural patterns. Scholars such as Andrew Lang, Jane Harrison, Sabatino Moscati, Johannes Brøndsted, and Ruth Benedict, to name just a few, have searched literary sources for ethnographic data. In "The Ethnographic Novel: Finding the Insider's Voice," anthropologist Janet Tallman discusses and contrasts the viewpoints of the writer and the ethnographer. Defining and redefining the concepts of the ethnographic novel, she points to the obvious parallels between the seemingly conflicting scientific, objective observer who stands outside the text and the subjective man of letters who invariably leaves traces of himself within the text. Through an analysis of the novel *The Water House* by the Brazilian writer Antonio Olinto, Tallman demonstrates how a literary work can explore cultures, history, and sociolinguistic patterns and how fiction, like contemporary ethnography, places the literary at the service of the scientific and the scientific at the service of the literary.

The next two essays in the volume consider literary texts as vestiges of culture and social discourse. In "'Splendid Disciplines': American Indian Women's Ethnographic Literature," Roseanne Hoefel discusses *Waterlily*, a novel by Ella Cara Deloria, an ethnographer herself and Franz Boas' collaborator in the anthropological studies of her people, the Lakota Sioux. In her exploration of the novel and the oral history narratives of three Yukon native elders who worked with Julie Cruikshank, an anthropologist and ethnographer, Hoefel demonstrates the powerful nexus between literature and ethnography. She sees the connection between the two as a hybridized art form which enlarges the understanding and deepens the appreciation of the rich worlds these formidable American Indian women inhabited throughout the twentieth century. Calling into question our predisposition towards binary oppositions, Hoefel's essay emphasizes how tenuous the distinctions between ethnographer and writer, observer and interpreter are and how important that we accept the shifting boundaries. In my own essay, "A Woman's Work Is Never Done: Business and Family Politics in *Umbertina* and 'Rosa in Television Land,'" the fictional lives of two representative Italian-American women, Umbertina Longobardi and Rosa Della Rosa, unveil the cultural dynamics of Italian familial relations. In their sporadic episodes of rebellion, Umbertina and Rosa subvert the predominant domestic ideology of female subservience and negotiate with the Italian cultural dictates of familial duty, personal integrity, and social responsibility for autonomy and self-fulfillment. Viewing the texts as sources of ethnographic data and looking at the dynamics of Italian kinship and affinal ties, I trace the emergence of the two Italian immigrant women from the shadows of the private domestic sphere into the public sphere of business and document the possibilities for social reorganization in the New World.

Theories of ritual and related studies of liminality by Victor Turner, David Kertzer, Mary Douglas, and others succeed in providing an innovative look at the poetry and drama discussed in the next group of essays. The poetry of Native American writer Judith Minty serves as the medium for Janet Heller's exploration of the similarity between the process of writing and the generation of new rituals in her essay "Rituals to Cope with Change in Women's Lives: Judith Minty's *Dancing the Fault*." The concepts of ritual as defined by Kertzer, Gluckman, and Turner inform the dynamic process of ceremonial rituals in Minty's poetry. The transformative power of these rituals is evident in the way they increase human capability, impose order, and sometimes playfully deconstruct both power and order. Such rituals, as Minty's poetry suggests, resemble art in mingling orderliness and the volatility of creative play. Using anthropological approaches to ritual, Heller examines the social dynamics of inter/intra-personal behavior in Minty's poetry and explains the ways in which Native Americans reconcile the tension emanating from the interpenetration of the human and the natural world.

Drama and performance continues the discussion of ritual and its relationship to real-life social drama and its re-enactment on the stage. For all of these essays, the stage becomes the forum to examine, criticize, and explore the rigidity of oppressive traditions in hopes of reinscribing them within flexible margins of culture that may provide a venue for reconceiving and altering those traditions. In "The Subversion of Ritual in the Theatre of Paloma Pedrero," Susan Berardini discusses the ways in which collective celebrations of Carnival, St. John's Night, and other traditions in the plays of Pedrero become private rituals that facilitate the exploration and public manifestations of sexual and professional identity. Rituals constitute a means of communication for Pedrero's protagonists and are often vehicles of liberation. Pedrero's subversion of ritual, Berardini suggests, destabilizes the sense of community and identity enjoyed by her public and encourages a reinterpretation of the old models. Richard Grinnell's "'And Love Thee After': Necrophilia on the Jacobean Stage" discusses Mary Douglas' definition of social order which, she argues, flourishes only when cultural boundaries are held in check. Grinnell suggests that stage necrophilia became a tool used by dramatists to understand and cope with the cultural upheaval of the early seventeenth century, especially in the social arena. The margins of culture already in place were beginning to disintegrate, and necrophilia on stage provided an opportunity for playwrights to shock, to mark the transitional states of empowerment between men and women, and to point to the refashionable boundaries of a society in flux. Finally, Jan Gross' "Staging the Social Drama of Maghrebi Women in the Theatre of Fatima Gallaire" examines Victor Turner's definition of social change as it is manifested in the stage dramas of the Franco-Algerian writer. Struggling to reconcile personal integrity with communal responsibility, Gallaire's female protagonists explore and experiment with the power of the collective action within traditional societal structures. Gross notes that despite, or perhaps because of, their inferior status or liminality, the Muslim women of all ages and life experiences in Gallaire's plays exemplify theatre's unique power to project beyond normative sociocultural life into culture's more inventive and often therapeutic "subjunctive mood." In these essays, social and ceremonial rituals serve as vehicles for the reinterpretation of societal mores reflected in the dramatic performance occurring on a given occasion or in a particular place and draw attention to what lies "outside" the performance by looking "inside" the text.

The last three essays deal with women travelers and the ways in which texts can and do fall somewhere between anthropology, travelogue, and literature, suggesting that observer/recorder objectivity and ultimately category/classification is compromised by the fluctuating status of both the authors and the texts. Again the hybrid nature of these texts and their interpretation challenge the traditional binary structure of opposition and force a more complex cultural and political analysis. Lizabeth Paravisini-Gebert's essay "Oriental Imprisonments: Habaneras as Seen by Nineteenth-Century Women Travel Writers" analyzes various accounts of travel to the Caribbean region by women during a period that represented both the apogee of the British empire and of American apprenticeship in imperial ways that followed the Monroe Doctrine of 1823. English and American visitors to Cuba in the latter half of the nineteenth century and their subsequent observations are the basis of the essay which documents the ways in which the efforts to explain Havana, its customs, and more tellingly, its women often result in misunderstandings at once amusing and disturbing for what they reveal about the tensions between imperial centrality and colonial marginality. In "Travelers Possessed: Generic Hybrids and the Caribbean," Ivette Romero-Cesareo comments on the stylistic shifting of categories and the hybrid status of texts by novelist/folklorist Zora Neale Hurston, dancer/choreographer/anthropologist Katherine Dunham, and nurse/entrepreneur Mary Seacole. The essay documents these women's own recognition of a fluctuating status, especially concerning race and the perceptions of their own authority/authorship as researchers/observers. Romero-Cesareo contends that these women's own sense of objectivity alternates with the people they study and that the resulting conflicting viewpoints undermine a definitive classification of author and text. The collection culminates with Mario Cesareo's "Anthropology and Literature: Of Bedfellows and Illegitimate Offspring." More theoretical than any of the essays in the collection, Cesareo examines the essays within the context of post-modern practices of literary textualization as we move away from anthropological materiality. He comments on the problems of interdisciplinarity and proposes hybridity as the construction that dispels the tension of the interdisciplinary in academia. Perhaps, hybridity is what lies in the space "between" anthropology and literature. Cesareo positions and repositions the two disciplines, commenting specifically on writing as anthropology and anthropology as travel writing and politicizing the foray into the interdisciplinary. He concludes that "anthropology does not *encounter* literature … it is engendered by it."

References

Ashley, K. A. (1990). *Victor Turner and the Construction of Cultural Criticism: Between Anthropology and Literature*. Bloomington: Indiana University Press.

Benson, P. (Ed.). (1993). *Anthropology and Literature*. Urbane: University of Illinois Press.

Dennis, P. and Aycock, W. (Eds). (1989). *Literature and Anthropology*. Lubbock: Texas Tech University Press.

Graff, G. and Robbins, B. (1992). Cultural Criticism. In S. Grenblatt and G. Gunn (Eds), *Redrawing the Boundaries* (pp. 419–36). New York: Modern Language Association of America.

Hall, S. (1992). Race, Culture, and Communications: Looking Backward and Forward at Cultural Studies. *Rethinking Marxism*, 5 (1), 10–18.

Jacobson, D. (1991). *Reading Ethnography*. New York: State University of New York Press.

Leavitt, J. (1997). *Poetry and Prophecy: The Anthropology of Inspiration*. Ann Arbor: University of Michigan Press.

Poyatos, F. (Ed.). (1988). *Literary Anthropology*. Amsterdam: Benjamins.

Tarn, N. (1991). *Views from the Weaving Mountain: Selected Essays in Poetics and Anthropology*. Albuquerque, New Mexico: University of New Mexico.

Part I

Anthropology and literature as ethnography

Chapter 1

The ethnographic novel
Finding the insider's voice

Janet Tallman

Back in the mid-1960s I decided to follow my BA in literature with a PhD in anthropology. In my first graduate class a classmate asked our famous teacher, a woman who had done ground breaking work in African ethnography, what she saw as the difference between an ethnography and a novel. The teacher answered brusquely, with impatience and disdain: "If you don't know that, you don't belong here."

My classmate dropped out after the first quarter, became a leader in the anti-war movement, and co-founded the women's liberation movement on the West Coast. The teacher retired. I have gone on to spend more than thirty years pondering the differences between the ethnography and the novel. In my teaching and writing, I have used world literature, children's literature and mystery novels to explore cultures, and I have studied the aesthetics of ethnographies.

Through the years I have not been alone in thinking about the relationship of anthropology and literature. The re-examination of anthropological texts has brought up complex questions about science and art, projection and distortion, truth and fiction. Many voices in this conversation have addressed the purposes and shortcomings of the writers of ethnography, their class, gender and cultural biases, their status as outsiders, and their ways of structuring their texts (see Benson, 1993; Clifford and Marcus, 1986; Marcus and Fischer, 1986).

Some contributors to this dialogue have explored the use of the ethnographic novel for conveying anthropological information (Fernea, 1989). Others have suggested ways to bring fictional devices or the fictional material of a studied culture into the ethnographic text (see Dennis and Ayocks, 1989; Van Maanen, 1993). Still others have blurred the distinctions altogether. Dan Rose, for example, has envisioned "the dissolution of boundaries between literature, sociology, anthropology, critical theory, philosophy, cinematography, computer science and so on" (1993, p. 220) and called for "a polyphonic, heteroglossic, multigenre construction" (1993, p. 218) to replace the old ethnography.

The separation between the ethnographer and the novelist may be somewhat artificial. In many ways they are similar. Both tend to stand apart, consciously marginalized vis-à-vis the cultures they describe, self-alienated, disciplining themselves to make the familiar strange and the strange familiar. Both attempt to put into words the results of their observations and their ruminations on what they have observed.

Both draw on conventions and traditions of writers before them, ethnographers usually more explicitly than novelists.

Yet they are different as well. Ethnographers have given themselves the task of describing a culture in such a way that other observers might come to similar conclusions were they to explore the same culture; novelists strive for a fresh, unique, original description of life and of individuals. Ethnographers want to generalize and novelists particularize a time, place or people. For novelists, "a single, creative, and willful voice is shaping the work" (Van Maanen, 1993, p. 134) while the ethnographer must avoid personal voice and fiction or else "the status of ethnography as scientific or factual description, analogous to journalistic reporting, must come into question" (Marcus and Fischer, 1986, p. 76).

The relationship between the ethnographer and the novelist becomes blurred in the ethnographic novel. Elizabeth Fernea mentions two forms of these novels, "one written by an outsider about an *other*, and an ethnographic novel written by an artist from within the culture" (1989, p. 154). The best known example of a novel written from outside about an *other* is Elizabeth Bowen's African novel *Return to Laughter* (1954). An example of an ethnographic novel written by an artist from within will be explored later in this paper.

I would broaden Fernea's definition to add that an ethnographic novel, from either insider or outsider, is one that conveys significant information about the culture or cultures from which the novel originates. The artist writing from within a culture need not be and usually is not self-consciously anthropological, and yet this special sort of writer intuitively weaves into the story, character, theme, setting, and style details of the culture from which the book emerges.

Over the years I have discovered and taught many novels, which I call ethnographic or culturally rich, written by insiders. One is Leslie Marmon Silko's account of Laguna Pueblo culture in *Ceremony* (1986). Here she talks about the psychic wounding of a man caught between two cultures, white and Laguna, and his healing as he learns to balance them. Another is Ivo Andric's depiction of multicultural coexistence in Bosnia over several hundred years in *The Bridge on the Drina* (1945), a book with powerful resonances when read today. Mildred Taylor's semi-auto-biographical children's novel, *Roll of Thunder, Hear my Cry* (1976), tells of an African-American girl's coming of age in the racist America of the rural South in the thirties. Paco Ignacio Taibo III's *An Easy Thing* (1990), a detective novel, gives a dark and detailed portrait of the corrupt and alienating atmosphere of modern Mexico City. I have used these and similar culturally rich novels alongside ethnographies to contrast the novelist's and ethnographer's perspective.

In an insightful passage comparing the novelist with the ethnographer and the ethnographic novel with ethnography, Fernea writes,

> The ethnographic novel had some advantages over the standard ethnography. The novelist need not shun conflict, anger, hatred, or passion, and may often become a participant in the drama of the novel in a way denied the ethnographer, who has in the past been at pains to observe carefully and not to become too

involved. Such involvement, existentially or textually, has been seen to mar the scholarly value of the work and violate the code of objectivity by which the ethnographer/researcher has been expected to abide. It is the relative freedom of the novelist that makes this form so fresh a source of insight into the cultures of others. (1989, p. 154)

I would take Fernea's point a little further. The ethnographic novel written by someone from within the culture has a point of view unsullied by the culture-boundness and the blind-spots that accompany any outsider, no matter how well-trained. Of course, the insider still has a biased point of view, influenced by class, gender, age, and whatever other social categories are operative. Yet the insider novelist can have an authenticity, a knowledge of the culture, impossible for the anthropologist. As I have written elsewhere,

> Like anthropologists, writers are curious about the underpinnings of daily life, the taken-for-granted assumptions that order our social world. Writers can uncover cultural assumptions by looking within themselves as well as by watching others. They have access to cultural knowledge unavailable to the anthropologist, because they live fully in the culture that serves as the source of their writing. They share language, history, values, assumptions as members of the group. On the other hand anthropologists must construct the understanding of norms and values from external data, by observing ordinary behavior and by learning to act in the new culture appropriately.
>
> (Tallman, 1992, p. 5)

Stepping back from my comparison, I want to point out that students of culture can learn from both ethnographers and writers. In addition, ethnographers can expand their own knowledge by defining themselves against the novelist's perspective. They can use novels as field notes and uncover rich ethnographic data from a careful analysis of the vision presented by the creative insider, the novelist. Writers' descriptions of patterns of social behavior can complement and supplant field work, while writers can add voices that might not otherwise be heard, voices that might not emerge through the ordinary field work process, but still are needed for understanding of the culture under consideration.

An ethnographic novel

Given these points about the ethnographer and writer, ethnography and the ethnographic novel, I would now like to explore one such novel in depth. The novel serves as an entry point to certain cultures in two ways. First, it is based on and parallel to historical and cultural studies of the people in the book. Second, it serves as an imaginative field study itself for someone doing sociolinguistic analysis. In addition, it brings to the reader's awareness characters who, in their life stories, reveal possibilities open to people of those times and places. I will first introduce this novel, talking about those aspects which make it so culturally rich. Next I will trace the historical setting in which its characters lived and which they helped shape. Lastly, I will demonstrate how the novel in its complex detail can serve as the foundation for a sociolinguistic study of the languages and cultural patterns which flow through it.

The novel

The ethnographic novel I am exploring is *The Water House*, translated from Portuguese into English by Dorothy Heapy and first published in America in 1985. It came out originally in Brazil as *A Casa de Agua* in 1969. The author is Antonio Olinto, a Brazilian writer, literary critic, cultural analyst, poet, and historian, as well as a Brazilian diplomat in Lagos. Since 1955 he has published a number of novels, several collections of essays on European writers and on poetics, books of poetry, and historical and ethnographic essays on Brazilian ethnic issues. Two novels and one poetry book have been translated into English.

The Water House covers seventy years in the life of an African-Brazilian family. It opens in 1898 as the family, led by the matriarch Catarina, an emancipated Yoruba slave, begins the long journey back to her homeland near Lagos. It ends in 1968 with the liberation of an African nation near Nigeria (Olinto, translated 1985, 1969). Though fiction, the novel is based on historical fact. It revises and develops the story of several generations of the Da Rochas, a successful family known in both Lagos and Brazil, to which Olinto is related through his mother (Akere, 1987, p. 187; Boadi-Siaw, 1993, p. 429; Mba, 1987, pp. 356–7, 359, fn. p. 363; Olinto, translated 1985, 1969, dedication page).

The central character in *The Water House* is Mariana, granddaughter of Catarina, daughter of Catarina's daughter Epifania. The book recounts Mariana's story as she leaves her childhood behind in Brazil, comes of age in Lagos, marries, gives birth to and adopts children, establishes herself as a very successful business woman, and brings up her children to be professionals and national leaders. She influences several generations of nephews, nieces, in-laws, grandchildren, friends, and neighbors with her business success, religious dedication, wisdom, family loyalty, and progressive outlook (Olinto, translated 1985, 1969).

The Water House is a culturally rich ethnographic novel. Olinto's experience as a writer of ethnographic studies is reflected in the novel. He includes excellent detail about music, dance, food, social events, marriages, funerals, and other rites of passage. The book is especially rich with information about religious rituals and practices, in particular about the blending of African and Roman Catholic religions. A study which focused only on the religious expressions described in this novel would glean enough for a substantive ethnographic description in anthropology and religion.

Not only does Olinto describe the details of his cultures, he uses their forms to give creative shape to his novel. He writes in a style that imitates *oriki*, "a primitive, daily, conversational poetry deriving from the western African language, Yoruba"

(Olinto, translated 1985, 1969, book jacket). *Oriki* is also a form of prayer that Mariana practiced constantly.

The Water House is an ethnographic novel written by a complex insider, and it is rich in cultural meanings. Inasmuch as it is a portrait of Mariana, it is a life history as well. The life history is a form ethnographers recently have been exploring for reporting the results of their field work. In *Anthropology as Cultural Critique* Marcus and Fischer give the following definition:

> [L]ife histories become the means to explore the discourses of particular strata of a society and arenas of political competition between strata, and to ask questions about the processes of cultural hegemony, as well as about the didactic norms of character, maturation and morality which become mass-cultural models. Life history here is no longer simply a narrative frame for stringing together life-cycle rituals, socialization patterns, and a generational history as experienced by one individual; nor is it left to unique individuals. Indeed, life history deconstructs in the fullest sense: not making the subject disappear, but rather illuminating the social and constructive elements of an individual that make him or her potent in social context. Insofar as a life is the locus of experience, it is important to specify the cultural meanings that figure and compose it. (1986, p. 183)

The Water House fits this description. Mariana's evolution from childhood to old age is fully grounded in an historically rich and culturally explicit context. Mariana as subject does not disappear but carries for the reader the embodiment of her times. With her grandmother's memories and reflections, along with her own stream-of-consciousness, *oriki*-shaped, commentary on the unfolding of her life, she evokes a powerful experience of slavery, emancipation, multiculturalism, and post-colonial awakening in both Brazil and Lagos/Nigeria.

Historical background of *The Water House*

I consider it part of Olinto's skill as a writer that through his novel he inspired me to study more about Yoruba culture, about the slave trade between Lagos and Brazil, about the return of Brazilian former slaves to Lagos, and about the role of Lagos in the struggle for independence in West Africa. The more I studied, the more I realized how accurately Olinto had reconstructed his cultures. His characters were grounded in their times and places, culturally believable, historically correct.

In uncovering the background of the novel, I investigated nineteenth-century plantation economy in Brazil and the changes in the slave trade from mid-century to emancipation in 1888 (Burns, 1980). In *The Water House* this period included the events of Catarina's enslavement in Lagos, her arrival in Brazil, and her return to Africa. I also explored historical events of the twentieth century, especially the independence struggle and post-colonialism in Africa. This was the time when Mariana lived and flourished.

By the nineteenth century trade routes between Bahia and Lagos were well established. Slaves passed from Africa to the New World, and many products went back and forth between Lagos and Bahia. A common event of slave times was the middle passage, an experience central to the life of every enslaved African who survived the journey between the ports of the slave trade from Africa to the Americas.

In *The Water House*, Catarina's memories only briefly dwelt on her journey to Brazil. What Catarina did remember was her uncle's betrayal and greed in Lagos, the great slave port. He tricked her into coming from her home village to Lagos for a visit, and then he sold her to traders.

In Catarina's uncle's world, traders made profits by figuring the death rates of their human cargo and their own financial returns on their investments (Conrad, 1986, pp. 36–8). Both Africans and Europeans made money from human bondage. When a slave bought for $4.00 in Africa could fetch $130.00 in Bahia (Lamb, 1987, p. 300), many were tempted to make their fortune this way. Catarina's uncle, though morally corrupted by greed, was not unusually evil when measured by the ethos that prevailed at the height of the slave trade.

The materials that passed on these trade routes were the same as those that formed the foundation of first Catarina's and then Mariana's success in the market. To Lagos went *aguardente de cana* (sugar cane rum), provisions and tobacco, and from Lagos came palm oil, cola nuts and cloth (Cunha, 1985, pp. 117–19).

Many of the slaves coming to Brazil stayed in and near the state of Bahia, where plantation economies based on sugar and coffee had need for much slave labor (Burns, 1980, p. 30, p. 40). Since the passage from Lagos to Bahia was relatively short, many Yoruba sold or kidnapped into slavery from the Lagos area found friends and neighbors in Bahia, where they were able to maintain their language, their culture, and their religion. This cultural continuity over several generations made easier their return to Lagos after manumission and emancipation.

After emancipation, as they worked to fulfill Catarina's dream to return to the land from which she was sold, Catarina and her family found in Bahia the friends and community to support them. Their Yoruba compatriots taught them how to become traders, where to find ships for Lagos, and how to travel. These were the people who facilitated their return to Africa, and many came with them or had gone before them to form their community in Lagos.

Catarina's return to her native land with her daughter and grandchildren was a much happier passage than her trip to Brazil. She returned with many other Brazilian Yoruba to Lagos, a dynamic and bustling political and economic center made strong by the slave trade (Aderibigbe, 1985, p. 46; Elegbede-Fernandez, 1952, p. 9). Upon her return, she found herself in the middle of a hierarchical social structure founded on ethnicity and power.

At the top, and least numerous, were the British colonial overseers, who had achieved dominion in Lagos in 1861. Next to them were the Saros, Yoruba who had returned from slavery and civil service in Sierra Leone and often served as clerks in the British administration (Elegbede-Fernandez, 1952, pp. 7–9; Mba, 1987, pp. 355–56). The returning Brazilian former slaves were third in the hierarchy and more numerous that the Saros. This group included many people of the Bahia community. Lagos had a strong Brazilian Yoruba community that, like the Saros, had a powerful impact on the development of the city (Akere, 1987, p. 181). Last and most numerous were the indigenous people of Lagos, denigrated by the other three groups (Aderibigbe, 1985, p. 46; Akere, 1987, p. 181).

The returning Brazilians brought much in the way of agricultural expertise (Boadi-Siaw, 1993, pp. 432–3), and they satisfied the city's needs for artisans and carpenters as well as small businesses (Aderibigbe, 1985, p. 53; Mbe, 1987, p. 356). Returning Saros and Brazilians brought back a type of architecture, the *sobrado*, a two story timber house that was to change the face of Lagos and to spread throughout the area as a symbol of power among chiefs (Akere, 1987, p. 186; Hull, 1979, pp. 68–9). In *The Water House*, Mariana built for herself, her family, and dependents several of these houses in Lagos and in the surrounding area, thus expressing her own economic power, matching that of the chiefs.

Brazilian returnees often prospered as small capitalists and independent business people (Lamb, 1987, p. 307). The freed slaves had learned small scale trading in Brazil, and they brought their skills to Lagos (Boadi-Siaw, 1993, p. 438). Catarina and later Mariana used trading skills learned in Bahia to build a strong business in Lagos. Mariana in particular made a fortune with her business acumen, starting with her decision to sell water from her Water House. No one begrudged them their success. As one writer pointed out, this was a society and an environment where "outstanding, powerful, intelligent [and] highly successful women," women like Catarina and Mariana, were able to flourish (Mba, 1987, p. 362).

Sociolinguistic analysis: omi/agua/water in Mariana's world

In studying *The Water House* I focused on Mariana and the ways she and those around her acquired and used language in the multilingual, multicultural settings in which they found themselves. On almost every page, Olinto describes speech patterns of characters and communities in Brazil and Africa. He shows the sensitivity of a well-trained sociolinguist as he documents the codes and language shifting, public and private domains, psychological and cultural attitudes to multiple languages. He also shows the artistry of the writer, blending this information so subtly into the narrative that it never becomes obtrusive.

Using Olinto's detailed descriptions of language and language use, I will first describe how Mariana expanded her linguistic repertoire throughout her life and then explore how she passed on her love of language to her children by her teaching and by example.

Mariana's languages

What drew me most to the character of Mariana was her ability to pick up and use the languages of her environment with pleasure, curiosity, and an absence of negative judgment. She always looked outward and forward, ready to mingle with those of any culture she met. This openness began in her childhood and was at the foundation of her success throughout her life.

In 1898, at the start of *The Water House*, the child Mariana was traveling through Brazil toward the coast, to Bahia. Portuguese was her native language and the language of her church and education. In her year and a half in the markets of Bahia and on the six-month boat trip to Lagos, she easily acquired Yoruba, her grandmother Catarina's language and the language of the Brazilian Africans around her.

When Mariana and her family arrived in Lagos, they found it dominated by the Yoruba under the colonial rule of the English, who regulated the legal and political life of the area. They met an Ibo population that communicated with the Yoruba in English. English speaking Irish Catholic priests and nuns served the Brazilians in their religious and educational life. Mariana soon acquired English, especially after she started her business and had to deal with the British colonial administration.

Moving into adulthood, Maria began to travel in the interests of trading. Everywhere she went she made contact with different ethnic and language groups. She established her business in areas dominated by the French, now known as Dahomey, at the edge of German Togo. As she did business outside Lagos, she found that the priests, teachers, and government officials were from France, the doctors were German, and the military people, who ran a small base near the city, were Portuguese. The Ewe and Fon were the Africans who dominated the area. She also found a small Yoruba and Portuguese-speaking group of Brazilian returnees. In this complex and changing political, linguistic, and geographical milieu, Mariana made a good life. At every stage she incorporated and used new languages. In this, she differed from her grandmother, who rejected her masters' Portuguese and only used Yoruba, and her mother, who clung to Brazilian Portuguese long after she came to Africa.

Having no linguistic chauvinism in her, Mariana did not resist any new language. On the contrary, she was eager and ready to learn the ways of speaking of those around her. For example, when the English colonial administrators declared that all business in Lagos would be conducted in English, Mariana did not join in the protests. She understood movements of history and immediately arranged English classes for those who wanted to learn.

Mariana had a linguistic repertoire that was complex and tailored to the whole range of activities that preoccupied her from childhood to old age. She could shift her languages as needed for her business and political dealings, and she had a range of languages to accompany her roles as daughter, granddaughter, trader, mother, sister, religious practitioner, wife, friend, and political leader.

Portuguese, Mariana's first language, remained her strongest and most private language even as the Portuguese-speaking people around her grew old and died. She learned to read and write in Portuguese. It was the language of her Catholic religious practice, and it linked her to her childhood in Brazil. She added other languages to her repertoire, but Portuguese was associated with a long sequence of memories from her childhood and emigration.

Yoruba was the language she shared with Catarina, her grandmother, and the language of her new religious life as she adopted African forms of worship and prayer. Yoruba was the language of the street; it surrounded her daily. She used it at parties, weddings, and social gatherings. Through Yoruba she interacted with other Africans and used it in the market place and in political discussions.

Mariana picked up Ewe and Fon through her business dealings and social life, and with these languages she could participate fully in the political and cultural life in her territory. She interacted with the Ewe and Fon political leaders of her time and played a leadership role herself.

Portuguese and Yoruba were grounded in Mariana's childhood and family. English and French, along with Yoruba, were the languages of business; through them she established her success, working with government regulations and policies. She wrote an extensive correspondence in English, French, and Portuguese and learned German as well.

Mariana's children

Mariana's understanding of the importance of multiple languages in developing a full life did not stop with herself. She trained her children from early childhood to follow her example. Mariana knew that her children must speak English and French if they were to be well educated. She and her husband spoke English at home for their sake. Because of their proficiency in French and English, the children acquired European educations that provided them with the tools for professional lives in law, medicine, teaching, and politics. Her children spoke English and French as first languages and learned Yoruba from the community around them. Mariana insisted that they know Portuguese as well. As her children matured and established their own lives, their Portuguese connections enhanced hers. Both her brother and her son married Portuguese-speaking women and used that language to share with her their family life. Her adopted son studied in France, there meeting the great Brazilian writer, Jorge Amado. At her son's suggestion, Mariana read Amado's novels, thus keeping her Brazilian Portuguese alive.

Mariana's children grew up in a Yoruba-speaking community, and though educated in other languages, some of them returned to Yoruba and their African identity. Her daughter, who studied medicine in Europe and became a doctor, used Yoruba in her medical practice and eventually married a Yoruba lawyer. Mariana's adopted son was Yoruba. He learned French and Portuguese and chose as his life's work teaching Yoruba in Brazil.

Mariana and her family picked and chose among the varied language groups and ethnicities of Brazil and Africa. Their choices reflected their identities and affiliations, and through their languages they created new selves and new nations. The European languages, Portuguese, English, and French, were the languages of colonialism, but they were also the languages of education, business, and politics, the languages which led to liberation and independent government. Yoruba, Ewe, and Fon carried strong tribal identities, yet Mariana and her son, both deeply engaged in the politics of independence, used these languages to forge African unity.

Sociolinguistic summary

In reading about Mariana's life, her relationships with her large, extended, multi-generational family, her successes as a business woman, and her political influence, we see the complex interweaving of languages and social life. Because of her gift for languages and her drive to learn, her intelligence and her abilities as a business person, Mariana fulfilled herself. In addition, she helped many of those around her to transform themselves. Her tolerance for others and her willingness to take on their perspectives—linguistic, religious, political, and economic—brought her to the end of her life wealthy, beloved, and respected. Mariana had become known throughout her region, in Brazil, and as far away as the Gold Coast.

Conclusion

In my exploration of the relationship between ethnographies and novels, I have discovered and described a fine example of an ethnographic novel. *The Water House* is rich in sociolinguistic, historical, and cultural information. Olinto's continuous recounting of language patterns, especially for Mariana but also for the rest of his characters, carries information about cultural identity and assimilation. Olinto captures the spirit of the times in Bahia and in Lagos. Finally, without using anthropological techniques or ethnographic discipline, Olinto presents us with a picture rich in political, economic, religious, educational, and general cultural data.

In addition to recounting the riches of an ethnographic novel, I examined the question my classmate posed about the differences between the ethnography and the novel. In exploring that question, I looked for similarities as well as differences and went on to contrast the relationship to cultural material of the writer and the anthropologist. I outlined the complementary perspectives of the ethnographer, who describes a culture from without, and the novelist, who is capable of creating a vision of a culture from within. In so doing, I finally answered to my own satisfaction that question my classmate put to our teacher so long ago.

I unexpectedly resolved another issue that I realized was embedded in my teacher's response to my classmate. Her dismissive answer indicated that she clearly valued the ethnography above the novel, perhaps because it was the product of an organized and precise investigation, based on a tradition of cultural study, refined with the discoveries and travails of fieldwork and participant-observation.

I too value ethnographies. By means of a systematic and disciplined method and account, the ethnographer gives readers a way of understanding the underlying assumptions of a new and strange culture, as seen from the outside. However, my appreciation of ethnographies does not rule out the possibility of my learning from a novel written by an insider, rich in ethnographic detail, as I try to grasp the patterns of a culture.

Writers can look from different angles at the same phenomena the ethnographer sees. The writer can create, through imagination and art, a picture of a culture with its own coherence, as seen from the inside, with its underlying assumptions taken for granted but present and available for discovery. Such writers provide field data from which anthropologists can build the theories and explanations that are the focus of ethnography.

In addition, these novels bring to the study of culture indigenous voices often absent in the anthropological literature. Anthropology carries the imprint of Northern European academics who study cultures as different from their own as possible. Until these limits are transcended, the discipline will represent only a small and distorted sample of human behavior as seen through the eyes of the outsider-spectator. Ethnographic novels help to regain a balance in cultural accounting, conveying an insider's voice.

In my own study of cultures, practicing the discipline of anthropology, I find that fieldwork and ethnographies take me only part of the way. I have many starting points. I find abundant information in films, food, fashions, music, architecture, biography, travelogue, sports, dance, visual art, and histories as well as novels and ethnographies.

In the final analysis I go back to the point made by Dan Rose at the beginning of this paper. To do justice to the complexity of the human condition and to the material available around us about cultures of the world, we will have to create a new ethnography that will be "a polyphonic, heteroglossic multigenre construction" (1993, p. 218). One part of this multigenre construction will be ethnographic novels and to the mix will be added history, folklore, philosophy, music, and other creative and complex expressions of ideas and images, visions and dreams that give human life meaning.

References

Adefuye, A., Agiri, B., and Osuntoku, J. (Eds). (1987). *History of the Peoples of Nigeria*. Lagos, Nigeria: Lantern.

Aderibigbe, A.B. (Ed.). (1985). *Lagos: The Development of an African City*. Nigeria: Longman.

Akere, F. (1987). Linguistic Assimilation in Socio-historical Dimensions in Urban and Sub-urban Lagos. In A. Adefuye, B. Agiri, and J. Osuntoku, (Eds), *History of the Peoples of Nigeria* (pp. 165–92). Lagos, Nigeria: Lantern.

Andric, I. (1945). *The Bridge on the Drina*. Chicago: University of Chicago Press.

Benson, P. (Ed.). (1993). *Anthropology and Literature*. Urbana, University of Illinois Press.

Boadi-Siaw, S.Y. (1993). Brazilian Returnees of West Africa. In J. Harris (Ed.), *Global Dimensions of the African Diaspora* (pp. 421–39). Washington, D.C.: Howard University Press.

Bohannan, P. (1964). *Africa and the Africans*. New York: Natural History.

Bowen, E.S. [Bohannan, L.]. (1954). *Return to Laughter*. London: Gollancz.

Burns, B. (1980). *A History of Brazil* (2nd ed.). New York: Columbia University Press.

Clifford, J. and Marcus, G. (Eds). (1986). *Writing Culture: The Poetics and Politics of Ethnography*. Berkeley: University of California Press.

Conrad, R.E. (1986). *World of Sorrow: The African Slave Trade to Brazil*. Baton Rouge: Louisiana State University Press.

Cunha, M.C. da. (1985). *Negros, estrangeiros: Os escravos libertos e sua volta a Africa* [*The Blacks, the Strangers: The Freed Slaves and their Return to Africa*]. Sao Paulo: Brasiliense.

Dennis, P. and Ayocks, W. (Eds). (1989). *Literature and Anthropology*. Lubbock, Texas: Texas Tech Press.

Elegbede-Fernandez, Princess A.P. (1952). *Lagos: A Legacy of Honor*. Ibadan, Nigeria: Spectrum Books.

Fernea, E. (1989). The Case of *Sitt Marie Rose*: An Ethnographic Novel from the Middle East. In P. Dennis and W. Ayocks (Eds), *Literature and Anthropology* (pp. 153–64). Lubbock, Texas: Texas Tech Press.

Hull, R.W. (1979). *African Cities and Towns Before the European Conquest*. New York: Norton.

Lamb, D. (1987). *The Africans*. New York: Vintage.

Marcus, G., and Fischer, M.M.J. (Eds). (1986). *Anthropology as Cultural Critique*. Chicago: University of Chicago Press.

Mba, N. (1987). Literature as a Source of Nigerian History: Case Study of *The Water House* and the Brazilians in Lagos. In A. Adefuye, B. Agiri, and J. Osuntoku (Eds), *History of the Peoples of Nigeria* (pp. 351–64). Lagos, Nigeria: Lantern.

Olinto, A. (1969, 1985). *The Water House* (D. Heapy, translator). New York: Carroll and Graf.

Oliver, R. and Page, J.D. (1962). *A Short History of Africa*. Baltimore: Penguin.

Rose, D. (1993). Ethnography as a Form of Life: The Written Word and the Work of the World. In P. Benson, (Ed.), *Anthropology and Literature* (pp. 192–224). Urbana: University of Illinois Press.

Silko, L.M. (1977). *Ceremony*. New York: Penguin.

Taibo, P.I. III. (1990). *An Easy Thing*. New York: Penguin.

Tallman, J. (1992). Talking Cultures: The Writer and the Anthropologist. Unpublished manuscript presented at the Fourteenth Annual Conference of the Association for Integrated Studies, Pomona, CA., November.

Taylor, M. (1976). *Roll of Thunder, Hear my Cry*. New York: Bantam.

Van Maanen, J. (1993). *Tales of the Field: On Writing Ethnography*. Chicago: University of Chicago Press.

Chapter 2

"Splendid disciplines"
American Indian women's ethnographic literature

Roseanne L. Hoefel

Twentieth-century American Indian Literature has repeatedly borne witness to the permeability of genre boundaries in literary works which defy simple categorization: N. Scott Momaday's multi-genre *The Way to Rainy Mountain*, Leslie Silko and Joy Harjo's prose poetry and landscape photography collections (*Sacred Water* and *Secrets from the Center of the World*, respectively), Linda Hogan's blending of history, legal discourse, and fiction in her novel *Mean Spirit*, Mourning Dove's negotiation of sentimental and romance novel traditions, conversion testimony, and anthropology in *Cogewea* are only a few cases in point. This rich literary tradition's origins in oral expressive forms such as myths, legends, stories, songs, and rituals makes for fertile ground to explore the nexus between literature and ethnography. Arnold Krupat in his historical overview of this link, "Ethnography and Literature," observes that scholars had to make a conscious effort to separate the two, "to distinguish between art and science, the imagined and the real, fact and fiction," a constructed difference he locates in the eighteenth century (with Thomas Jefferson's *Notes on the State of Virginia*) (pp. 62–3).

An especially fruitful place to begin is with an ethnographer herself, Ella Cara Deloria, who collaborated with Franz Boas in extensive anthropological studies of her people, the Lakota Sioux. As Paula Gunn Allen contends, Ella Deloria extends the tradition of the American Indian woman as repository and purveyor of culture. We have seen how the position of the woman in the mythic structure of tribal cosmologies has allowed her historically to develop a storytelling function within her community. What may not be so apparent, perhaps, is the process by which she emerges as a conscious writer (1983, p. 140).

Born of mixed ancestry in 1889 as the daughter of a Yankton Sioux who became an Episcopal priest and raised her among the Tetons while missioning at the Standing Rock Reservation, Deloria was raised by Christian parents who spoke both English and Lakota. Formally educated first at the Wakpala mission school and later at the All Saints' Boarding School in Sioux Falls, South Dakota (Prater, 1995, p. 41), Deloria eventually spent two years at Oberlin followed by two at Columbia where she earned a BS in 1915 and worked with Franz Boas translating Lakota George Bushotter's collection of stories (spelled by Boas Bush-Otter in a correspondence dated September 17, 1935). After several years of teaching, she began anthropological field research under Franz Boas's tutelage in her late thirties.

Though largely productive, this working relationship was stressful for Deloria. In 1929 again at Boas's request, she finished the translation of George Sword's account of the Sun Dance about which she gathered more information. But she was not able to corroborate Sword's personification of particular natural phenomenon, much to Boas's disappointment. Later, Deloria declined Boas's invitation in 1936, due to familial obligations, to rework the South Dakota stories she had collected; yet he sent her the following year former Pine Ridge physician James Walker's manuscript asking her to authenticate it by interviewing elders at that reservation and Rosebud. She was unable to find anyone who remembered the symbolism of the ritual acts Walker detailed decades earlier in *The Sun Dance* but was bound not to reveal until his informants were deceased due to their secret nature. After concerted efforts to no avail, Boas condescendingly scolded Deloria: "I do not know how serious an effort you have made to get the material I want ... on the whole I confess I am not well satisfied with what you got for me during the last few months" (Letter from Boas, 6/1/38). The paucity of corroborating evidence, however, left her only to conclude that the materials in question "were the work of a clever storyteller" (Letter to Boas, 5/12/39).

Despite this impasse, Deloria continued to record thousands of pages in both Lakota and English on all facets of traditional life: Sioux kinship roles, tepee and camp circle social systems, praying for power, education by example, and the economics of giving, among other aspects. In addition to her 1932 collection of myths and legends *Dakota Texts*, she translated and compiled extensive editorial notes for Gideon and Samuel Pond's Santee myths from their missionary days, and Bushotter and Sword's texts, all of which constitute invaluable data on Lakota semantics. In *Dakota Texts* alone, she includes free translation of all 64 stories told directly to her by storytellers, which she transcribed in Lakota; she also provides supplementary literal translations for the first sixteen to more clearly evoke Lakota thought patterns, customs, and metaphors. In 1941, she and Boas published *Dakota Grammar*, a three-dialect dictionary wherein she presents kinship terminology, among other things, and she produced an unpublished Sioux ethnography, *Camp Circle Society*.

Such was the process, thus, by which Deloria "emerged as a conscious writer." An "accomplished ethnologist who sought to record and preserve traditional Sioux ways through this imaginative recreation of life in the camp circle" (DeMallie, 1988, p. ix), Deloria unveils the Dakota kinship system complete with the duties, mores, expectations, and respect network which support it in her novel *Waterlily*. In February, 1938, Deloria wrote to Boas distinguishing between her multiple observations of "folklore" and the evolution of fiction-writing which she noted was more involved than retelling a traditional plot in a "highly personalized way" (Walker, 1983, p. 22). Cognizant of the many facets of oral creativity characterizing "a vital traditional community" (p. 23), Deloria gradually developed her own aesthetic norms for literary production. Her anthropological research enabled her to describe the Lakota's own system of two major and two minor genres.

The two major categories are the ohunkakan and the woyakapi. Ohunkakan were tales regarded as having some fictional elements, whereas the woyakapi were stories about actual happenings. Each of these divisions has a subdivision. The first group of ohunkakan are situated in a mythic past when the world as we know it was still in the process of formation; the second group involve more recent but still amazing events. All of the woyakapi are told as though they had occurred within the historical memory of the tribe (p. 25).

It is not surprising that these various elements would culminate in her own work of fiction. Her editor, anthropologist Ruth Benedict, helped her reduce the original 1944 *Waterlily* manuscript by half, though finding a publisher for a book which did not concern the war effort was difficult. Until the University of Nebraska Press produced the full text in 1988, the nation had missed out on an entire world seen and told from a woman's vantage point. Here, we will explore the historical reconstruction of that world which informs this ethnological novel. "We shall go back to a time prior to white settlement of the western plains, when native custom and thought were all there was, and we shall examine certain of the most significant elements in the old life" (Deloria, 1944).

This passage from Ella Cara Deloria's anthropological publication of the same year, *Speaking of Indians*, intended for church groups as an accessible introduction to North American Indians in pre- and post-reservation contexts, captures her keen sense of a "scheme of life that worked" previously because it preserved traditional values. Understandably, then, Deloria emphasizes in this ethnographical narrative that the pivotal goal in Dakota life was to be a good relative, the honoring of kinship rules and obligations thus serving as the gauge of one's humanness:

> To be a good Dakota, then, was to be humanized, civilized. And to be civilized was to keep the rules imposed by kinship for achieving civility, good manners, and a sense of responsibility toward every individual dealt with. Thus only was it possible to live communally with success; that is to say, with a minimum of friction and a maximum of good will.
>
> (Deloria, 1988, p. x)

When the novel's protagonist, Blue Bird, prepares to birth her first child, she recalls the fateful day when she was young and a raiding war party disrupted her joyful childhood, killing or dispersing her entire family, except her grandmother. Together these two bereaved people are adopted by a sympathetic Teton camp circle. Soon after that tragedy, when Blue Bird naively elopes with Star Elk, we learn about the various grades of honorable marriage, hers having barely qualified, a fate assuaged by the women's patience and understanding regarding her motherless circumstance. As this gifted narrator endears us to our first female protagonist, we are grateful for kinship laws which facilitate Blue Bird's welcome by "correct in-laws" who try to compensate for Star Elk's lazy, possessive, jealous, and increasingly morose nature. Ironically, his peers' ridicule and elders' disapproval—intended to pressure him to be a better husband—lead to his worst blunder: throwing Blue Bird away publicly without cause, a blatant violation of Dakota propriety. Since, in a kinship system which values mutual respect and civility, only weaklings vented their anger and temper in public, Star Elk is banished as a fool; Blue Bird thereby gains her freedom after her daughter Waterlily's birth, though at the cost of his shaming her.

As John Prater (1995) contends, Deloria's portrait of the camp circle of the plains does encompass "both happiness and tragedy in a patterned, meaningful manner" (p. 44). He argues further that Star Elk's character demonstrates "the range of human behavior" and serves as a catalyst for "human agency." To be sure, at this same juncture, Deloria beautifully teaches readers about Dakota prayer to the Great Spirit (Wakan Tanka) when Blue Bird courageously and independently tries to revive her dying daughter; she expresses her gratitude for the healing she trusts will be forthcoming by leaving her father's venerated otter skin. Shortly thereafter, Blue Bird is miraculously reunited with a long-lost surviving cousin, Black Eagle, whose son Little Chief becomes Waterlily's lifelong friend.

The unfolding of Blue Bird's life offers a rich ethnological study whereby Deloria instructs readers about the spiritual as well as the societal and how these dimensions, ideally, reinforce each other. We learn throughout the course of the novel's events that, for instance, making moccasins for another honors the recipient and his family; that curiosity is impolite; that sisters are loyal and loving, and brothers strive to make sisters happy; that humility and sincerity in prayer make a lasting impression on children; that kindness, gentleness, and observance of kinship roles merit love and respect; that hospitality and generosity are essential to a good life; that paternal aunts have the privilege of making portable cradles for a newborn (in this case, Blue Bird's with her new husband, Rainbow); and that a hunka ceremony elevates the status of a child—beloved, as was the case with Waterlily, because "to have something given away in one's name was the greatest compliment one could have. It was better than to receive" (Deloria, 1988, p. 77).

Certainly, Deloria's ethnographic studies inform this emphasis. On March 8, 1939, J.B. Reuter, Manager of People's Finance and Thrift Company, wrote to Franz Boas seeking funding for Deloria's meticulously outlined research project which he enclosed and which, in my view, demonstrates how passionately Deloria desired to make known her people's most prized cultural practices. The proposal, given how closely her plan parallels the portraits painted vibrantly in her fictional account, merits extensive quotation here:

> Proposed Line of Research (on Dakota Sioux)
> Considerable material on the old Dakota religion and its practices has already been collected by Miss Ella Deloria, and is now in manuscript form. Such rites as the following would appear in such a book on Dakota native ritual, by description in words and drawings. Of general tribal concern would be:
>
> 1 The Buffalo ceremony (Puberty rites wherein a girl was taught moral standards, through a colorful sort of pageantry);
> 2 The Hunka ceremony (an honoring rite, very elaborate, much desired by individuals as a means of elevation to a kind of nobility upon assuming certain definite obligations to the tribal circle);

3 The Virgin's Fire (For maintaining the standards of strict chastity);
4 The redistribution, at the close of the elaborate ghost-keeping rite.
5 The Sundance. The most extensive and significant of all the ceremonies, filled with exact regulations as to ways of doing, costuming, etc. The whys of all the details of this series of rites lasting several days.

(Franz Boas Collection)

And, as Julian Rice (1984) posits regarding *Dakota Texts*: "In these traditions greed is a shameful sin and generosity perhaps the primary virtue" (p. 208). As we shall see, the principles which arise in the well-known story Blood-Clot Boy—wherein "ceremonies, ordeals, and love" make creative power possible—apply to Waterlily, as well: "The story has established kinship on the basis of generosity. The Lakota ceremonies emphasize sacrifice and sharing as necessary acts of relationship" (Rice, 1984, p. 211).

Another prominent ethnographic theme which prevails in this novel hails from "The Man Who Married a Buffalo Woman," also from *Dakota Texts*, the primary lesson of which, according to Julian Rice, is "steadfast love, humility, and patience rather than the forced application of autonomous will" (1984, p. 213). For example, as Blue Bird's son comes into his own, readers discover the care and patience wise elders exercise with maturing boys; that ridicule of "young ambition" might kill it (Deloria, 1988, p. 88) and that it is crucial to avoid making adolescents feel self-conscious about the changes they are experiencing; that his rights of passage—counting coup, joining a war party, securing a buffalo—are to be lauded, just as Waterlily's emergence into womanhood was recognized by the prestigious Buffalo ceremony. Again, the buffalo symbolism is instructive:

Because he sacrificed himself completely for the people, feeding, clothing and providing ceremonial objects, the buffalo was the symbol of generosity. And because generosity is a necessary prerequisite for the survival of the group, the buffalo was also a symbol of fertility, generation, and renewal.

(Rice, 1984, pp. 208–9)

Understandably, then, the buffalo image is central to both genders in coming of age, serving as it does for the entire camp circle as a reminder and model of fundamental values.

Likewise in exemplary fashion, Rainbow's own excellence is awarded by election to the selective Kit Fox society:

A warrior was bidden who had achieved his four feathers designating four major war deeds; or a man of peace was bidden who was industrious and had some outstanding skill. In addition, every candidate must have a record of consistent hospitality and generosity, which were the qualities that marked a good citizen of the camp circle.

(Deloria, 1988, p. 96)

He, too, is an exemplar of obedience to social kinship ties as we witness in his dedication to his kola (friend) Palani:

> [F]ellowhood, a solemn friendship pact that must endure forever. 'Fellows' were men of comparable standing and ability who were drawn together by like tastes and by a mutual respect and admiration for each other's character and personal charm. 'The best I have is for my fellow' was their code from the time they pledged eternal loyalty. (p. 99)

As Thomas Matchie points out, "ceremonies may prevent conflict" as when the Dakota and Omaha meet here. "Rather than shame each other 'by seeming competition' (p. 109), they watch each other perform as virtual brothers" (Matchie, 1994, p. 143). Indeed, this camaraderie is essential if they are to withstand the larger alien forces discussed at this ceremonial gathering: "Long-Knife soldiers," "stockades," "big-holy-iron booms" (Deloria, 1988, p. 107). This traditional strong bond, combined with the implicit coalition-for-survival, automatically made their families surrogates for each other—a boon which will sustain Waterlily much later, too, when she needs to return to family during a winter of hardship.

Such extended familial regard, Deloria's novel shows, ritually manifests itself at the macro-level during the Sun Dance where all Dakotas—even traditional enemies—are welcomed in friendship to bear witness to the men who had pledged vows which require tremendous physical sacrifice after a period of fasting and dancing in the heat, and to the women who wailed for their suffering or ransomed them by making a counter-offer to the Great Spirit. The story of Blood-Clot Boy's own tremendous suffering and endurance suggests itself again (see Rice, 1984, pp. 209–13). Deloria explains other rites as well: The Virgin's Fire, to protect a woman's reputation from unfounded rumors; the laborious ghost-keeping ceremony, which required a long-term custodial commitment, as was the case in Leaping Fawn's devotion to her beloved grandmother's soul. Both rituals show the primacy of community and spiritual humility as antidotes to the false trap or delusion of "self-reliance" which the *Dakota Texts* pertaining to wasichus (whites) caution against (see Rice, p. 214).

Without a doubt, Deloria's own self-abnegating priorities parallel those of Waterlily, whom Prater (1995) describes as a "composite character" (p. 47). Her amazing reply to Boas's 1936 offer of $100 per month to rework her stories at Columbia bespeaks the seriousness with which she managed her own kinship duties: caring for two younger siblings after her mother's death in 1916 and for her aging father in 1929:

> I am responsible for providing a roof for my sister as well as for me. … I cannot just leave her and go off. That would not be right. Besides, we have no home at all. I live in my car … all our things are in it. And if I go anywhere, I find it cheapest to go in my car; and take my sister with me. I love her, I can not do otherwise than give her a home of sorts.
>
> (Letter to Boas, 2/7/36)

On every score, then, Deloria in her fiction deeply knows whereof she speaks.

Waterlily later exemplifies selflessness of similar sort when Good Hunter offers to buy her—the most honorable of marriage proposals—for their son, Sacred Horse. The timely offer of horses which could replace those which were killed before Black Eagle could redistribute them at the Ghost feast, compounded Waterlily's dilemma. Significantly, neither the men nor women pressure or even overtly expect Waterlily to accept against her will, yet her mother reminds her that to be a good relative is all, and Waterlily bends to the "nobility of kinship loyalty" (Deloria, 1988, p. 153). Nevertheless, her role in a rewarding gift-giving ceremony intended to extend and prolong her grandmother's hospitality came at a high price: her lingering homesickness for her own family after going to live with her new husband's at the mere age of eighteen. Though Sacred Horse is kind, considerate, and patient, and his family warmly welcoming, Waterlily's strict observance of kinship rules combines with being out of her element (i.e., in the sense that she is away from her immediate family) to keep her from blossoming in their midst.

But Deloria uses this space of discomfort to demonstrate the important role of gendered duties in sustaining community, in this case surrounding the multiple tasks of preparing a cache of buffalo meat as an anticipatory survival strategy against encroaching whites. Here, the narrative describes the treading, drying, blanching, and tenderizing, as well as the artistic encoding of the parfleche packaging:

> Throughout this work, the women kept together and apart from the men. Waterlily saw her husband from a distance during the day and they might speak in passing or converse if they had to work at something together. But it was customary for men and women to keep with their own kind in public. The married did not demand one another's exclusive attention. (1988, p. 171)

Nor was it customary to express affection in public. Only when Waterlily takes courtesy food to her social parents for their infant's naming feast and she is completely at ease does Sacred Horse come happily to know her spirit and spunk.

Again the personal details of Waterlily's life story intersect with ethnography when we are taught about the kinship appeal as a Yankton way of settling scores, to wit a murderer of one's kin is adopted into the tribe to replace the victim, because—as an elder teaches the understandably speechless Waterlily and Sacred Horse—"there is no more powerful agent for ensuring goodwill and smothering the flame of hate than the kinship of humans." Here, significantly, we witness once more the "oral creativity that characterized a vital community," as Deloria wrote in the letter to Boas mentioned earlier. This story within the novel, like those in *Dakota Texts* to which Rice alludes, offers "a synchronic view of the world in which the historical understanding is necessarily contained within an external vision of human behavior, metaphysical relation, and spiritual development" (Rice, 1984, p. 205). The power of such customs as this elder relates, as well as those which were legally forbidden in 1931, lives on—to borrow Rice's priceless phrase (p. 207)—in the "word-dance" of these stories.

In this light, readers realize that the tragedy of epidemics is doubled when kin are separated in an effort to stop the spread of disease, as when Good Hunter sent his family away once their encampment became contaminated by smallpox, what Matchie refers to as "an internal type of violence spread externally through the white man's blankets" (Matchie, 1994, p. 147). Eventually, only six remained, Sacred Horse and several children not among them; but after a war party killed four more, Waterlily returned her wounded sister-in-law, Echo—who had been scalped—home and prepared to leave her husband's family. They assured her they would always love and never neglect her or the baby she was expecting. Her cousin, a male collateral relative, promised Lowanla, his younger brother, as her future husband so that the expected child could "have for father one who is father to him already, and not a total, unrelated stranger" (Deloria, 1988, p. 211). This generous interchange illustrates in practice the theory surrounding extended kinship networks the narrator discussed earlier. Waterlily's son was born in the Moon of Bursting Buds (April), the same day her father-in-law died, and she married Lowanla, the talented singer and staunch Sun Dancer to whom she had been attracted in her youth. Thus, while history haunts Waterlily with a war party massacre similar to the one her own mother's family had endured, it also revisits her with the apparently fated union for which she had yearned, yet, selflessly put aside, and which, we discover later, Lowanla had also coveted. No small wonder Deloria is foremost among those authors Annette James and Theresa Halsey (1997) deem "unequivocal in her affirmation of 'Indian-ness'…. [one who has] set in motion a dynamic wherein native women reasserted their traditional role as 'voice of the people'" (p. 313).

Deloria offers a multi-generational female perspective in an ethnological narrative that defies simple classification. What Arnold Krupat (1988) calls "an ethnographic novel" (p. 22) Robert Berner (1989) refers to as "interpretive anthropol[ogy]" (p. 722), Matchie (1994) deems a "rather successful psychological as well as cultural novel" (p. 145), and Prater (1995) suggests is the "varied intercourse" made possible by Deloria's own multicultural heritage (pp. 40, 46). Considering that Deloria's transcription and translation of a large number of texts in the Lakota and Dakota dialects encompassed various genres: "traditional myths, anecdotes, autobiographies, political speeches, conversation, humorous stories, and aphorisms" (Deloria, 1988, p. 236), it is not surprising that we meet several, if not all, of these genres in the course of the novel, if not the autobiographical in the conventional sense, then certainly the ethnobiographical: this work richly documents the life of her ethnohistorically situated community. Raymond DeMallie's assessment rings solid:

> In conception it is fundamentally a work of ethnographic description, but in its method it is narrative fiction, a plot invented to provide a plausible range of situations that reveal how cultural ideals shaped the behavior of individual Sioux people in social interactions. (p. 241)

Interwoven are Deloria's 20 plus years of study of such anthropologists as George Bushotter and George Sword, as well as her own interviews and personal input (p. 242). Another pivotal ingredient, I would add, is Deloria's supreme love for her people and her undying respect and admiration for their stamina and grace, to which she movingly alludes in *Speaking of Indians*: "Nobody knows and appreciates the fact any more than Indians themselves that there were splendid disciplines in the old culture to sustain and strengthen its people" (1944, p. 149). These elements cumulatively proffer the intellectual and cultural world of the nineteenth-century Sioux. As Julian Rice (1984) writes in his introduction to the memorably entitled "Why the Lakota Still Have Their Own," "Since the themes of Lakota stories emphasize the dominant, perhaps the predominant virtue of wacantognaka (generosity), a storyteller manifests that virtue by giving or transmitting the values and vision of the story to his [sic] listeners" (p. 205). We have in Deloria a storyteller of unsurpassed wacantognaka whose ethnological novel of values and vision has offered a richer world to her readers who might do well to retrieve their/our own "splendid disciplines," the postmodern double-entendre of which serves this multi-genre context well.

Cruikshank and ethnobiography

One anthropologist and writer of impressive repute who in the past twenty years has pursued her own "splendid disciplines" to all of our enrichment is Julie Cruikshank, an ethnographer who has collaborated with Yukon Native elders over a period of two decades. Like Deloria, she has produced ethnographic literature which asserts the truth value of oral narratives, blending and preserving tribal traditions in a way that resists the stasis of the written word. But, whereas Deloria posited fiction as an alternative to standard ethnography, Cruikshank compiled the oral narratives of the female octogenarians with whom she had worked for ten to seventeen years in a newly emerging hybrid genre which, for lack of a pre-existing comprehensive term, we will call ethnobiography. Like Deloria, Cruikshank understood the intricacies of writing about knowledge which was meant to be learned over many years of listening and experiencing, rather than shared with an anonymous public. Cruikshank followed Paula Gunn Allen's injunction to "honor by knowing," and the result of her labor of love, *Life Lived Like A Story: Life Stories of Three Yukon Native Elders* (1990) assumes the challenge Gunn Allen set forth in 1983: "We can chart the transition from reliance on primarily oral forms to the conscious transformation of those forms into literary genres by examining ethnographic biographies, life stories, and native traditions" (pp. 140–1). Cruikshank and the Yukon matriarchy with whom she closely, carefully, and innovatively collaborated appreciated the value of an analysis which provided "important information about the historical and cultural development of women within American Indian societies" (Allen *et al.*, 1983, p. 141).

Constituting another link between oral tradition and written literary forms, not unlike earlier "as-told-to" autobiographies, these ethnobiographies allow for the women's self-definition. To be sure these "life stories illuminate the process by which oral tradition informs and structures the narrative, … [and] reflects and extends the oral tradition through the coherence of several levels of narrative" (Allen, 1983,

p. 142). In the Yukon life histories, stories enlighten events; writing is supplement to telling and serves as an extension of voice, as Cruikshank reflects in a recent retrospective essay (1995).

In *Life Lived Like a Story*, we meet three Yukon elders who forge a new genre rooted in the stories of their own and, by inextricable connection, their communities' lives. This innovative literary species weds, thus, autobiography and ethnography, each of which stems from an oral tradition wherein storytelling both offers a context for relating the past and enables social, cultural, and economic adaptation over considerable time. Forewarned in the *Preface* to part with the notion of autobiography as a "universal form of explaining experience" (Cruikshank, 1990, p. x), readers eagerly anticipate instead the transliterated oral narratives, songs, and nomenclature which render and interpret Angela Sidney, Kitty Smith, and Annie Ned's life histories. Common to each history are those themes Gretchen Bataille and Kathleen Sands found in various American Indian women's autobiography, as Cruikshank aptly summarizes: landscape, mythology, the everyday, and generational continuity (p. 2).

> Another shared feature is that each narrative exacts of the reader genuine listening skills: Whenever I ask her what it is that children actually learn from these stories, she replies by repeating the story for me. The messages, she suggests, are implicit, self-evident; the text, she would argue, should speak for itself.

Julie Cruikshank's introduction contextualizes these women's cultural background to facilitate these stories' fair "hearing." We learn here, for example, of the sequestration of menstruating women whose spatial separation ensured the acquisition of "ritual and practical knowledge unavailable to men" (1990, p. 11). We also discover Cruikshank reckoning with anthropology's ethical quandaries inherent in the juxtaposed methods of observation and participation (p. 13). Elsewhere Cruikshank has elucidated the contrasting theoretical frameworks of oral tradition and western science. Claiming that the former is a distinct tradition in its own right rather than merely an adjunct of the latter, Cruikshank calls the question: "Can someone trained in a western rationalist framework really make any claims to understand cognition which considers time, space, causality, materiality as secondary characteristics of the universe?" (1981, p. 67). She is cognizant of the distance between what Arnold Krupat describes in *Ethnocriticism* as:

> epistemological rationalism that valorizes categories like the empirical and material as "real," and the very different epistemologies of others—ones which, to the Western eye, appear irrationalist, magical, or whatever, but which, indeed, may appear so only because they radically refuse the dualistic and circumferential categories of the West. (1992, p. 26)

Remarkably, as Cruikshank respectfully collaborated with these Yukon women for over ten years outside a university framework and from within these elders' own spaces, she modified her own objectives to accommodate their goals of "legitimizing" their oral histories by putting them on paper and thus into the school curriculum of succeeding generations (1990, p. 16). Indeed, using Jan Vansina's succinct definition of oral tradition, "oral testimony transmitted verbally from one generation to the next or more" (1971, p. 444), Cruikshank adapted the structure of this compilation with the Yukon elders' priority in mind, by interweaving their stories with their individual narrative skills via reconstructed traditional narratives, many of which they learned from matrilineal kin (e.g., uncles, grandfathers) (1971, p. 443). As such, each woman's multiple stories may be parallel or concurrent, rather than sequential or chronological, one characteristic among many which authenticates the story-telling, though it has been somewhat removed from its oral context. These unique autobiographies, thus, serve as an integral link between oral tradition and written literary form, as Paula Gunn Allen and her co-editors claim more generally (1983, p. 142). The Yukon narratives are clearly among those "recent autobiographies" which, co-editor Gretchen Bataille contends, "reflect a far more conscious attempt to present a story of an individual Indian woman and her relation with the tribe, with other native people, and with non-Indians" (p. 87). Cruikshank's introductory notes for each of the narrative sets assists with this complex, perhaps unfamiliar approach. This accompanying apparatus assiduously enables the Western-trained reader to transgress what Krupat calls "a naiveté perpetuating the worst imperial arrogance" (1992, p. 181).

In Part I, for instance, Angela Sidney's "My Stories are My Wealth," we understand more fully the urgency not only of Mrs. Sidney's story, but of her very life, having lost four siblings in an epidemic during the Klondike Gold Rush of the late nineteenth century. Importantly, as initiates to this unique and complex ethnobiographical portrait, we find ourselves in the position of Tagish children alluded to in the epigraph to this paper, children whose responsibility it was/is "to learn what each of the greetings, exchanges, songs and dances meant" (Cruikshank, 1990, p. 32); this is the least we can do as co-beneficiaries of the rich oral inheritance Mrs. Sidney has left her grand-children.

As Cruikshank explains in a chapter of the recent *When Our Words Return: Writing, Hearing, and Remembering Oral Traditions of Alaska and the Yukon*, Mrs. Sydney deems the oral tradition a useful part of "the equipment for living" (Morrow and Schneider, 1995, p. 53). She taught Cruikshank when and how to record her tellings and the way to "mean" with stories, for the oral tradition—as Mrs. Sydney so memorably claims—is good to "think with." The result of their seventeen-year dialogue (1974–91) was manifold: together they produced a brief life history for her family members and booklets of narrative, family and place names. In *Life Lived Like a Story*, Mrs. (because that is the common respect term in the Yukon) Sydney begins with her family history (shag-on), the headnote to which tellingly equates her history with her mother's: "The way you should tell your history is this way: first, my own history—that's the same as my mother's in Indian way—" (p. 37). This tripartite history is followed by three creation stories and an introduction to her parents, which constitutes an oral family tree complete with kinship ties, dates, and place names. Spiralling inward is a layer of four of her parents' stories, such as "The

Discovery of Gold" which, among other principles, demonstrates the invariable downfall and inevitable suppression and death which accompany material greed.

As with each of the Yukon elder's accounts, factual highlights of Mrs. Sidney's childhood alternate with stories—mostly didactic—from that period of their lives. Distinct to hers, though, is the component on travels between the ages of ten and thirteen, wherein the various destinations and landscapes literally chart the course of her pre-pubescence. Their significance in her development is reinforced by the "Stories and Place Names" section which immediately follows it, much as the "Potlatch Song" (Chapter 10) adds a culturally enriching dimension to Chapter 9: "Potlatches." This chapter is both a tribute to the potlatch's value and a lament of its loss with the passing of an older generation. Mrs. Sidney's puberty narrative, likewise, dovetails with the cautionary and anticipatory stories concerning types of husbands and "A Stolen Woman's" resourcefulness in restoring herself to her original family and eluding her captors in the process, variations of the story punctuating her accounts of her own marriage and children. Here, she clearly articulates her regret over the "white people ... changing everything," for instance "burning the afterbirth" rather than placing it in a tree or a gopher's nest to symbolically en-gender the infant's later success as a hunter (p. 129).

Of Mrs. Sidney's seven children, only three survived. Though the narrative does not explicitly state that she underwent a hysterectomy (or sterilization?) at the young age of 27, it indicates that this irreversible operation occurred without her knowledge and against her will:

> Then I had Ida, my last one. Ida was a year old when I had my operation. Even so, if I knew what it was about I wouldn't have let them do it …. But I didn't know. The doctor talked to my husband. 'What do you want, your children or your wife?' 'My wife,' he said. 'I love my children, but the ones I've never seen, I can't help. I love my wife. I'd rather be without them.' So they decided. My husband is the one who signed the papers—I didn't even know what they were going to do. I can't have any more children…. I never found out till long time after. I used to blame the Old Man for it. 'It's all your fault!' I said. He said, 'I love you, that's why. We've never seen those children. We don't know them. You've got to fight for the ones we've got now.'
>
> (Cruikshank, 1990, p. 134)

She relates this painful story while explaining the adoption of Beatrice, the child she eventually lost to illness in 1943 after the arrival of the army. Biography and ethnography frequently merge, even—perhaps especially—in the midst of an ordeal, when she consciously links the story of her life, in this case her son Pete's five-year absence while serving in the war, to the story her aunt told her when she was ten, and which she then "gave to Pete" (p. 139): "Five years he's gone—just like that Kaax'achgook story I told you" (p. 135). In the middle of her song, Mrs. Sidney addresses Cruikshank and other listeners/readers simultaneously:

That's the song I sing for you.
I'm going to tell you about it and tell you why I can sing it
And why we call it Pete Sidney Song.
I'll tell you that when I finish this story. (p. 142)

But Angela Sidney generously is telling us more, in the refrain "I gave up hope and then I dreamed I was home" which resonates with the miracle of any familial reunion in defiance of great odds, and in reiterating how her tribe came to "own that song"; as Cruikshank explains, even Mrs. Sidney had to pursue her own ethnographic research with coastal elders when others questioned if she had rights to that song (1995). To be sure, the first-person plural which closes the hymn, "That's why we claim that song" (Cruikshank, 1990, p. 145), beautifully embodies both ethno- and biographical rights, for she heard her "father tell it to the boys" (pp. 139, 143). In her final chapter, Mrs. Sidney movingly renders both her extended family's cooperative efforts to honor the graves of her deceased beloved and her reflections on her Baha'i religion, her encounter with and belief in Malal, the "Indian doctor" who prophesied the fire of sickness that would decimate her people, her own illnesses and near-death experiences, and the power of prayer and steadfastness of faith.

In this ethnobiography, then, like the two which follow, oral tradition tells us more about the present than the past. While we learn about the turbulent influx of gold prospectors, the establishment of ecclesiastical residential schools, international fur trade, Alaska highway construction, an unstable mining economy, and expansion of government infrastructure, the stories on another level become points of departure for the discussion of these women's personal development and their effort to interpret and connect an otherwise unrelated range of events, as Cruikshank points out (1995, pp. 53–75). For example, born around 1890, roughly 12 years before Mrs. Sidney, Kitty Smith stood apart from other women of her day in her well-known success as a trapper and in her perspective on husband and children "as an extension of her already active and busy life" (Cruikshank, 1990. p. 161). Her life stories probe the implications of a woman's independence:

> Characteristically, such a woman is placed in a circumstance in which independence is forced on her and she must think her way out of a difficult situation. Frequently, the plot evolves around a woman who is "stolen" away from her human community and taken to an unfamiliar world where she manages either to escape or to send help to her human relatives. In other cases, she is abandoned because of some real or perceived misdemeanor and is forced to provide her own living. Usually, such a protagonist is able to turn the tables by not only surviving but also providing for the economic well-being of other people. (p. 172)

Mrs. Smith clearly marches to her own beat regarding conventional expectations of female behavior, as well:

Her husband urged her to marry again when he was dying, but she said no, she preferred her independence now that she was older: 'I tell him, no. I can't take men no more. I can make my own living.' Should be you're on your own. Nobody can boss you around then. You do what you want. My grandchild can look after me. (p. 173)

Kitty Smith deploys stories, then, to explore women's roles and friendships, her travels and observations, and the grandmother–grandchild bond, all of which—according to Cruikshank—are priorities which "shape her narrative" (p. 174), enhancing what Cruikshank refers to elsewhere as the "cultural dimensions" of knowledge (1981, p. 86).

Like Mrs. Sidney's, Mrs. Smith's life account opens with family and tribal history, the latter in the form of origin and transformation stories. After a brief history of her husband's people, she tells two stories which demonstrate justice in the face of wrong-doing and courage as a key to survival. Perhaps these are antidotes to the break-up of Indian marriages when one partner leaves for a white, as was the case in the preceding "My Husband's People." Her rendering, like those of the two other elders, embodies Cruikshank's taxonomy of the strengths of oral narratives:

1   these stories persist in spite of tremendous change;
2   while those of a particular region demonstrate noticeable consistency, they also allow for individual variation;
3   they regularly integrate historical events;
4   they offer, as the latter story posits, "technology" in a broad sense (i.e., tips for survival);
5   they endure over a lifetime or several generations; and
6   they provide the most significant source of history, given the paucity of written documents in oral cultures. (1981, pp. 71–2)

Such characteristics make their tellings especially conducive to an ethnocritical approach that embraces, as Krupat claims by citing Talal Asad, "learning to live another form of life" (1992, p. 185).[1]

Another common feature is the rich symbolism of the natural world, often lending a deep and resonant "mythographic" dimension to the landscape (1981, p. 81). For example, like Mrs. Sidney's, the heart of Mrs. Smith's ethnobiography resides in her own and her tribal childhood stories, the glacier narratives indicative of the landscape as dynamic rather than static; these constitute a dramatic "use of nature to reflect on culture, enmeshing human activities and behavioral taboos in a living and active landscape" (Cruikshank, 1990, p. 169). Central, too, is the transition to woman-hood, eased by the mythic "Wolf Helper" and other daughter-to-wife tales. The collage which follows offers a particularly memorable echo effect: highlights from her marriage, a time when she exercised considerable independence and earned $1,800 in one winter from trapping, on one occasion successfully securing a live fox. This legendary coup lingers in our minds as we read section 10, aptly entitled

"The Resourceful Woman," the headnote to which captures Kitty Smith's autono-mous sensibility: "'This is a story about a woman alone. She's so smart she didn't even need a husband!'" (p. 233). Conflicted allegiance of the married woman to her own family or her husband's arises in this series, a common version of which resides in "A Stolen Woman." This tribute to woman's keen wit and skillful cunning gives readers an ounce of hope as we bear painful witness in the next chapter to the litany of her personal losses: the two children from her first marriage and four of her six from the second.

Remarkably, she remains undefeated, near impermeable. After chastising a "government man" for ruining the Yukon and suggesting he's trespassing: "'How the hell you're coming here, then? Nobody called you to come here'" (p. 251), she contrasts herself and her own rights to be there:

'Me, my grandpa's country, here. My grandma's. My roots grow in jackpine roots all. That's why I stay here. I don't go to your grandpa's country and make fire. No. My grandma's country I make fire. Don't burn. If I be near your grandma's country, it's all right you tell me.' (p. 251)

In relating this story to her grandson, who is baffled by her outspokenness to this "big shot," she proclaims:

'I'm bigshot, too. I belong to Yukon. I never go to his country. I'm born here. I branch here! The government got all this country, how big it is. He don't pay five cents, he got him all. Nobody kicks me out. No, sir! My roots grow in jackpine roots.' (p. 252)

Their easy-going and mutually fulfilling relationship makes the final section of "true stories" entitled "Grandmothers and Grandsons" a fitting close to her ethnobio-graphical retrospective, which went to press a year after she died in 1989. Her triumphant claim to the land crystallizes the cultural integrity of the landscape to which Cruikshank alludes: "In the north where a small population has lived for centuries, the natural environment has historical, social, economic and intellectual dimensions as well as physical aspects" (1981, p. 81).

Also an excellent hunter, twice-married and mother of eight is Mrs. Annie Ned, a contemporary of Mrs. Smith. Both her father and second husband were shamans, and she also possessed special powers, the discussion of which is impossible, else she would lose them. Her priority in sharing her life story is two-fold: "What she learned as a child and what she can teach as an elder" (p. 265). These do not include the mishaps of her life which most autobiographers might emphasize: accidents which broke her leg or nearly blinded her, the loss of her home in a fire, for instance. Whereas Kitty Smith adeptly used dialogue to structure much of her narrative, Annie Ned's main concern in this collaborative ethnobiography is that Cruikshank "get the words right" (p. 267), for she believes the power of words increase with their repetition. Indeed, only "accurate repetition," in her view, enables the "authority to speak about the past" (p. 268). And her epistemology here sheds instructive light upon the intersection of ethnography and biography: she contends that authority hails from two sources. First is "received wisdom from the elders" about which she states: "This is not just my story—lots of people tell that story. Just like now they go to school, old time we come to our grandpa. Whoever is old tells the same way. That's why we put this on paper" (p. 268).

As Cruikshank surmises about oral tradition as a distinctive and worthy approach to knowledge, "knowledge has both linguistic and cultural components" (1981, p. 86). According to Annie Ned, the second source of knowledge rests in "direct experience," from having witnessed specific events; she's cautious, thus, not to speak beyond her ken and to emphasize, in addition to the above goals, the skills needed to survive. For Mrs. Ned, singing was one of those tools: with a deep and powerful voice even in her nineties, she is known as one of the best singers in the southern Yukon, one who knows and tells the creator, origin, and reason for the songs in her repertoire, as the five songs in Chapter 8 attest. As Krupat contends, "Contemporary singing and storytelling goes on in communities that use those performances as means of affirming and validating their identities as communities—communities, which, insofar as they are traditionally oriented, do not separate those stories from their performers, audiences, and occasions" (1992, p. 187). He argues further that these intrinsic links obliterate any "reason to develop [a] distinctive category of criticism about them." That is, "Indian people ... have no need to produce a body of knowledge about it that is separate and apart from it"; such commentary, according to Krupat, inheres in and emerges from the art, rather than rectifying or commodi-fying "it" (1992, pp. 187–8).

Consider, e.g., the myth criticism and regionalist perspective embedded in Mrs. Ned's ethnobiography. Giving repeated credit where it is due for the stories in her opening family history, Mrs. Ned regrets the discovery of gold which changed everything, including the nomadic culture, to an era where "people stay where they stay" (1990, p. 280). And where they stay, the vast Yukon, has its own history in the innovatively interwoven Beaverman and Crow creation myths, wherein "the sky came down to the earth at the horizon and it was possible for people to be stolen away to the 'far side,' where everything was perpetual darkness and winter" (1990, p. 272). For those unfamiliar with these origin stories, Cruikshank's introductory context regarding human and animal negotiation is invaluable. As with Angela Sidney's, Annie Ned's family history of her husband is literally and figuratively grounded in the region, with various place names commemorating one of the earliest trade routes between the coast and interior, Kusawa Lake. The succeeding formal narratives affiliated with this long, winding lake interrogate the risks of isolation and abandonment for wayfarers in "unfamiliar territory" (1990, p. 273) particularly probing the unclear ethnic borders of the Athapaskan and Tlingit. For these women, as Carter Revard suggests in his study of history, myth, and identity among native peoples, "the notions of cosmos, country, self, and home are inseparable" (quoted in Krupat, 1992, p. 210).

Undoubtedly these are among the stories to which Mrs. Ned refers in the headnote to the next section as ones "to make your mind strong" (1990, p. 311). Because "old ladies tell stories about what they see, that's how they teach kids" (p. 314), she relates the memory of her grandfather's potlatch for her mother, who died when she was six. She candidly expresses missing the grandmother who raised her, who taught her how to snare and make traps. Thus she tells us in the section which follows, entitled "Since I Got Smart": "My grandmother told me everything. That's the one I tell you this time, all this" (p. 315). To be sure, Annie Ned's primary goal is to educate the next generations, who, if they listen and learn, could also be(come) smart, aware, and incrementally self-sufficient at the age of nine or ten. Uncomfortable focusing on her self, *per se*, she instead demonstrates how she learned, usually in the form of oratory, speeches thereby structuring much of her account. Even her "Marriage" chapter is not self-centered, as one might imagine in typical autobiography, but rather presented as an impersonal illustration of old-time self-sufficiency and self-reliance:

> I stayed with Grandma at Jojo [Mendenhall River]. I stayed home, looked after kids, I sold sewing to Sewell's store and in Taylor and Drury's store—moccasins, mitts, coats. When moose are fat, I go hunting with my uncles: I cut meat, dry meat, make tallow, make grease. When you kill moose, you got to pack baby up the hill. These young ladies, I don't think they could make it: 'I'm tired … got to get the car …' It's true, I think, what old people did! Then I would go fishing at Klukshu—put up maybe five hundred fish so we won't go short. Some people put up one thousand fish! (p. 324)

Mrs. Ned's ethnographic modeling takes precedence over a conventional ego-centric focus, to wit, she doesn't even discuss her thirty-year third marriage to a white, and much of her adult life—including emotions and affections—she embeds in community songs. Frequently, she intertwines the ancestors' traditions with her own experience—again merging "splendid disciplines," in this case ethnography with biography—for example, in the closing chapter, warning us of the impact our actions have upon the land and its animal inhabitants. The final breath group of "Caribou" suggests her own causal analysis of these allegedly inexplicable shifts:

> After Skookum Jim found gold, everything changed.
> White people came to this country.
> White people learned everything from Indians.
> Now they want the whole thing, the land!
> I've got sixty-four grandchildren in this Yukon.
> I worry about them, what's going to happen?
> White people, where's their grandpa? their grandma?
> Indians should have their own land. (p. 338)

Clearly, Mrs. Ned's firm sense of the implicit remedy has the last word in her ethnobiographic narrative; she has definitely "got the words right." Because oral narrative is integral to indigenous intellectual traditions, Cruikshank and, by extension, readers, "[take] seriously" what these women "say about their lives rather than treating their words simply as an illustration of some other process" (p. 1). Remarkably, the persistence of stories over time constitutes the essential and dynamic fabric of education. The initiates' own learning is enhanced by Cruikshank's astute taxonomy of the elders' pedagogical strategies, e.g., of "The Stolen Woman" and "Moldy Head" stories which explore social contradictions and the myths they evoke, and dramatize cultural ideals, difficult choices, and alternative approaches (which may differ in sequence along gender lines). As a Hopi friend suggested to Larry Evers, we, too, learn to "go along with the stor[ies]," which is to say, to trust them and what they have to teach us, including how to listen to them (pp. 71–5).

Each Yukon narrator's performance of her oral traditions is historically situated, with the teller, audience, and meanings shifting accordingly. While narratives can serve as commemorations, they also proffer culturally specific and highly personal commentary, as Cruikshank observed (1995, pp. 53–75). These women's stories not only "say," they do. Cruikshank is thereby able to incisively assess narrative behavioral modeling and the pregnancy of meaning for physical space and place which simultaneously root memory, orator, and community as the tripartite context for these ethnobiographies.

What Allen suggests regarding women's autobiography certainly obtains with these ethnobiographies: they offer "insight into the values of the American Indian woman writer and the process by which she identifies herself and extends and shapes her art to express her particular cultural heritage" (1983, p. 143). Without a doubt, the quintessential motif of connection—to nature, to others, to the land—bespeaks these narratives' penultimate theme of kinship systems. As Morrow and Schneider surmise, "oral tradition is less about tellers and texts than about relationships" (which prompt "all telling, remembering, and hearing") (1995, p. 224). A dynamic genre, ethnobiographical narrative is "always accomplishing" just as we are "always learning, rather than learned" (p. 225). Understandably, stories about each of these elements are the main mode of each elder's explanation. As Morrow and Schneider recommend, rather than take these ethnographic literary words into "intellectual captivity," we would do better to maintain "a sense of humility.... [understanding] that we cannot preserve and interpret but only participate and retell" in this now transliterated oral tradition (p. 225).

As Deloria, Cruikshank, and these Yukon elders' literary productions demonstrate, viewing ethnographic materials in literary terms does not detract from their importance as historical and cultural change documents. Rather this hybridized art enlarges our understanding and deepens our appreciation of the worlds these women inhabited throughout the twentieth century. As is the case with Deloria's ethnographic novel *Waterlily*, the cultural constructions inherent in these Yukon narratives generously make accessible to a wide and grateful readership, the rich worlds of formidable women, all of whom—like Blue Bird, Waterlily, and the women of their extended family and camp circle—have indeed lived and told their lives like a story.

Note

1   See Asad (1986) for a fuller discussion.

References

Allen, P.G. *et al.*, (Eds). (1983). *Studies in American Indian Literature*. New York: Modern Language Association.

Asad, T. (1986). The Concept of Cultural Translation in British Social Anthropology. In J. Clifford and G. Marcus (Eds), *Writing Culture: The Poetics and Politics of Ethnography* (pp. 141–64). Berkeley: University of California Press.

Berner, R. L. (1989). Review of *Waterlily*, by Ella Cara Deloria. *World Literature Today* (Autumn), p. 722.

Clifford, J. and Marcus, G. (Eds). (1986). *Writing Culture: The Poetics and Politics of Ethnography*. Berkeley: University of California Press.

Cruikshank, J. (1995). Pete's Song: Establishing Meanings through Story and Song. In P. Morrow and W. Schneider (Eds), *When Our Words Return*. Logan: Utah State University Press.

—— (1990). *Life Lived Like a Story: Life Stories of Three Yukon Native Elders*. Lincoln: University of Nebraska Press.

—— (1981). Legend and Landscape: Convergence of Oral and Scientific Traditions in the Yukon Territory. *Arctic Anthropology*, XVIII (2), pp. 67–93.

Deloria, E.C. (1988). *Waterlily*. Lincoln: University of Nebraska Press.

Deloria, E.C. and Boas, F. (1927–1934+). *Correspondence*. L. 71 items. Philadelphia: American Philosophical Society. Franz Boas Collection.

DeMallie, R. (1988). Afterword. In E.C. Deloria, *Waterlily*. Lincoln: University of Nebraska Press.

Evers, L. (1979). A Response: Going Along with the Story. *American Indian Quarterly* 5, pp. 71–5.

James, M.A. with Halsey, T. (1997). American Indian Women: At the Center of Indigenous Resistance in Contemporary North America. In A. McKlintock, A. Mufti, and E. Shohat (Eds), *Dangerous Liaisons: Gender, Nation and Postcolonial Perspective* (pp. 298–329). Minneapolis: University of Minnesota Press.

Krupat, A. (1992). *Ethnocriticism: Ethnography, History, Literature*. Berkeley: University of California Press.

—— (1988). Review of *Waterlily*, by Ella Cara Deloria. *Nation*, 2–9 July, pp. 22–3.

Matchie, T. (1994). Two Women of the Sioux: Ella Cara Deloria's *Waterlily* and Mary Crow Dog's *Lakota Woman*. *South Dakota Review* 32 (1, Spring), pp. 138–51.

Morrow, P., and Schneider, W. (Eds). (1995). *When our Words Return: Writing, Hearing, and Remembering Oral Traditions of Alaska and the Yukon*. Logan: Utah State University Press.

McClintok, A. *et al*. (Eds). (1997). *Dangerous Liaisons: Gender, Nation and Postcolonial Perspective*. Minneapolis: University of Minnesota Press.

Prater, J. (1995). Ella Deloria: Varied Intercourse. *Wicazo Sa Review* 11 (2, Fall), pp. 40–6.

Revard, C. (1980). History, Myth, and Identity among Osage and Other Peoples. *Denver Quarterly* 14, pp. 84–97.

Rice, J. (1984). Why the Lakota still have their own: Ella Deloria's *Dakota Texts*. *Western American Literature* 19 (3, Fall), pp. 205–17.

Swann, B. (Ed.). (1992). *On the Translation of Native American Literature*. Washington, DC: Smithsonian Institute Press.

Taylor, J.G. *et al.* (Eds). (1987). *A Literary History of the American West*. Fort Worth: Texas Christian University Press.

Vansina, J. (1971). Once Upon a Time: Oral Traditions as History in Africa. *Daedalus* 100 (2), pp. 442–68.

—— (1965). *Oral Tradition: A Study in Historical Methodology*. London: Routledge and Kegan Paul.

Walker, J. (1982). *Lakota Society*. R. DeMallie. (Ed.). Lincoln: University of Nebraska Press.

—— (1983). *Lakota Myth*. E. Jahner. (Ed.). Lincoln: University of Nebraska Press.

—— (1989). *Lakota Beliefs and Ritual*. R. DeMallie and E. Jahner (Eds). Lincoln: University of Nebraska Press..

Chapter 3

A woman's work is never done

Business and family politics in *Umbertina* and "Rosa in Television Land"

Rose De Angelis

Even though a woman's domestic work is seldom accorded a financial value or acknowledged as important, the routine of domestic housekeeping, domestic life itself, at times has served as a stepping stone towards social and economic advancement for the Italian-American woman. The Italian-American woman's search for autonomy and self-fulfillment has often emerged from the shadows of the private domestic spheres where "home work" improved her family's living conditions. Two women, Umbertina Longobardi in Helen Barolini's novel *Umbertina* and Rosa Della Rosa in Daniela Gioseffi's "Rosa in Television Land," underscore the Italian woman's business savvy and resourcefulness. As Umbertina and Rosa take an active role in the household economy, they subvert a domestic ideology that bespeaks a woman's innocence, ignorance, and submissiveness in a culture that has specified and limited the role of the female. Both women integrate the dynamics of family life and the economics of business. They negotiate with familial duty, personal integrity, and social responsibility as they struggle to achieve economic and familial goals. In a socio-cultural power system that oppresses and contains them, they reinscribe themselves, Rosa to a lesser degree, in a new social order written and enforced by them, even while they are denied the public recognition granted to men.

The sixteen-year-old goat girl, Umbertina, in Helen Barolini's novel is the hybrid product of her ancient pagan ancestors, the Bruttii, and her present Christian culture; as such, she has the power to interpret nature, as if, the narrator tells us, it schooled her thoughts: "[S]he saw and read the language of nature and read its portents. What did she need with books when all the world was about her?" (Barolini, 1979, p. 26). This is the woman the villagers of Castagna say will "be the man of her family" (Barolini, p. 23), the shepherdess who interprets her injuries during an unexpected storm as a sign from God not "to think further of Giosue" (Barolini, p. 35) and to renounce her whimsical dreams of romantic love with the charcoal maker for economic security with Serafino Longobardi.[1]

An American "sojourner," Serafino's emigration is prompted by the political, social, and economic malaise of rural Southern Italy, a region abandoned by a government which did not understand, at times disregarded, and sometimes feared the integration and participation of the South in a unified Italy.[2] Serafino returns from his American sojourn with the money to buy land and to marry a village woman. Offering to purchase the marriage linen and willing to forfeit the dowry "in a culture where a dowry was mandatory if a daughter was ever to marry," *l'emigrante* secures Umbertina as his bride (Mangione and Morreale, 1992, p. 94).[3] As was the custom, Umbertina travels from her father's house to her husband's house via the traditional route of the arranged marriage. However, as Serafino's pragmatic young wife, she immediately begins freeing herself from the constraints of male surveillance, more prominent in a culture where the male is perceived as the primary enforcer, and precipitates the emigration to America for the same security that had prompted her to marry Serafino. The narrator notes that "though Serafino marveled at her willingness to go, it had all been decided in her long before, at the time she agreed to be his wife" (Barolini, p. 47). Respectful affection, not passion, characterizes Umbertina's marriage to Serafino, for her passion is directed toward economic security and self-fulfillment even though, as Anthony Tamburri suggests, "she ... realized that a woman could not be a whole person in a male-dominated society" and that "the female of her generation was most always subservient to the male" (1991, p. 364). Umbertina has internalized the traditional Italian concept of marriage/ merger where duty, responsibility, and financial security take precedence over love and physical satisfaction. Serafino "wanted to treat her as a girl-wife, to hold her on his knee ..., to caress her, but she did not want this from him. She brought him her strength and loyalty instead" (Barolini, p. 46). Marriage for Umbertina was "to start a family, ... not a *carosello*, a merry-go-round.... [It was] a woman's duty!" (Barolini, p. 132).

Taking with her the tin heart of past daydreams of romantic love, *la coperta matrimoniale* of her present, and the rosemary plant of her future, Umbertina arrives in America with Serafino and their children circa 1883.[4] Financially unable to make the trip upstate to where the expanse of land could recreate for them the agrarian lifestyle of their village in Castagna, they settle in the throng of tenement buildings on the Lower East Side known as the Mulberry District, "the first and largest of the nation's Italian enclaves" (Mangione and Morreale, p. 131), and take their place among the huddled masses of Mott Street where most of the Calabrians live. Most Italians thought of themselves, some still do, in terms of provincial identities. In America, they tended to settle in large Italian colonies, duplicating the customs and traditions of their particular Italian town or village (Alba, 1996). So it was not unusual for immigrants, like Umbertina, from a specific town or village, to be housed in one tenement, on one block, or an entire area where the similar regional dialect and surroundings created the illusion of being back home: "Thus Umbertina learned that she was in America but living in a little Italy, in streets filled with Italians arranged according to where they had come from in the old country" (Barolini, p. 59).

Umbertina, however, did not want to be back home; the same resolution that had prompted her journey out of the Old World and into the New World surfaces amidst the din of her surroundings. With conviction, Umbertina says, "We won't stay here.... We will get to the country" (Barolini, p. 60). It is this determination that will empower her and renew her talent for reading the language of her surroundings—a talent which tells her that in America she "need[ed] to be her own boss" (Barolini, p. 63). She begins taking in wash like many of the other immigrant women and saving every penny, for she, more than Serafino, knew that "money was the key to everything" (Barolini, p. 65). Virginia Yans-McLaughlin writes that "Italian women shared a preference for homework. ... [It] was acceptable because it did not take women away from their young and because it represented a comfortable extension" of their position in the household (1977, pp. 109–10). Homework did not threaten Serafino's position as breadwinner and head of household nor Umbertina's role as the traditional wife and mother, nurturer/lover to her husband and role model for the female child, the person who would establish the continuity of the Italian lifestyle for later generations. Yet, when Serafino suggests that they send her brother Beppino money for his passage to America, Umbertina defies all cultural standards of wifely behavior, assumes the Italian male rhetoric of authority, and lashes out at what she deems is his sentimental foolishness: "Let Beppino make his way as we did! ... He can work.... You are a fool! ... You have the sentiment and no brains to go with it!" (Barolini, pp. 68–9). Umbertina's verbal aggressions reflect the possibilities of change in the position, place, and power plays of affective relationships and forms of social organization in the New World. In time, these possibilities would become part of the social and cultural inventory of the Italian-American population from which other generations of Italian women would profit.

As the woman in charge, she fulfills the villagers' prophecy of being "the man of her family," empowering herself, disempowering Serafino (Barolini, p. 23). Umbertina disassembles a tradition which associates decision making with the male and public life, and, consequently, disassociates it from the female. She privately challenges the gender-specific role of *capo famiglia*, thereby undermining any essential understanding of a fixed male identity and the concomitant power generally associated with it within Italian society. Her behavior contests the culturally sanctioned beliefs about the powers of each sex, what anthropologist Helen Fisher calls the "sexual template" (1992, p. 218), and the traditional demarcations of sexual roles within both the Italian family and Italian culture. Italian familial relationships served as an organizing force for establishing the rules of conduct and power relations between the sexes not only within the particular family unit but also within the broader societal context. Her private defiance of cultural standards prescribed for the Italian woman sets the precedent for the public displacement of patriarchal privilege. Laura Anker notes,

> From the interaction of customary practices with new economic realities, women forged strategies of adaptation and protest that stressed the goals of family advancement and community welfare over purely individual needs and that defined success through the prism of the household responsibility rather than purely personal gain. These strategies, in turn, mediated transatlantic renegotiation of gender roles and family relationships. (1993, pp. 271–2)

Change, slow and gradual, as reflected in her sporadic episodes of rebellion, illustrates Umbertina's participation in what anthropologist George Foster calls "stripping down," a conscious or unconscious peeling away of the excess and sometimes stultifying layers of cultural paraphernalia (1960, p. 12). This "stripping down" allows her to "redress" herself in a way that is most profitable to her and to her family.

In America, Serafino finds comfort in the routine of a steady job, a glass of wine, and a game of cards; he enjoys all of the patriarchal privileges that come with being *il capo famiglia, de jure* if not *de facto*. As Colleen L. Johnson notes,

> The authority system which the Italians brought with them can only be described as patriarchal, where the immigrant father stood above other family members as the ultimate source of social control. His status was so elevated that he was described … as aloof, distant, and an object to be feared… . [H]is superior position was maintained by the enforcement of respect for his role as provider and protector of the family. (1978, p. 237)

Serafino's mode of conduct in private and public, however, differs from the cultural patterns brought to, followed, and reinforced in the New World by other Italian men. As Umbertina herself notes, "Serafino was not like the other men" (Barolini, p. 54): Serafino lacks ambition and drive. His complacency forces Umbertina "to take charge … whether it meant disrespect to her husband or not" (Barolini, p. 69), for the husband's authority did not go unqualified in Italian culture. It was contingent on several factors, one of which was his ability to be a good provider.

Serafino's resignation and deference signal the shift in gender roles—his now subordinate/defensive, hers now dominant/offensive—and the repositioning is confirmed by the pathos of his invocatory supplication, "What do you want from me, Signore Dio!" (Barolini, p. 69). Serafino's inability to improve his family's economic situation provides Umbertina with an opportunity to establish herself as the head of household even if she does so within the parameters of personal decorum and public scrutiny, and she does not relinquish her familial goals even after the loss of their savings at the hands of an unscrupulous fellow countryman.[5] She takes matters into her own hands and has Anna Giordani, a visiting nurse and a compatriot of sorts, write to her *paesani* in Cato, New York, to inquire about work for Serafino.[6]

With the assurance of a job for her husband, Umbertina demonstrates the enterprising spirit which will fulfill her dreams for economic advancement and self-fulfillment: she sells her precious *coperta matrimoniale*. The centerpiece and pride of her domestic life, the most important piece of her dowry, finances her family's trip out of the slums and into a "new, fresh world" where, she thought, they could "start fresh" (Barolini, pp. 77, 76). The sale emphasizes the traditional role of the Italian woman as selfless martyr, the woman who would sacrifice anything for the good of her family, but, at the same time, it reinforces her role as the purveyor of financial security, the stronghold of the Italian male, challenges the established mores in the Italian familial-social structure, and blurs the once clearly defined distinctions in the Old World between men and women, public and private.

In the New World, Umbertina places domestic life and female privilege on a par with that of public life and the male prerogative and overwrites the traditional behavior of the Italian woman with words and actions usually attributed to men.

Domestic life, with Umbertina in control, serves as the impetus for her family's economic prosperity. The switch in roles, renegotiated and transformed by the migration process, is evident in the way she apprises Serafino of her plans for the family. She *tells* him, "The first thing we will do is get a piece of land to grow our food" (Barolini, p. 77). Serafino's deference to her comes in part because of his "easygoing" personality, but mostly because, as the narrator notes, Umbertina "would have done what she wanted anyway," for "she was more intelligent than he" (Barolini, p. 93). As she asserts her business and decision-making skills, usually thought as male prerogatives, Umbertina subverts an economic system, whether Italian or American, that links dominance to the "control over the production and distribution of valued goods," a dominance which is historically the domain of men and normally increases as their control is consolidated (Tiffany, 1979, p. 2).

In Cato, domestic life continues serving as the springboard for economic success. Umbertina's *panini* with vegetables and meat, which she prepared for Serafino's lunch as part of her wifely duties, titillate the palates of his co-workers, and when they suggest paying for similar lunches, she immediately sees the financial implications and capitalizes on their offer. Umbertina takes the "Italian wife's clearly defined household responsibility ... [of] preparing and purchasing food" (Yans-McLaughlin, 1977, p. 108) and turns it into a business venture, one which establishes her family's future social and economic status. She soon turns homemade lunches into the Longobardi *groceria*; and what she lacks in schooling, she compensates with "great powers of concentration[,] memory," and hard work (Barolini, p. 90).[7] "As both family and grocery store grew, Serafino ... let his wife take [complete] charge" (Barolini, p. 93).

Miriam Cohen writes that "agrarian society ... was in large part organized around the household. All members of the family contributed to the family's income in one way or another" (1977, p. 121). Coming from an agrarian society, Umbertina understood that a successful enterprise depended on each member of the family doing his or her own part. Like many other Southern Italians, she organized the family into a working unit (Yans-McLaghlin, 1977). Her daughters helped in the store, and the older boys, Jake and Ben, worked during the day after finishing a basic elementary education. Jake, having finished eighth grade, "took a job on the streetcar by day to add to the family earnings, which all went back into the store, and studied a business course by night. Then Ben did likewise" (Barolini, p. 96).[8] Humbert Nelli notes that

> [p]arents expected respect and obedience from children, who assumed responsibilities at an early age. Families were large and the numerous children, especially the boys, were looked upon as economic assets... . [M]ost—if not all—of the wages earned were turned over to the parents. (1983, p. 134)

In Italian society, it was usually the mother who had control of the pursestrings.[9]

In Cato, Umbertina "gave orders and directed the family" and the family business (Barolini, p. 93). Phrases like "the girls would be stationed" and "nothing was left to chance" underscore the martial tactics with which she managed work and family (Barolini, p.108). Over the years, a retail grocery had turned into a wholesale business under her generalship, yet she maintained and encouraged the visible and public nature of traditional social ties between husband and wife, male and female, even as she continued making every public and private decision affecting the lives of her immediate and extended family, married or single, male or female, to the end of her life. As Anthony Tamburri has justly noted, the sign on the business, Umbertina's business, reads "S. Longobardi and Sons," and, at his death, Serafino's obituary credits him, not Umbertina, with establishing the family fortune (1991, p. 363). None-theless, Umbertina's story is one of triumph: she achieves her dreams, which were for personal and financial success, not public recognition: "It was a man's world, they said, and this had never troubled her [or stopped her] when she was actually in command and actively wielding her own will" (Barolini, p. 127). When her daughter Carla asks her about love and happiness, Umbertina answers saying, "The important thing is to find your place. Everything depends on that. You find your place, you work, and like planting seeds, everything grows" (Barolini, p. 133). In a culture which established the woman's place for her, Umbertina had recontextualized the woman's place and her relationship to it, integrating public and private, family and business. She had created a place for herself, germinated her seeds, and watched as both her family and business grew.

While Daniela Gioseffi's main character Rosa in the short story "Rosa in Television Land" does not possess Umbertina's domineering and adventurous spirit, she does share the same sense of family commitment and domestic space within which she must create her fortune, though it never reaches the extent of Umbertina's. Moreover, if Umbertina "read[s] the language of nature" (Barolini, p. 26), Rosa knows about human nature, "now and then offering a bit of wisdom to" her co-workers who always "nod[ded] their head[s] in affirmation" (Gioseffi, 1991, pp. 22–3). In adhering to her cultural heritage, Rosa subscribes to an androcentric view of marriage where it is assumed that the woman's life will revolve around home and family, and she reinforces the traditional demarcations of male and female roles firmly established in Italy and transported to America.

> When the other women complain of their husbands' behavior, she always states
> … 'A man, he no can cry too mucha; is a woman's work to cry, to worry, to make
> a nice housa, cooka da food and lova da bambinos.'
>
> (Gioseffi, p. 21)

Rosa, with hair forming a "bun at the back of her neck" and wearing practical "black oxford heels" and a "black dress and coat" (Gioseffi, p. 20), fits the description of the traditional Italian woman often used in the ethno-marketing of Italian products.[10] She arrives in America with her mother and older sister at the end of World War I. As Humbert S. Nelli (1983) and others have noted, a large percentage of the early immigration was male.[11] Some of these "sojourners" saw America as a seasonal adventure, a place where they could make money and return home; others, like

Rosa's father, came hoping to become a permanent member of the community after earning enough money to send for their families. Like Umbertina and many other immigrants before her, Rosa endures the hardships of the ocean crossing in steerage and settles in the Italian enclave at Mulberry Street.[12] Conditions in the tenements of the Lower East Side were no different thirty-five years later for Rosa than they had been for Umbertina. In her 1919 study of the Italian women in industry, Louise Odencrantz noted that, even though some improvements had been made, "[s]eventy per cent of all the persons in these Italian households were living under congested conditions" (1919, p. 15), some living in apartments with no windows, no running water, and no toilets (Gabaccia, 1984). After reuniting in America, the Della Rosa family, mother, father, Rosa, her sister Helena, and three brothers, "lived in a small, crowded apartment, huddling around a coal stove in freezing winter and fanning themselves for relief on the fire escape in sweltering summer" (Gioseffi, 1991 p. 21). Later, her parents, half frozen in the inclement weather, would die within two days of each other in one of those apartments. Having never made the distinction, like Rosa, "between hard-earned social security and welfare or charity," they died in abject poverty (Gioseffi, 1991 p. 21). Rosa, like her parents and many other Italian immigrant families before and after them, adheres to the collective imperative of *la bella figura* (the good image) which, according to Anthony LaRuffa, "is linked to two very important values in traditional Italian and Italian-American societies: honor and pride" (1988, p. 4). Conscious of family honor and ethnic pride, "Rosa never considers staying home and collecting social security, as it would be shameful to take government funds" (Gioseffi, 1991 p. 21); and so, at seventy-eight, she is still traveling her daily route to work.

Like many other children of immigrants, Rosa started working at an early age to lift the financial burden under which her family struggled in New York. Poor economic and social conditions place Rosa's father in the unpleasant position of worrying about her virginity and family honor, for unlike Umbertina and many other immigrant women who worked at home, Rosa goes out of the home and finds employment as a factory worker where she is beyond the reach of her father's watchful chaperonage. "New York City provided … employment opportunity for women, offering many jobs in small-scale industries…. Such labor did not require knowledge of English and made use of traditional skills that were easily learned or were extensions of household skills" (Cohen, 1977 p. 122). Rosa's limited education and lack of language skills, therefore, do not undermine her earning potential at the workplace, and her willingness, like that of many other exploited immigrant women and children, to work for low wages increases her success in securing a job. Amongst the immigrant groups, "the Italian girl [underbid] her fellow-workers in every occupation she [entered]" (Odencrantz, p. 4). Even though Rosa would never be financially successful, she would at least achieve economic stability, for she "earned money for the family table" (Gioseffi, p. 24). As Miriam Cohen notes, during the first decades of the twentieth century, "45.5 percent of Italian women over sixteen years of age were gainfully employed, a higher percentage than all other ethnic groups surveyed" (p.123). Later, after the death of her husband, factory work would enable

Rosa and her ailing sister, for whom she had assumed responsibility, to survive with pride. Factory work, which rose significantly after immigration restrictions diminished the possibility of boarders and legislation outlawed home work, also aided in shifting generational relationships (Smith, 1978). In the New World, "[t]he separation of production from the home ... [made] parents ... potentially more dependent on the help of their children" (Smith, p. 219). The change in the locus of work in America, from home to a manufacturing industry, would redefine power relationships between parents and their children, for the contact with people other than those with familial and affinal connections, new cultural perspectives, and new experiences would loosen the ties of kinship which emphasized obligation, support, and control of and for one's own family instead of the American emphasis on the individual and independence from the family of origin.

"Home work" becomes for Rosa, as it had years earlier for Umbertina, the catalyst for self-fulfillment and economic advancement, if only temporarily. Rosa's aging and ailing sister desperately needs a hospital bed, one that Rosa cannot afford with her meager salary. Since Rosa fits the description of the typical Italian matriarch, Domenica, one of her co-workers, suggests that she consider doing a commercial for her nephew Don. Rosa's strong sense of moral responsibility prompts her to take Don's offer and portray "everybody's sweet old grandmother," even though she "feels embarrassed by the public admission of her need for money" and tries masking her private need with a public denial (Gioseffi, p. 22). Subscribing to the cultural mandate of *la bella figura*, she says, "Uma no needa money. Uma save lidda by lidda. But, uma be so glad to meet you nephew!" (Gioseffi, p. 22). Self-fulfillment for Rosa, as it did for Umbertina, comes from meeting family responsibility; and family and financial obligations thrust Rosa, a woman of strong traditions and ultimate reserve, into the public arena of television commercials and monetary profit. The shift in routine brings her to experience the American dream—one almost forgotten, but not quite, for Rosa, who shares Umbertina's indomitable spirit, never let her soul "writhe in the agonies of ambition" or have her "miseries and longings" crush her hopes (Gioseffi, p. 24). Many of the Italian immigrants coming to America in search of a better life were bitterly disillusioned with what they found and sought every opportunity to go back to their homeland. Between the years of both Umbertina's and Rosa's arrival in America (1880–1924), of the nearly "4.5 million Italians who arrived in the United States ... , fewer than half remained" (Mangione and Morreale, p. 159).

The television commercial becomes her ticket out of Red Hook and into the "America [her] family was promised by the ticket salesman who came to [their] village" (Gioseffi, p. 25). Ticket salesmen, labor recruiters, and steamship agents were often described as "merchants of human flesh" (Mangione and Morreale, p. 71). Agents, some unscrupulous, would create visions of an America "paved with streets of gold," a paradisaical oasis from the backbreaking work in their hometown where all they could hope for was a short reprieve from certain poverty, but the mirage of the American dream that few Italian immigrants would ever experience would soon vanish upon their arrival in the New World. On her trip to Morristown, where she would film the commercial, Rosa sees the trees of "Apulia's olive groves" and the "[b]lue sky" *della patria sua* (Gioseffi, p. 25). She says, "Dis isa America uma dream when um holda my Mamma's skirt ona da cold oceana!" (Gioseffi, p. 25). Her domestic role as the traditional Italian matriarch, a role which usually limits the woman's potential and confines her to the private sphere of the home, becomes not only the source of her business venture but the force behind its success. The commercial takes Rosa into the public arena of the media as the head of household and chief breadwinner responsible for her family's well-being. More importantly, domestic life makes the American dream come alive for Rosa. In Morristown, she is surrounded by the glory of green pastures, easy living, and good food. With absolute satisfaction, she says, "At lasta, uma see America ina my family's dreams" (Gioseffi, pp. 25–6).

Unlike Umbertina, who becomes a major staple in the Cato community, creating her own personal and financial success and empowering herself, Rosa capitalizes on an opportunity provided for her, and her empowerment is mediated and temporary. In fact, once the filming of the commercial is over, she returns to the private sphere of the home where her sister's wheezing and a "half-eaten piece of anisette toast" reminds her that dreams are just fanciful flights from reality (Gioseffi, p. 28). Nonetheless, from the commercial, she will make more than she "make[s] in a month at the factory" (Gioseffi, p. 23), and her earnings will contribute to the financial and physical well-being of *la famiglia*. The new hospital bed will make life easier for both Rosa and her sister, and it will give Rosa a sense of personal fulfillment, for, like Umbertina, meeting her familial responsibilities is synonymous with self-fulfillment. Rosa and Umbertina take domestic life and turn it into an opportunity to realize the American dream which for so many other immigrants remained just a dream; and even though Rosa sees "the food of her dreams behind the house of her dreams shoveled into a huge plastic mouth" (Gioseffi, p. 27), finally, she, like Umbertina, triumphs, though neither of them receives any public recognition for their accomplishments, big and small. Umbertina and Rosa succeed in defining themselves as active agents, rather than passive victims of their gender and ethnicity, empower themselves through personal and collective organization, and transform the dependent and subservient relationship of family and domestic life into ethnic self-definition, financial success, and personal fulfillment.

Notes

1 See *From Sacred to Secular* for a discussion of Umbertina's replacement of religious values with the more material ones of capitalism in hopes of attaining the American dream (Bonomo Albright, 1995).

2 Many Italian immigrants who traveled to America fully intended to return to their native land. Sociologists call these immigrant travelers "sojourners." The sojourner phenomenon delayed their full integration into and acceptance of American life and placed them at a disadvantage with regard to other immigrant groups (Alba, 1996).

3 Most Italian families provided a dowry (*il corredo*) of one kind or another for their daughters. Even the poorest families provided a basic trousseau of embroidered and crocheted linens. In the past, a substantial dowry became an attractive commodity for a

prospective husband and allowed the young woman to "marry well" (La Ruffa, 1988; Cellini, 1978). As Leo Cellini notes, "emigration [was] an asset to marriageability" (p. 283). A woman offering a chance to immigrate to America or remain on American soil became perhaps even more attractive than a substantial dowry for a man looking to "settle down."

4   According to *Rodale's Illustrated Encyclopedia of Herbs*, rosemary symbolizes love, friendship, and remembrance, but, more importantly, it signifies that a woman heads the household (1987, pp. 428–9). Therefore, Umbertina's taking of the rosemary plant on her voyage foreshadows her eventual displacement of Serafino as head of household. The Longobardi family became one of the thousands who made the journey to America. "At the end of the 1870s, an annual average of 117,596 Italians, chiefly farm workers, emigrated to other nations" (Mangione and Morreale, p. 69). 307, 309 immigrants came to America between the years 1881–90 (Nelli, p. 41).

5   At the end of the nineteenth century, American banking institutions did not cultivate an immigrant clientele; therefore, a number of Italians opened exchange offices and small banks in New York's Italian enclaves. Inevitably, the lack of a federally secured and centralized system led to abuses and bankruptcy, resulting in the loss of the life savings of many an immigrant family who had trusted one of their own (Federal Writers' Project, 1938).

6   Anna Giordani, a nurse for the Board of Health's Italian Department in the novel, represents the second-generation Italian, usually better educated and financially secure, who dedicated himself/herself to the service of others. Social workers found the resignation with which many of their political and spiritual brethren accepted the employment, housing, and educational conditions perplexing and sought to "civilize" the immigrants. The immigrants, in turn, disliked the force and patronizing spirit with which these people implemented change. As Alberto Pecorini notes, "Social workers [were] well-intentioned but they for[got] that they were dealing with human beings" (1974, p. 192).

7   L. J. Iorizzo's study of credit reports at Harvard University's R.G. Dun Collection found that in the nineteenth century only 7 per cent of all merchants were Italian American women (1994, p. 278).

8   Although many Italian immigrants eventually complied with compulsory-education laws, many, out of economic need and insecurity, withdrew their children from school as soon as they reached the legal working age, some even sooner, and put them to work (Federal, 1938; Cordasco and Bucchioni, 1974). Humbert Nelli notes that from 1899 to 1910, Italians "had among the highest illiteracy rate of all the Southern- and Eastern-European groups (p. 146). More recently, a 1990 CUNY study showed that Italians had the third-highest dropout rate, with 15.5 of Italian Americans in the United States having less than an eighth-grade education (Lee, p. B4). The study indicates that many Italians still believe that the benefits of getting a good education do not outweigh those of working and earning money.

9   Umbertina's control of the finances extended outside of her immediate family. When her older boys married, they came to live with their wives under her roof where she "doled out" and "supervised" the money they earned (Barolini, p. 110). It was not uncommon for the Italian matriarch to maintain control of her children, and sometimes even their finances, after they had reached adulthood and married and had children of their own.

10 For a discussion of ethnic marketing and advertising, see *Mammas, Papas, Traditions, and Secrets: The Marketing of Italian Americans* (Mitrano and Mitrano, 1996).

11 Over one million Italians emigrated to America between 1911 and 1920; 80 per cent were from Southern Italy, and nearly 85 per cent were men with a background in agricultural labor (Nelli, pp. 41–2).

12 Even after the Passenger Act of 1902 and several investigations into the inhuman conditions in which these immigrants were forced to travel, steerage passage was still

one of the dreaded elements of trans-Atlantic emigration, what Mangione and Morreale call *la via dolorosa*. Men, women, and children traveled literally next to the steering equipment below the ship's water line in overcrowded and unsanitary conditions (pp. 103–4; Cordasco and Bucchioni, 1974).

13 Granted, the commercial in which Rosa participates reinforces certain stereotypes that impede what Richard Alba (1985) calls the "regeneration" and "transformation" of Italian American identity and perpetuates visual and aural imagery that affect the public opinion of and reaction to Italian Americans (Mitrano and Mitrano, 1994); however, a discussion of the media's impact on the definition of Italian American identity goes beyond the confines of this chapter.

References

Alba, R.D. (1985). *Italian Americans: Twilight of Ethnicity*. Englewood Cliffs, NJ: Prentice-Hall.
—— (1996). Italian Americans: A Century of Ethnic Change. In S. Pedraza, and R.G. Rumbaut (Eds), *Origins and Destinies: Immigration, Race, and Ethnicity in America* (pp. 172–81). Belmont, CA: Wadsworth.

Albright, B.C. (1995). From Sacred to Secular in *Umbertina* and *A Piece of Earth*. *MELUS*, 20 (2), 93–103.

Anker, L. (1993). Immigrant Voices from the Federal Writers Project: The Connecticut Ethnic Survey, 1937–1940. In J. Gilbert, A. Gilman, D.M. Scott, and J.W. Scott (Eds), *The Mythmaking Frame of Mind* (pp. 270–302). Belmont, CA: Wadsworth.

Barolini, H. (1979). *Umbertina*. New York: Bantam.

Cellini, L. (1978). Emigration, the Italian Family, and Changing Roles. In B.B. Caroli, R.F. Harney, and L.F. Tomasi (Eds), *The Italian Immigrant Woman in North America* (pp. 273–87). Toronto: The Multicultural History Society of Toronto.

Cohen, M. (1977). Italian-American Women in New York City, 1900–1950: Work and School. In M. Cantor, and B. Laurie (Eds), *Class, Sex, and the Woman Worker* (pp. 120–43). Westport, CT: Greenwood.

Cordasco, F., and Bucchioni, E. (1974). *The Italians: Social Backgrounds of an American Group*. Clifton, NJ: Augustus M. Kelley Publishers.

Federal Writers' Project. (1938). *The Italians of New York*. New York: Random House.

Fisher, H. (1992). *Anatomy of Love*. New York: Norton.

Foster, G. (1960). *Culture and Conquest*. Chicago: Quadrangle Books.

Gabaccia, D.R. (1984). *From Sicily to Elizabeth Street*. Albany: State University of New York Press.

Gardaphe, F.L. (1996). *Italian Signs, American Streets*. Durham: Duke University Press.

Gioseffi, D. (1991). Rosa in Television Land. In A.J. Tamburri, P.A. Giordano, and F.L. Gardaphe (Eds), *From the Margin: Writings in Italian Americana* (pp. 20–8). Indiana: Purdue University Press.

Kowalchik, C., and Hylton, W.H. (Eds). (1987). *Rodale's Illustrated Encyclopedia of Herbs*. Pennsylvania: Rodale Press.

Iorizzo, L.J. (1994). Research Note on the R.G. Dun Collection, Baker Library. *Italian Americana*, 12 (2), 278–80.

Johnson. C.L. (1978). The Maternal Role in the Contemporary Italian-American Family. In B.B. Caroli, R.F. Harney, and L.F. Tomasi (Eds), *The Italian Immigrant Woman in North America* (pp. 234–44). Toronto: The Multicultural History Society of Ontario.

La Ruffa, A.L. (1988). *Monte Carmelo*. New York: Gordon and Breach.

Lee, F.R. (1990, May 1). 20% Dropout Rate Found For Italian Americans. *The New York Times*, p. B4.

Mangione, J., and Morreale, B. (1992). *La Storia: Five Centuries of the Italian American Experience*. New York: Harper Collins.

Mitrano, J.R., and Mitrano, J.G. (1996). Mammas, Papas, Traditions, and Secrets: The Marketing of Italian Americans. In M.J. Bona, and A.J. Tamburri (Eds), *Through the Looking Glass: Italian and Italian/American Images in the Media* (pp. 71–84). Staten Island, NY: American Italian Historical Association.

Nelli, H.S. (1983). *From Immigrants to Ethnics: The Italian Americans*. New York: Oxford University Press.

Odencrantz, L.C. (1919). *Italian Women in Industry*. New York: Russell Sage Foundation.

Pecorini, A. (1974). The Italian in America, 1891–1914. In C. Cordasco, and E. Bucchioni (Eds), *The Italians: Social Backgrounds of an American Group* (pp. 167–86). Clifton, NJ: Augustus M. Kelley Publishers.

Smith, J.E. (1978). Italian Mothers, American Daughters: Changes in Work and Family Roles. In B.B. Caroli, R.F. Harney, and L.F. Tomasi (Eds), *The Italian Immigrant Woman in North America* (pp. 206–21). Toronto: The Multicultural History Society of Ontario.

Tamburri, A.J. (1991). *Umbertina*: The Italian/American Woman's Experience. In A.J. Tamburri, P.A. Giordano, and F.L. Gardaphe (Eds), *From the Margin: Writings in Italian Americana* (pp. 357–73). Indiana: Purdue University Press.

Tiffany, S. W. (1979). Introduction: Theoretical Issues in the Anthropological Study of Women. In S.W. Tiffany (Ed.), *Women and Society: An Anthropological Reader* (pp. 1–35). Montreal, Canada: Eden Press Women's Publications.

Vecchio, D. (1995). Connecting Spheres: Women's Work and Women's Lives in Milwaukee's Italian Third Ward. *Italian Americana*, 13 (2), 217–26.

Yans-McLaughlin, V. (1977). A Flexible Tradition: South Italian Immigrants Confront a New Work Experience. In R.L. Ehrlich (Ed.), *Immigrants in Industrial America 1850–1920* (pp. 67–84). Charlottesville, VA: University Press of Virginia.

—— (1977). Italian Women and Work: Experience and Perception. In M. Cantor, and B. Laurie (Eds), *Class, Sex, and the Woman Worker* (pp. 101–19). Westport, CT: Greenwood.

Part II

Anthropology, ritual and literature

Chapter 4

Rituals to cope with change in women's lives

Judith Minty's *Dancing the Fault*

Janet Ruth Heller

In *Dancing the Fault*, a book of concise poems published in 1991, Native American writer Judith Minty focuses on the theme of change, especially changes in family relationships as the children grow up and the parents age. These changes create dichotomies and tension, which require creativity to resolve. She describes rituals that her family and friends have evolved to cope with life's challenges and to build a bridge between human consciousness and nature. The images in *Dancing the Fault* often derive from Native American beliefs about the interpenetration of the human and natural worlds. I will draw on current anthropological approaches to ritual to illuminate Minty's poems.

Anthopologist David I. Kertzer (1988) has defined ritual as "action wrapped in a web of symbolism" (p. 9). This observation applies to Minty's poems, which embed rituals in a matrix of repeated symbols, such as rivers, birds, and winter landscapes. While rituals are often "formal, patterned, and stereotyped public performances" (Evans, 1996, p. 1120), individuals can also generate their own informal ceremonies. Minty describes many informal rites, especially those of her family. Kertzer believes that rituals and other symbols help to "define the individual's sense of self" and also express our society's "emotionally charged interdependence" (pp. 6, 9). He does not distinguish between religious and secular rituals. Researchers and theorists like Max Gluckman and Victor W. Turner have emphasized that ritual is "a dynamic process—symbolically, spatially, and temporally reorganizing society and lived experience" (Evans, p. 1121). Rituals are often attempts to increase human power over the environment, to impose order on the chaos of everyday life. Turner (1982) argues that rituals are important in healing social and psychological disruption in large and small groups. He believes that, in modern societies, symbolic means of redressing crises have "moved out of the domains of law and religion into those of the various arts" (p. 11). In Minty's family, rituals and the act of writing poetry ease the pain of daughters' leaving home, husband and wife being separated by jobs in different states, and the aging process. Yet, according to Turner, rituals also have playful, anti-structural aspects. These activities include ceremonial sports, masks, clowning, carnivals, trickster tales, and word games. Such ceremonies resemble art in mingling order and earnest work with the novelty and volatility of creative play. *Dancing the Fault* recognizes the similarity between the process of writing poetry and the generation of new rituals. Both may result in what Turner calls "unprecedented insights and even ... new symbols and meanings" (p. 79). Both have a transformative power and help humans to cope with life crises.

Minty's poems focus on Michigan landscapes and the evolution of individual and family rituals. She told the editors of *Contemporary Authors*, "I speak of my region, the land, and the people who are important to me. Water is a mystic power, and certain animals, the moon and sun, take part in the ritual" (Kinsman, 1975, p. 378). Minty is also interested in psychological issues, especially those raised by close friendships and family ties. "My concerns involve attempting to bridge the conscious [and the] unconscious and to articulate the unity between two worlds: the human, and what we call 'the natural world'" (Straub, 1987, p. 303). She often juxtaposes a change of seasons with events in a person's life. Richmond Lattimore (1974) has called her work "intensely personal" (p. 468), but Minty's compelling themes like parent/child relationships, the place of humans in nature, and the connection between the conscious and the unconscious give her poems universal appeal.

The title *Dancing the Fault* refers to the San Andreas Fault and the poet's splitting her time between her teaching job in California and her heartland home in Michigan. Minty has danced different faults ever since her childhood when her family spent the school year in Detroit and summers in the North Woods of Michigan. Being part Native American (her maternal grandfather was a Mohawk) has also forced her to mediate between that heritage and her paternal Finnish roots. In an interview with Karen Carlton (1985), Minty reveals, "There has been that awareness and investigation of migration, of splitting the self, of duality, ever since the beginning" (p. 97). Carlton sees Minty as a "wanderer" in her life and poetry (pp. 96, 98–9). Minty herself stresses that life requires adaptation to change and frequent movement. She likes lakes and rivers because of their "constant motion" (p. 99). Her appointments as a visiting professor and poet-in-residence at the University of Oregon, Syracuse University in New York, the University of California, Santa Cruz, and elsewhere have left her feeling "uprooted" from her midwestern heartland. Yet her uprootedness gives her a fresh perspective on her surroundings: "the eye clear in new air" ("Six Poems for Nine Crows," *Dancing the Fault*, p. 55). In many ways, modern civilization requires Americans to be wanderers and to constantly adjust to dualities and new environments, so this theme is universal.

Though Minty was not raised in the Native American tradition, she has made an effort as an adult to understand Indian beliefs and legends. The North Woods of Michigan where she has lived for part of the year since her childhood "was originally Ottawa/Iroquois/Chippewa land. Because I spent so much time there, I began to learn the Indian history of the region." She attributes her feeling of closeness to animals like deer and bear to this heritage ("An Interview with Judith Minty," 1981, pp. 104–5; see also "The Nature of Writing," 1996, p. 5).

Minty begins *Dancing the Fault* with a poem about her relationship with her own father, "Meeting My Father at the River." She recalls her father's last fishing trip and his pleasure when she witnesses his catching a trout. The words exchanged between the father and daughter here are simple but convey respect and ease. "He calls, 'I got one!'" and she responds in kind: "'Good one,' I cry, and wave." Reading the poem, one senses that this warm father–daughter interaction during a fishing expedition has been repeated often: Minty describes her father as he "leans with grace in hip boots/ for the ritual of netting,/ stepping sure as a young man again" (p. 5). Words like "again" and, especially, "ritual" emphasize the frequency of these actions and the quasi-sacred nature of the parent–child bond. The poem also captures a moment when an older person transcends time, a frequent theme in *Dancing the Fault*. In "Easter Saturday," Minty returns to the fishing ritual by recounting another trip, but with her lover this time. While the title and the act of fishing emphasize a Christian framework, the poem itself celebrates a natural ceremony.[1] Minty was raised as a Roman Catholic, but she has drifted away from that tradition. The lover acts more like a teacher than the father did, pointing out the hidden fish to his companion: the trout are hard to detect because they

> drift below the surface, brown
> shadows over moss—his voice, his arm
> guiding so I could see too.

This fishing poem has more touching in it than the one about her father. The two lovers touch, the wind "skimmed the water like a hand passing" (p. 20), and after he has caught several trout, she holds them appreciatively in her hands before she cooks them. This ritual of fishing, teaching, touching, and eating binds the lovers on a Christian holiday and is clearly as significant for them as any church service. The lovers' informal secular ritual contains many of the elements of a public Christian service, including teaching and eating, but embeds them in a personal celebration.

Such natural rituals link many of the poems in *Dancing the Fault*. A large number of poems focus on Minty's bonds to her two daughters, Lora and Ann. In "Ironing," Minty irons her daughter's floral blouse, which she has cleaned after a bloody car accident. While her daughter sleeps in the hospital, Minty recalls the scene of the accident, with shattered glass everywhere. She compares her woman's act of ironing to the movement of tree branches in a wind. Both actions are natural responses to stress, attempts to re-establish order in a chaotic world. Similarly, in "Celebrating the Mass," Minty and her teenaged daughter cope with the accident by creating their own ritual: the mother braids her daughter's hair into cornrows.[2] Feeling helpless in the hospital, they empower themselves by this braiding, which links them to countless "other mothers who have done this" in rural areas and big cities after their chores are done. The act of touching, so important to Minty's poetry, enables the mother and injured child to "learn each other again" (p. 19). Note that the title refers to a Catholic ritual, but the poem focuses on a natural sacrament. Again, the writer emphasizes a movement away from what Evans has termed "stereotyped public performances" toward private, flexible, familial ceremonies.

The middle section of *Dancing the Fault* consists of seventeen poems entitled "Letters to My Daughters." The act of letter writing is another important ritual for Minty. The poem/letters enable her to communicate with her children on a deeper and more archetypal level than most conversations. They enable her to discuss the pain of loss and change in the comforting framework of art, which captures moments of insight and, through rhythm and sounds, transforms difficult experiences into beauty. The poems also seek to heal friction and reconcile differences between the mother and her daughters. Thus, "Letters to My Daughters" has the therapeutic function (see Turner, 1982) of ritual.

Many of these poem/letters emphasize family rituals that have grown out of love and intimacy. For example, in the fourth letter, Minty describes the ritual of daughters bringing flowers to their mothers. Minty's own mother made her return and apologize for picking a neighbor's pansies. However, Minty portrays herself as more sympathetic to her two daughters when they bring her flowers. She whimsically eats the yellow violet that the older girl has found, and she puts the younger girl's scentless daisies in a vase and pretends to smell them. These responses are typical of the playful, anti-structural aspects of ritual that Turner analyzes. Minty emphasizes that it is important to appreciate a child's effort to "honor" a mother with flowers and "never ask ... where you picked them" (p. 28). Another mother–daughter ritual is cooking, celebrated by Minty in the fourteenth letter. She personifies the kitchen, which "sings with the warmth of our making." The kitchen is not just a place for cooking but also for important conversations among the women and other key activities, such as reading or writing letters. Minty's husband, understanding how central the kitchen is to the women's lives, has constructed a bird feeder and purposely "planted it outside [the] kitchen window," where the poet watches juncos and a loving male and female cardinal (p. 38). Thus, even the natural world can enter the family kitchen. Note that the birds' intimacy resembles that of the humans. Another family ritual is naming pets. In the fifth letter, Minty cares for the old dog and cat during the winter and remembers her daughters' naming them when the children and animals were young. As a new act of naming, one of the daughters "has called me by my first name" (p. 29). By referring to her mother as "Judith," the daughter subtly changes their relationship.

Still other family rituals are unconscious imitations of our ancestors. In the sixteenth of the "Letters to My Daughters," Minty focuses on a visit by her parents to their home. While three generations of women sit together indoors, she notices that her daughter's gestures resemble those of the grandmother. The poet yearns to know what her mother was like as a girl and realizes that the shared gestures give hints of the woman's mystery:

> In this straining, I grow lonely for the girl
> locked inside my mother, the one you and I never met,
> except in these feathery hands of ours, or how we walk
> across a room, or sleep curled to the fabric of our men. (p. 40)

The inheritance here is both simple and profound, including birdlike movements and commitment to heterosexual relationships. Minty may also be curious about the Mohawk heritage on her mother's side of the family, as well as want to know her mother at a younger age.

Kertzer (1988) points out that, in some societies, "clans and lineages were themselves defined in terms of common ritual practices" (p. 18). This is clearly the case for the three generations of women in the sixteenth of the "Letters to My Daughters." According to Kertzer, rites "give meaning to our world in part by linking the past to the present and the present to the future." Furthermore, ritual gives us "a sense of continuity" by identifying underlying patterns (Kertzer, pp. 9–10).

A major change in the family occurs when Minty's older daughter leaves for college in Boston. But the mother and child create a ritual for this, too: in the sixth of the "Letters to My Daughters," Minty drives her eldest from Michigan to her new city. This new separation has replaced Native American puberty rites involving hunting, vigils, and visions. Leaving home for college, like earlier separation rituals, has all the unpredictability and potential for exploring "wish, desire, possibility" that Turner (1982) identifies in more primitive liminal experiences (pp. 82–3). As usual, Minty respects her child's right to choose a different kind of life. The girl cries, "No more wilderness," and desires "roots far away/ as an ocean." Though the mother loves the Michigan wilderness, she helps her daughter "transplant" herself. The poem's imagery, however, undercuts the child's attempt to escape wilderness: Minty portrays the daughter as a plant that is "pruning" itself away from the family and wants to "root" itself elsewhere. So the "transplanted" child takes her wilderness with her, unaware. Depressed after leaving her daughter in Boston, Minty drives home alone, imagining that the French Revolution's guillotine has severed her hand (the child) from her arm (p. 30). This poem fits Turner's pattern of people using rituals when agreeing to differ and separate (p. 10).

On a visit to her daughter, Minty listens to the male law students at a nearby table in a Boston restaurant. She worries that her daughter will marry someone like these men, who are too far away from nature and manual labor to make good husbands and fathers. The eleventh of the "Letters to My Daughters" articulates these unspoken fears.

> Their hands, I want to tell you. Beware of hands
> too pale and soft. These hands have forgotten
> the bark of trees. They have never sanded wood to its skin,
> never felt rope slide across the palm. These fingers
> have never reached into the earth, never touched
> the heart of a deer. (p. 35)

Such citified men do not understand life's essence because they are out of touch with natural experiences and removed from nature. Activities like woodworking, gardening, and hunting serve as the raw material for the evolution of ceremonies that bind a loving family.

One major theme of these poems is parents' dreams for their children. In the first letter, Minty recalls her great-grandfather's wish "that his son/ would be an engineer," in contrast to his own job as a blacksmith. In the next generations, we find even more refinement: both Minty and her father enjoy playing the violin. However, Minty has avoided pushing her own daughters. The poem ends, "[W]e never spoke of dreams" (p. 25). When she does express an ambition for her children, it is a more general desire that they live life to the fullest. For example, the second letter urges her daughters not to be afraid to follow strange gypsy men, whose "fire" (p. 26) represents their passion. Some of these letters emphasize the contrast between our self-image and reality. Minty describes her fantasy: "I still think of myself as young./ I am still the child." She imagines herself a slim teenager in her hometown. However, the reality is that she is a middle-aged woman living elsewhere and a parent with a different body: "Now I grow fat and my eyes are wrong" (p. 27). Yet she still experiences the excitement of a younger woman when she hears about sex crimes. This poem questions our assumptions about age by pointing out that our mental and emotional age may differ markedly from our body's age. Like her father in "Meeting My Father at the River," Judith Minty transcends time for a moment here.

Minty often uses nature imagery to reflect changes in the human sphere. This interpenetration of the human and natural worlds may arise from her Native American heritage. Basil Johnston (1987) points out that Native Americans "gained a reverence for the mystery of life which animated all things" (p. vii). According to Robert E. Ritzenthaler and Pat Ritzenthaler (1983), "The world of the Woodland Indian was filled with a host of spirits (*manido*; plural *manidog*), which inhabited trees, plants, birds, animals, and cosmic phenomena" (p. 85). Furthermore, many Native Americans believe that these spirits have "intelligence, emotions, and free will comparable to those of man" (Driver, 1961, p. 480). George and Louise Spindler (1977) argue that boundaries between people and nature dissolve in many Native American traditions. "For the Menomini the separation between mind and body, man and animal, spiritual forces and material forces, natural and supernatural is absent in their framework of belief and rationality" (p. 412). Thus, Native Americans consider their visions to be actual occurrences. Young people were often sent out on vision quests to connect themselves to sources of natural and supernatural power. Judith Minty's poems reflect her own vision quest to understand the mysteries of modern life.

Furthermore, Minty tries to help her readers to re-connect with nature. In the Foreword to *Yellow Dog Journal* (1991), Deena Metzger describes taking a walk in the woods with her friend and fellow poet.

> When Judith Minty walks in the woods she meets the woods on its [sic] own terms. Consequently, the woods are in her and she is in them; she allows herself to become part of the mud, the light, the wind, and the bear.

According to Metzger, Minty's poems "teach us how to enter the woods. They teach us that the woods are a sacred world from which we have exiled ourselves and into which we may sometimes return." To re-enter the natural world, we need to share Minty's "awareness and ... open heart." These are traits that the poet fosters in her readers.

Because Minty attempts to break down the barriers between people and their environment, personification of nature is frequent in *Dancing the Fault*. For example, during a thunderstorm, "trees shake their fists at the lake" and the cool wind comforts the speaker like a parent or grandmother: "a breath/ on my skin, the hand passing over my forehead" ("The Cottage Poems: Lake Michigan," Part 2—The Storm, p. 46). Migrating monarch butterflies "tremble against shore/ like children tearing away" ("The Cottage Poems: Lake Michigan," Part 3—Monarchs, p. 47). Often, nature expresses the moods and emotions of the female persona. In "Waves," the speaker and the lake move from stillness to restlessness. The lake begins with "hands/ still as a woman waiting," but the next day the lake "stirs, shakes/ white froths of hair./ I feel the mood of this stretching,/ this swinging of arms" ("The Cottage Poems," Part 4, p. 48). Similarly, after a rainstorm the persona and various birds emerge from a sleeplike state: "We are all surfacing from dream,/ shaking our heads" ("The Mount Pleasant Journal," p. 52). Sometimes Minty transforms one element of nature into another—and back again. In "Six Poems for Nine Crows," the speaker watches as "sparrows drift from the maple/ like brown leaves," and later a maple tree caught in storm winds "flaps its wings and turns wild" (pp. 55–6). Minty's images blur the distinction between what is animate and inanimate because she emphasizes the spirit in all of nature. For example, the third section of "A Sense of Place" narrates her encounter with a bear when she returns to the Yellow Dog River where she fished with her father:

> When the bear came to me, I already knew
> that trees walk at night, that the river speaks,
> and the wind knows everything. (p. 69)

The world of *Dancing the Fault* is in constant flux, due to the peripatetic movements of the central character, the transforming powers of her imagination, and the *manidog* present in all things.

The interpenetration of the human and the natural world is also evident in the prose poem "Trying to Remember." Here, Minty refers to the different seasons of the year to interweave three themes: the passage of time in a friendship between two women, male–female passion for two lovers, and memories of sitting in her grandmother's lap as a child. These memories are also linked by the ritual act of touching: the speaker in the poem holds her friend's letter in her hand, she touches her lover's hand while they eat and remembers their intercourse ("hands fluttering, spiralling cries"), the first snow of the year falls on her face, and her grandmother's loving "fingers traced lacy patterns on my skin" (pp. 12–15). Touching is an important means of communion in *Dancing the Fault*. The first snowfall seems to represent middle age, which the two friends are approaching. Another unifying device in the poem is respect for one's ancestors: both the friend and the lover tell the persona their grandmothers' pronouncements about the first snowfall and the need to honor bread, respectively. As she writes her poem, Minty's persona tries to recall her own grandmother's words on that summer day long ago. This is another theme in *Dancing the Fault*: the desire to recover the past, to communicate with people remote in time or space.

A related theme is the persona's quest to understand the language of the natural world. The epigraph of "The Gray Whale" emphasizes the belief that "certain species of whales could communicate across hemispheres" (p. 64) in past centuries. The poem ends by focusing on five whales like "dancers leaping in unison" who "touch" one another and "sigh" in their own language. But the human observers cannot comprehend this gamboling: "All this we've lost./ All this forgotten" (Part 3— Following by Boat, p. 66). While many people may consider the natural world remote from human spheres, Minty repeatedly tries to connect with landscapes, animals, and birds and mourns when she is unable to understand or merge with their *manidog*.

Another poem that uses natural images to symbolize change is the last of the "Letters to My Daughters," letter seventeen. As usual, the poet portrays her children as plants. Minty tries to explain to herself and her daughters why it is so painful to leave the home where the girls "blossomed to women." She warns her children to remember, "Nothing remains as it was. If you know this, you can/ begin again, with pure joy in the uprooting" (p. 41). The ritual of packing boxes to move from one home to another helps the poet to accept change and to understand that change is an essential part of life, just as plants may be "uprooted."

At times, the persona ritually merges with nature. This could be due to the influence of Native American legends, which are "peopled by anthropomorphic animals, birds, and fish, creatures that became the totems of various clans" (Ritzenthaler and Ritzenthaler, 1983, p. 129). For example, Minty's prose poem "Purple Finches" ends, "She puts her fingers to the glass and enters their rhythm. She steps inside their color" (p. 21). This is a moment of insight when the poet and the birds merge in a mystical union. Similarly, the mother in "Ironing" repeats "I am a tree" twice. In California, three human observers, including the poet, merge with a surfacing gray whale: "the four of us joined each time in the air" ("The Gray Whale," Part 2—The Fisherman Calling, p. 65). The fisherman in this poem, like Minty's lover in "Easter Saturday," teaches the less experienced women about the natural world by helping them to see the whale. More midwestern bird imagery dominates the eighth of the "Letters to My Daughters," in which Minty compares herself to the mother robin outside the kitchen window, who tirelessly protects and feeds her babies but knows when to leave the nest and allow her children to mature on their own. Minty realizes that, like the robin, she must respect her college daughters' new independence. However, unlike the robins, her daughters have moments of regression, which Minty also respects.

> Summer, and you two here. Boarders
> who sleep till noon while I take your messages
> and wash your empty glasses and stack your clothes
> and mutter and scratch for time at my desk. (p. 32)

The mother/daughter relationship has grown more remote: the girls seem like "boarders." But Minty accepts this paradoxical closeness and simultaneous separation.

A more unusual merger of woman and nature occurs in the thirteenth of the "Letters to My Daughters." Minty remembers her father's story about wolves threatening a human family's home during a blizzard. But she tells her daughters a different tale about women who allow the wolf to enter them.

> We never know how to send it away
> so we take it in, in here, into this body, this cage.
> And when the fire dwindles, when the door flies open,
> we rush toward the moon. Fur bristling on our shoulders,
> we send shrill cries out through the night. (p. 37)

Instead of fighting the wolves or cowering in fear of them, the women in this poem merge with the beasts, defying the standard boundaries, acknowledging the wildness within themselves.[3] This union may be influenced by Native American legends about Wenebojo and a pack of wolves who perform magic and give him food. One of the wolves becomes his younger brother (see Ritzenthaler and Ritzenthaler, 1983, pp. 129–31). Turner (1982) insists, "There is often some element of risk or danger in the atmosphere of living ritual. And something numinous" (p. 95). The danger of such rites is clear in Minty's poem. In an interview with Karen Carlton, Minty explains that one needs to cope with a painful life experience like the death of a relative by

> transform[ing] it into animals and Aztec goddesses. All of life is transformation. If we can go back and forth, into and out of the earth, into the sea to join with whales, then we've done a better job of getting through than we might have otherwise. (p. 98)

This ability to merge with what frightens and dismays us enables us to both accept the painful reality and to transcend it with our imagination.

Though Minty taught for years at Humboldt State University in California, imagery of the midwest dominates these poems. A recurring theme is the transition from fierce midwestern winters to the warmth of spring. For example, "Snow in April" contrasts the optimistic view of young people that spring has come to stay with the older generation's foreboding that winter may return. Although the "Sons and daughters act smug," their parents' predictions are fulfilled: "But the old ones are restless. / They tell the tales over again, / even as the ground turns white" (p. 22). The older generation's pessimism about snow represents a more knowledgeable perspective on life in general: perfection rarely lasts, and spring has the unpredictability of any liminal experience.

Throughout *Dancing the Fault* Minty refers to her ritual of collecting bird feathers (see "The Mount Pleasant Journal," p. 54 and "Six Poems for Nine Crows," p. 55).

She seems to feel a special kinship with these winged creatures that may have roots in her Native American heritage or in the Romantic poems of Shelley and Keats. Traditionally, poets have identified with birds because, like writers, they create songs. When Minty and her friend exchange letters, she compares this to the actions of birds: "Our words spin over trees, trill in strands, a sparrow's song" ("Trying to Remember," p. 12). Minty preserves this theme in the opening stanza of "Meditation on Friendship: Driving to the Baths in a Blizzard with Deena":

> Once, what left our hands made birdsongs:
> the voice of stones, a song like a loon's
> skimming the frozen pond.
> In that motion, our arms were wings.
> We carried the notes inside. (p. 60)

In contrast, "Hawk" describes her superstitious reaction to finding a "Dead hawk outside my bedroom window. / ... / I laid low for three days, / didn't leave the house." But even here, the poet merges with the ominous bird: she takes for her own the hawk's "tail feathers and feet" and notes the resemblance between her clenched hand and the bird's claws (p. 67).

Minty also intertwines the themes of infertility and adoption with analogies to nature. In the tenth of her "Letters to My Daughters," she compares her adoption of her older daughter to her younger child's dreams that the sprouts in her first garden have suddenly matured and produced ripened fruit, ready to harvest. The adopted child is the parents' "dream," and the parents learn to accept the fact that their sudden "harvest" is "the child not of our own mating" (p. 34). They learn this through another ritual: waking at night and trying to find the crying baby in their bed, though they know she is in a downstairs room. In the fifteenth letter, Minty recalls how she "cried for babies" during the winter. Now her children, who have left home, are old enough to be mothers. As part of her yearly ritual, she searches for signs of spring in the Michigan woods and finds them in the lowly skunk cabbage, which she personifies.

> I bend to touch the first blooms:
> waxen blossom, shy child folded inside.
> I take in the heat of growth, the perfect circles
> around each flower, and feel the whole earth
> pregnant under my boots, under the stubborn snow. (p. 39)

This poem ends with an image of potential: the entire earth is fertile, though this may be hidden, and she has hope for the future.[4]

Another theme in Dancing the Fault is how Minty copes with being a fairly well-known poet and how this affects her marriage. In the seventh of the "Letters to My Daughters," she sketches a typical day at home, stressing the ritual of waiting for and opening her mail. She receives "two love letters" from younger men. Her husband "pretends disinterest," but she catches him trying to write something for her. Minty ends the poem ironically: her husband really has weak competition because "those young men are only in love with poetry" (p. 31). The fan mail brings excitement to the poet, but the letters are not the center of her life. Similarly, in "Raining All Across the Country," Minty, watching the rain in California, phones her husband back in Michigan, where it is also raining. The cold rain links the couple like a ceremony: "It marries us again." His voice enters her body and "flows like blood to my arms, my legs" (p. 71). Though separated by half a continent, they can still merge and preserve their union.

The volume ends with "Christine, On Her Way to China: An Earthquake Poem," which describes a shopping expedition with a friend in Eureka, California, during an earthquake. Minty writes that she and her friend "knew we danced the fault" (p. 72). The fault here represents all of the dichotomies that Minty explores in *Dancing the Fault*: youth and age, change and stasis, male and female, summer and winter, city and forest, human and animal, European American and Mohawk, California and Michigan. Like Christine, who has traveled from the midwest to California and is about to fly to China, humans and the earth itself are in constant motion. Minty ends the poem with the advice to "make adventure from these briefest shifts and passings" (p. 73). This is consistent with her attitude toward change throughout this book: shifts and losses in life need to be faced as challenges, not as prompts for despair. Every human faces some threatening fault and must learn to "dance" despite the stress and danger.

Notes

1   Native Americans had important fishing rituals that governed how fish were caught, transported, killed, cooked, and eaten. These ceremonies ended with singing and dancing (see Driver, 1961, p. 82).

2   The ritual resembles funeral customs of the Woodland Indians. See Robert E. Ritzenthaler and Pat Ritzenthaler, 1983, p. 40, and Frances Densmore, 1929, p. 73.

3   A similar process occurs in Minty's earlier poems about women merging with bears and wolves in *Yellow Dog Journal* (1991b). See Fall, poem #23 and poem #29, and Spring, poem #25. Shirley Clay Scott (1985) points out, "Desire manifests itself, from her early poems on, in imagery of light or fire and wildness" (p. 93). Scott sees death and desire as inextricably linked in Minty's poems.

4   Marilyn Zorn (1979) argues that this poem likens women to the earth. "Women's power to nurture parallels the earth's and includes growth toward and away from the time of fertility—spring and winter—the complete life cycle" (p. 39). Harold E. Driver (1961) points out that Native Americans often had ceremonies for the first wild plant food of the season, such as berries. While boys had hunting rituals, girls had ceremonies centered around plant products (pp. 83, 85). The fifteenth of the "Letters to My Daughters" may link Minty to these traditions.

References

Carlton, K. (1985). Interview with Judith Minty. In E. Dallman, and M. Friedberg (Eds), *Woman Poet: The Midwest* (pp. 96–9). Reno: Women-in-Literature.

Collier, H. (1985). Judith Minty: Biographical Notes. In E. Dallman and M. Friedberg (Eds), *Woman Poet: The Midwest* (pp. 100–1). Reno: Women-in-Literature.

Dallman, E., and Friedberg, M. (Eds). (1985). *Woman Poet: The Midwest*. Reno: Women-in-Literature.

Densmore, F. (1929). *Chippewa Customs*. Smithsonian Institution Bureau of American Ethnology Bulletin 86. Washington, DC: United States Government Printing Office.

Driver, H.E. (1961). *Indians of North America*. Chicago: The University of Chicago Press.

Evans, E.S. (1996). Ritual. In D. Levinson and M. Ember (Eds), *Encyclopedia of Cultural Anthropology* (vol. 3, pp. 1120–3). New York: Henry Holt.

Johnston, B. (1987). *Ojibway Ceremonies*. Illus. D. Beyer; Toronto: McClelland and Stewart. (Original work published 1982).

Kertzer, D.I. (1988). *Ritual, Politics, and Power*. New Haven and London: Yale University Press.

Kinsman, C.D. (Ed.). (1975). Judith Minty. *Contemporary Authors*. Detroit: Gale Research (vols. 49–52, p. 378).

Lattimore, R. (1974, Autumn). Poetry Chronicle. Includes review of Judith Minty's *Lake Songs and Other Fears*. *The Hudson Review*, 27(3), 460–74.

Metzger, D. (1991). Foreword. *Yellow Dog Journal*. By Judith Minty. Berkeley CA: Parallax Press, 1991. No pagination given. (Original work published 1979).

Minty, J. (1981, Fall). An Interview with Judith Minty. Interview with Karla Hammond. *Hawaii Review*, No. 12, 103–12.

—— (1991a). *Dancing the Fault*. Contemporary Poetry Series. Orlando: University of Central Florida Press.

—— (1991b). *Yellow Dog Journal*. Berkeley CA: Parallax Press. No pagination given. (Original work published 1979).

—— (1996, July 29–August 11). The Nature of Writing. Interview with Marc J. Sheehan. *Capital Times*, pp. 5–6.

Monaghan, P. (1991, September 1). Review of Judith Minty's *Dancing the Fault*. *Booklist*, 23–4.

Ritzenthaler, R.E., and Ritzenthaler, P. (1983). *The Woodland Indians of the Western Great Lakes*. Milwaukee: Milwaukee Public Museum. (Original work published 1970).

Scott, S.C. (1985). *Dancing the Fault*: The Poetry of Judith Minty. In E. Dallman, and M. Friedberg (Eds), *Woman Poet: The Midwest* (pp. 92–5). Reno: Women-in-Literature.

Spindler, G., and Spindler, L. (1977). The Menominee. In G. Spindler and L. Spindler (Eds), *Native North American Cultures: Four Cases* (pp. 361–454). New York: Holt, Rinehart and Winston.

Straub, D.A. (Ed.). (1987). Judith Minty. *Contemporary Authors*. New Revision Series. Detroit: Gale Research (vol. 21, pp. 302–3).

Turner, V.W. (1982). *From Ritual to Theatre: The Human Seriousness of Play*. New York: Performing Arts Journal.

Zorn, M. (1979, Summer). Mother Lore: A Sequence for Daughters: Review of Judith Minty's *Letters to My Daughters*. *Great Lakes Review* 6 (1), 37–9.

Chapter 5

The subversion of ritual in the theatre of Paloma Pedrero

Susan P. Berardini

In *Ritual Theory, Ritual Practice*, Catherine Bell (1992) offers a thorough overview of the literature that has been generated on ritual as performance, and she concludes the following: "[R]itual comes to be seen as performance in the sense of symbolic acts specifically meant to have an impact on an audience and entreat their interpretative appropriation" (p. 42). Similarly, Sally F. Moore and Barbara G. Myerhoff (1977), in their introduction to *Secular Ritual*, allude to the theatrical character of collective rituals, which they define as a dramatic occasion that consists of symbolic behavior with some specific goal (p. 5). Moore and Myerhoff postulate that performance is one of the inherent qualities of ritual, which is "self-consciously 'acted' like a part in a play" (1977, p. 7). In short, the theatricality of ritual derives from the intentional use of the body at some predetermined time and place, and the fact that it is often performed with the purpose of being observed.

Myerhoff (1977) defines ritual as "an act or actions intentionally conducted by a group of people employing one or more symbols in a repetitive, formal, precise, highly stylized fashion" (p. 199). Richard Hornby (1986) notes that in both life and theatre, many types of rituals abound, such as ceremonies, initiations, games, and festivals. These activities are carried out on stage in two ways: either they are executed according to their traditional format, or they are not completed due to some interruption, perversion or corrupt manner in which they are performed. Hornby also notes that while the completed ritual inspires feelings of harmony, peace and happiness in the public, the imperfect ritual leaves one feeling disoriented and anxious due to the sense of discord that results (pp. 49–55).

In the theatre of the contemporary Spanish playwright Paloma Pedrero (b. 1957), uncompleted rituals prevail in the form of collective celebrations, rites of passage, and quasi-ceremonies. Beginning with her first and most controversial play, *La llamada de Lauren* (1984), Pedrero incorporates into her theatre traditions that are an integral part of Spanish collective identity.[1] *La llamada de Lauren* takes place during Carnival, a pre-Lenten festival characterized by people in costume reveling in the streets. In *El Carnaval*, Julio Caro Baroja (1979a) accurately summarizes the atmosphere of this celebration: "Romper el orden social, violentar al cuerpo, abandonar la propia personalidad equilibrada y hundirse en una especie de subconsciente colectivo. ¿Hay algo más dionisíaco en esencia?" ("Breaking social order, forcing the body, abandoning one's own balanced personality and sinking into a sort of collective subconscious. Is there anything more dionysian in essence?) (p. 146). [2] Carnival is a sensual event that consists of three days of festivities, disorder and social disruption. This festival is known above all for the tradition of dressing in costume, and Pedrero begins *La llamada de Lauren* with an elaboration of this ritual aspect. In the opening scene we see Pedro transform himself into the image of Lauren Bacall. His costume is complete with sexy lingerie, a seductive dress, stockings, high heels, make-up, a wig and a cotton-enhanced bustline. Pedro proposes that his wife Rosa dress as Humphrey Bogart, and the sexual inversion of the couple reflects yet another typical feature of Carnival. As Caró Baroja observes, "La más clásica inversión propia del Carnaval es la del hombre que se disfraza de mujer y la de la mujer que se viste de hombre" ("The most classic inversion related to Carnival is that of the man that disguises himself as a woman and that of a woman who dresses as a man") (p. 90). It is precisely during Carnival that Spanish society tolerates such unconventional acts as cross-dressing, but they are only permitted in a public and collective context. Additionally, Julia Kristeva (1969) notes that those who participate in Carnival lose their individuality while at the same time assuming a double ontology, given that participants are both actors/objects and spectators/subjects of the festival (p. 160). Pedro, on the contrary, maintains his individuality by conducting his own "Carnival" at home with the purpose of exploring and, apparently, expressing his true sexual identity. He breaks the rule, then, of socially-sanctioned collective and formalized ritual. Pedro proposes to Rosa that they make love with the sex roles reversed, and he demands that she penetrate him with a synthetic penis that he gives her for their wedding anniversary. [3] The idea is shocking not only to Rosa, but also to the spectator/reader of the play, due to Pedro's intense, sexually ambiguous behavior. Both Rosa as participant and the audience member as observer experience doubts regarding Pedro's sexual orientation. We are left wondering if he is homosexual, bisexual, a transvestite or merely a heterosexual enjoying a carnivalesque whim. It is through the context of Carnival that Pedrero maintains this disconcerting ambivalence. Pedro's vacilating explanations of his motives exacerbate the sense of ambiguity even further.

In "Code and Message of Carnival," Monica Rector (1984) suggests that the mask donned for Carnival reveals the hidden interests of the person who has chosen it:

> The costume (fantasy) exchanges what one is and what one would like to be. To be and to want to be change places. The world in reverse is what characterizes Carnival. The costume also reveals more than it hides; it represents a hidden wish, summarizing the person wearing the costume, the role it represents, and the one he would like to play. (p. 142)

Rector's observations shed valuable light on Pedro's behavior. The protagonist finally confesses to Rosa that he enjoys dressing and acting like a woman, and that throughout his life he has had to repress this part of his identity in order to conform to patriarchal norms. Ironically, Pedro has been wearing a "mask" all along, and it is only now, during Carnival, that his more authentic identity is unveiled. As Iride Lamartina-Lens (1990) states, "Through the donning of one mask, Pedro's other mask falls, and in a stirring moment of self-revelation, he is forced to admit his sexual ambivalence to Rosa and himself" (p. 466).

According to Mikhail Bakhtin (1984), Carnival permits people to abandon established norms briefly: "[O]ne might say that carnival celebrated temporary liberation from the prevailing truth and from the established order; it marked the suspension of all hierarchical rank, privileges, norms and prohibitions" (p. 10). Rector notes further that the unbridled freedom enjoyed during Carnival produces a catharsis that alleviates the daily frustrations of the participants. While such a purgation does indeed result for Pedro, his sexual liberation leaves Rosa in a state of crisis regarding their marriage. As Joan Torres-Pou (1992) observes, "[E]l disfraz de Pedro descubre su yo escondido y el de Rosa el carnaval a la que la somete la sociedad patriarcal" ("Pedro's mask exposes his hidden self and Rosa's [reveals] the carnival to which patriarchal society subjects her") (pp. 89–90).[4]

Pedrero continues her analysis of individual identity through the subversion of collective rituals in La noche dividida (1989).[5] This play focuses on the encounter of Sabina and Adolfo, two desperate, young people whose meeting takes on the tone of a "sanjuanada."[6] Sabina and Adolfo are dissatisfied with their personal and professional lives. While Sabina is extremely frustrated with the roles she receives as an actress, Adolfo, a Bible salesman, suffers from the constant pressure of having to promote his product in order to remain employed. Adolfo's identity crisis is fueled by his revulsion to the mediocrity of his all-consuming "career."

Adolfo visits Sabina with the intent of selling her a Bible, and throughout the play the actress repeatedly criticizes the shallowness of Adolfo's commercial identity: "Tú, tú tienes que ser algo más que tú y esos libracos …" (You, you must be more than you and those worthless books.") (Pedrero, 1989, p. 65). Adolfo finally recognizes his "deformación profesional" and abandons his sales objective, opting instead to enjoy a few drinks with Sabina.

Adolfo seems to make a definitive decision regarding his identity when, in a drunken state, he sets fire to a Bible on the floor and declares: "Ahora todos los Angeles están en el infierno … Adiós San Pablo. Adiós San Juan. Adiós San Mateo … Adolfo Guzmán os condena a la hoguera para purificar su alma …" (Now all the angels are in Hell … Good-bye Saint Paul. Good-bye Saint John. Good-bye Saint Matthew … Adolfo Guzmán condemns you to the bonfire to purify his soul …) (Pedrero, 1989, p. 74). The destruction of the Bible and the condemnation of the saints confirm Adolfo's rejection of his profession. By burning the Bible, Adolfo symbolically liberates himself from the professional identity that enslaves him. He also announces that it is "la noche de San Juan"—despite the fact that the play is set in September—and he begins to leap repeatedly over the flames. With this episode Pedrero incorporates a national holiday that is celebrated on June 23. Bonfires constitute the most famous tradition for St. John's Night. Jumping over the bonfire is a popular custom associated with this holiday, although the significance of the activity varies widely. One of the commonly held beliefs regarding this ritual features its performance as a preventative or curative measure against illness, curses, and other misfortunes. Caro Baroja (1979b) affirms that the St. John bonfires "[T]ienen un carácter fundamental preservativo, pues se cree que mediante ellas el hombre, los animales y las plantas pueden prosperar de un lado, librándose de toda clase de maleficios por otro" ("[T]hey have a fundamental preservative character, in that it is believed that through them man, animals and plants can prosper on the one hand, freeing themselves from all kinds of evil on the other" (p. 155). In the case of Adolfo, it is evident that the purpose of jumping over the fire is self-purification. Ironically, it is a question of purging himself of what has always been the religious focus of the celebration. The act of burning the Bible on St. John's Night also suggests the triumph of paganism over Christianity and a return to the underlying primitive nature of the festival, whose original rituals involved water, fire, and plants. As Wilma Newberry (1974) observes, "Most of the water, fire, and vegetation rites which are performed on the longest day and the shortest night of the year are pagan in origin but have been cloaked with the mantle of Christianity" (p. 241).

Leaping over the "bonfire" also gives Adolfo the opportunity to demonstrate his valor and physical talent. Newberry notes in general that the act of jumping over the flames represents "a typical Midsummer death/life encounter": "[I]n the leap over the flames the young men confront the destroying/creating aspects of fire in the appearance of momentary consumption by the flames, followed immediately by a renewal of life" (1974, p. 251). These notions correspond to Adolfo's interest in modifying his identity and beginning a new life. He is determined to overcome the "mediocrity" that, according to Virtudes Serrano, characterizes him as a Bible salesman.[7] In an effort to convince Sabina of his courage and physical skills, Adolfo announces that as a child he always won the prize for jumping over the St. John bonfires: "En mi pueblo siempre me daban el premio, el jamón … Casi me quemaba los talones pero seguía saltando. Eran fogatas más grandes que esta terraza. ¡Cien veces más! ¡Mil veces más! …" ("In my town they always gave me the prize ham … I almost burned my heals but I kept on jumping. The bonfires were bigger than this terrace. A hundred times bigger! A thousand times bigger!") (Pedrero, 1989, p. 74).

In *La noche dividida*, St. John's Night is transformed into an individual, antireligious ritual whose only agent is Adolfo. Sabina does not participate. On the contrary, the actress feels puzzled when Adolfo sets fire to the holy book, and she does not hesitate to extinguish it. The ritual does, however, provide Adolfo with a means of purging his professional frustration, and at the end of the play we see a man who is determined to break with his commercial identity. After the dramatic ritual of burning the Bible, Adolfo announces his decision to change his career: "Mañana cogeré un avión y me iré al lago Ness, haré un reportaje sobre el monstruo y lo venderé muy caro. Dejaré de vender biblias para siempre …" ("Tomorrow I'll take a plane to Loch Ness, I'll do a report on the monster and I'll sell it for a lot of money. I'll stop selling Bibles forever …") (Pedrero, 1989, pp. 75–6). It is evident that Adolfo desires to change his life. For that reason the selection of St. John's Night is especially appropriate, given that the correct date of the celebration coincides with the summer solstice and thus marks a time of change.

In addition to bonfires and seasonal change, St. John's Night has often been associated with romantic encounters and new love. As Newberry (1975) notes,

> Midsummer is traditionally a holiday for lovers, probably because of the ancient fertility rites practiced on Midsummer day and evening. It is pervaded with an atmosphere of magic conducive to the belief that Midsummer dreams will come true and that lovers will find fulfillment during this period of enchantment. (p. 47)

Such beliefs are dramatized in *La noche dividida* when Adolfo and Sabina attempt a mutual seduction while imbibing. Intoxication is an integral part of the St. John tradition in Spain, and Newberry notes that "the inebriation should be one which provides release, exhilaration, and a marked change from a fairly responsible existence during the rest of the year" (1975, p. 61). Sabina and Adolfo indulge in champagne to overcome their inhibitions, and after several glasses they begin to imitate the erotic behavior of the stray cats outside. Nevertheless, it is precisely because of their drunken state that the couple fails to consummate their relationship. They fall asleep as soon as they reach the bed and, in the end, all that remains is the illusion of the "sanjuanada."

La llamada de Lauren and *La noche dividida* offer excellent examples of the treatment of collective celebrations in the theatre of Paloma Pedrero. Carnival and St. John's Night are ancient Spanish traditions that form part of the national identity. With respect to Carnival, Caro Baroja (1979a) emphasizes the following: "Efectuar, pues, un análisis de las costumbres de Carnaval significa adentrarse en la conciencia (o subconsciencia) colectiva de muchos siglos, porque semejantes costumbres se han repetido año tras año, aquí y allá" ("To effect, therefore, an analysis of the Carnival customs is to penetrate the collective conscience (or subconscience) of many centuries, because similar customs have been repeated year after year, here and there") (p. 22). The same may be said about St. John's Night, as this holiday is also deeply rooted in Spanish culture.

Collective rituals generally foster feelings of community among the participants, as they unite people both physically and emotionally (Driver, 1991, p. 152).[8] Pedrero, however, subverts her country's traditions. Carnival and St. John's Night are transformed into private rituals that enable the performer to explore and express his own identity. Furthermore, the results of these rituals contrast sharply with the usual outcomes. While the carnivalesque fantasy permits Pedro to manifest hidden aspects of his sexuality, it is precisely through the burning of the sacred book on St. John's Night that Adolfo is able to "purify his soul." Through the alteration of popular customs, Pedrero destabilizes the sense of community and identity enjoyed by her public. She provokes her spectators with characters that deviate from tradition by the individualization of normally communal rituals. In short, the playwright employs the expressive capacity of such acts in order to facilitate the thematic and critical development of her works.

In *Besos de lobo* (1987) and *El color de agosto* (1989) we find examples of Pedrero's treatment of rites of passage, rituals whose purpose of fostering a sense of community coincides with those of the collective celebrations discussed above. Rites of passage mark biological and social milestones in life and achieve integration of the individual into society at different levels. According to Myerhoff (1982),

> Rites of passage are a category of rituals that mark the passages of an individual through the life cycle, from one state to another over time, from one role or social position to another, integrating the human and cultural experiences with biological destiny: birth, reproduction, and death (p. 109).

Rites of passage defined in this way arise occasionally in Pedrero's works in distorted forms and/or non-traditional contexts. Agustin's wake in *Besos de lobo* exemplifies this tendency. The play begins with Ana's return to her native town of Jara, after a lengthy absence, and the drama develops around her relationships with the men in her life. Her traditional father Augustin, her homosexual friend Luciano, her imaginary French boyfriend Raul, and Camilo, the head of the train station who tries unsuccessfully to court Ana, are numbered among them. Although the death of Agustin is not dramatized, the event is foreshadowed. Ana anticipates her father's death while they argue about her French boyfriend and Agustin's alcoholism, predicting that he will suffer a terrible, painful death (Pedrero, 1987b, p. 39).

The sixth scene of *Besos de lobo* begins with Augustin's wake. Although the funeral ritual generally constitutes a public event, Pedrero focuses on a private moment between Ana and her deceased father after the mourners have left. In a monologue that recalls that of Carmen in Miguel Delibes' *Cinco horas con Mario* (1966), Ana addresses to her father her thoughts on the ritual and the hypocrisy of the people expressing condolences. Ana also attempts a reconciliation with her father. Although the initial "staging" of the ritual suggests a traditional wake, given the candlelit coffin and the serious tone, the scene is suddenly transformed into a grotesque situation due to the comic humiliation suffered by the deceased. For example, Ana finds her father in the casket with one eye open: "¿Me está mirando? ... No, sólo tiene un ojo abierto. La bestia de la Paulina le ha dado un beso tan fuerte que le ha abierto un ojo" ("Are you looking at me? ... No, you just have one eye open. Pauline, that beast, kissed you so hard that she opened one of your eyes") (Pedrero, 1987b, p. 43). The anguish over Augustin's death is interrupted by such moments of macabre humor, and eventually Ana screams at the corpse: "¡No me guine el ojo!" ("Don't wink at me!") (Pedrero, 1987b, p. 43). Finally, she pleads with her father to open the other eye and pronounce her name. The comicality of the scene culminates when Ana's name is shouted from off-stage, visibly startling the protagonist. When Luciano enters with flowers, the ritual resumes a conventional tone that is reinforced by the mysterious circumstance that both of Augustin's eyes are closed when the scene ends.

Agustin's wake can be considered an uncompleted ritual due to the humorous interruptions. Pedrero transforms the most somber event of the plot into the funniest scene of the play, and in this way she broadens her criticism of the rigid, local traditions which tend to oppress Ana. Nevertheless, the wake does complete its function as a rite of passage because it marks Agustin's departure to another world.[9] As A. Paul Hare (1988) observes, funeral rituals provide a symbolic transition for the deceased and imply a change of status and roles for the family and other mourners (p. 152). In harmony with Hare's statement, and in reference to *Besos de lobo*, Torres-Pou notes, "[A] la muerte de su padre, la protagonista decide empezar a vivir de nuevo y abandona el pueblo en un acto de liberación y crecimiento emocional" ("[U]pon her father's death, the protagonist decides to begin a new life and abandon the town in an act of liberation and emotional growth") (1992, p. 91). Augustin's wake does indeed signal a moment of change in the life of Ana, who now finds herself completely free to leave town.

In *El color de agosto* rites of passage are incorporated within a non-traditional context, and they contribute to the play's thematic development. The action of this drama is generated by the reunion of two artist friends, María and Laura, after an eight-year separation. During these years María has become a successful painter and Laura, who was originally the more talented of the two, has abandoned her career. The two women reunite at María's apartment-studio, and it immediately becomes apparent that the most salient feature of their relationship is their intense personal and professional rivalry.

Rites of passage in *El color de agosto* emerge in both subtle and shocking forms. On one occasion, for example, Laura begins to obsess about her ex-lover Juan, contemplating a reunion with him and the revenge that she would launch. Laura reaches a highly emotional delirium, and María tries to calm her friend through a pseudo baptism at the fountain in her studio:

Maria   I'm going to wash your pretty face.
Laura   (Going toward the water, arm in arm with Maria) Wash away my thoughts. Can you do that?
Maria   I'll try. (She sprinkles water on Laura's face and on her hair.) How's that? How are those thoughts now? (Pedrero, 1994, p. 16)

Despite the customary baptismal elements (the fountain, water on the head), Pedrero employs the ritual in a non-religious context. The rite's function, however, approximates the tradition of the purification of the baptized individual. Baptism comprises an initiation rite through which the novitiate becomes a member of the church. It also represents the separation of the neophyte from his or her previous life, marred by original sin. In his commentary on the symbolism of baptismal water, Robert Bocock (1974) notes, "Water is being used as a symbol of death and resurrection, death to one state of life and being born again into another, in this case as a member of the Christian Church" (p. 129). Goals similar to those underlying Christian baptism define the ritual scene in *El color de agosto*, as Laura attempts to purge herself of obsession for Juan. Moreover, it seems that María wishes to purify her friend in order to receive her once again into her world, given the implication that Laura has lead a sinful life during her absence. Finally, María's marriage to Juan may provide her strongest motivation to help her friend stop tormenting herself over him.

The "baptism" of Laura is followed by a lesbian wedding scene, which constitutes a non-traditional representation of another rite of passage. María and Laura briefly adopt bridal roles while they contemplate and explore their relationship. María dons a white sheet, as if it were a wedding gown, and dresses Laura in similar fashion. They then act-out the ritual. First they imagine what the priest and guests would say during the ceremony, which is already marred by the rumor that both brides are "pregnant." They continue with a bridal dance, but the scene ends abruptly when María tries to kiss Laura, whose immediate withdrawal interrupts the ritual.

According to Myerhoff, rites of passage generally coincide with moments of crisis and constitute occasions in which a group teaches cultural values to the initiate, with the intent of integrating that individual into society. In *El color de agosto* María assumes the superior role in both of the rituals mentioned above; she interprets the role of "priest" in the "baptism" of Laura, and she subtly directs the action of the wedding scene so that it culminates in a kiss. The "baptism" may be viewed as a prerequisite ritual for the wedding scene because from María's perspective it serves to sever symbolically the love triangle that exists between the protagonists and Juan. As we have already seen in *La llamada de Lauren* and *La noche dividida*, Pedrero's rituals are realized typically by individuals in a private context, without the sacred elements or the significant shared interpretations inherent to a community celebration. As Myerhoff observes, such circumstances impede the integration that normally results from a rite of passage (1982, p. 126). Consequently, in *El color de agosto* María is unable to control Laura. This becomes evident particularly when Laura abandons her at the close of the play.

In addition to the subverted rites of passage found in *Besos de lobo* and *El color de agosto*, these plays are also distinguished by what Hornby considers "quasi-ceremonies"; that is, ritualized activities performed to satisfy some personal need. These "rituals" are often shocking to the audience/reader due to their empty, grotesque and/or obsessive nature (Hornby, 1986, pp. 61–3). As Hornby (1986) notes,

> Ceremonies that convey no meaning to an audience, that make no connections with a surrounding, stable culture, seem merely bizarre or exotic. Unlike true ceremony, which orients its watchers to a whole order of society and the universe, such quasi-ceremonies confuse and disorient, increasing rather than overcoming our feeling that the world is meaningless. (p. 62)

While the bizarre nature of quasi-ceremonies agitates and disorients Pedrero's public, a closer look at her plays will demonstrate that such "rituals" are not without purpose.

In *Besos de lobo* Ana and Luciano share a private ritual that consists of secret meetings during which they discuss Luciano's homosexuality and the "news" received by Ana from her French boyfriend. [10] The ritual is repeated with a fixed form: the two characters always meet by candlelight at Ana's house at 7:00 p.m. Furthermore, it is suggested that the ritual has been formalized by some kind of "pact," although the details of this agreement remain undisclosed.

Ana and Luciano's quasi-ceremony primarily serves one of the principle functions of ritual, to foster solidarity between the participants. According to Tom F. Driver (1991), "Out of the shared perceptions and ritualized 'ways' of a people, as these gradually take on symbolic functions, there comes into existence a shared 'world'" (p. 136). Through their meetings, Ana and Luciano establish their own "community" in which they seek refuge from the hostile world of the town and their own families. In the company of Luciano, for example, Ana escapes her father's daily reproaches regarding her boyfriend. Likewise, it is during the clandestine meetings that Luciano can avoid the local prejudices against his homosexuality. Ana and Luciano understand and support each other, and their quasi-ceremony permits them to realize not only their fantasies, but also their true identities. The ritual also allows them to legitimize their controversial sexual interests. As Moore and Myerhoff (1977) note, ceremonies serve to establish the legitimacy of certain people, organizations and perspectives (p. 4). Ana and Luciano validate their sexual preferences through their ritualized meetings; Luciano exhibits his homosexuality, and Ana can maintain her fantasy engagement with "Raul" while enjoying the solitary life of an introvert.

The most shocking quasi-ritual in Pedrero's theatre is found in El color de agosto, when the protagonists violently paint each other's naked bodies. Curiously, Laura recalls that this "ritual" was an entertaining childhood activity: "I do feel like painting. Now I'll paint you. I'll paint your body, like when we were little. I like your body in colors (She takes paint and smears María's legs.)" (Pedrero, 1994, p. 21). María and Laura now repeat the ritual with intense competition. While Laura insists that they paint each other naked, María demands that they use their hands when Laura offers her a brush. The ritual takes on a frenetic pace. The women paint each other aggressively, transforming themselves simultaneously into both painters and canvases. Thus they achieve a total (con)fusion of artist and work. The frenzy climaxes in an exchange of insults—"Whore!", "Faker!", "Whore! Filthy bitch!", "Whore. Pig. Liar." "Faker. Faker!"—and concludes with a desperate hug during which María's and Laura's colors mix (Pedrero, 1994, p. 22). As Mary Makris (1995) notes, this episode is staged as if it were a passionate sexual encounter: "In this scene, because of the insinuations of the stage directions and the accompanying verbal affirmations of sex and sexuality (the paintbrush as a phallic symbol, a womb, sterility and orgasms), the sex act implicitly emerges as a metaphor for artistic creation" (p. 21). [11]

In addition to dramatizing the creative process, the body-painting ritual seems to be executed with the intent of overcoming the inspirational drought suffered by both María and Laura during their separation. This condition is expressed through the metaphor of emptiness. [12] Laura initiates the ritual, for example, by painting Maria's abdomen red while declaring: "Hell. Hell is the empty womb … The red of sterility. Sterile womb at thirty-five." María responds with her own ritualistic chant while she paints large, black stripes on Laura's body: "Jail! Frustration hides itself behind the bars. Failure" (Pedrero, 1994, p. 21). When they conclude the ritual, María reiterates her lack of inspiration: "You left and took away all the ideas, all the water. You left me empty" (Pedrero, 1994, p. 22). María's emptiness contrasts throughout the play with the statue of Venus in her studio, which contains a live, caged bird in the mid-section. Not only does the bird represent fecundity, but the inspiration that cannot be freed, since the stripes painted by María on Laura's body correspond to those of the cage. María, like the statue, finds herself incapacitated and unable to free her artistic inspiration—that is, the metaphoric bird. It is clear that, in addition to creating a mythological reference, the sculpture of Venus constitutes a mise-en-abyme that constantly reflects the thematic currents of the play.

Although reluctant to admit it, María considers Laura her muse, and for this reason she contracts her as a model. She believes that Laura will free her inspiration, and this is suggested when María insists that Laura's hands be the model for those that will open the cage in her new painting of Venus. At the end of the drama, Laura contemplates the work and offers the following advice:

> Oh, by the way, the hands have to be hers. No, it doesn't matter that she has no arms. It's something like ... That's it! Wait a minute! *(Quickly.)* The figure in a downward motion trying to reach the lock with her mouth. The bird looking up with an open beak. *(At top speed.)* The light, only from behind. A white light. And on the floor ... pieces of broken body ... stains ...
>
> (Pedrero, 1994, p. 27)

Laura suggests that one has to free one's own inspiration. After she leaves, María follows her suggestions and opens the cage. As Carolyn Harris (1994) states: "La percepción de los personajes se ha alterado y entienden que para crear necesitan buscar la fuerza en ellas mismas, no en una relación de dependencia" ("The perception of the characters has been altered and they understand that in order to create they need to seek strength in themselves, not in a relationship of dependence") (p. 176).

As demonstrated by the examples discussed in this study, the theatre of Paloma Pedrero offers a wealth of rituals, ranging from collective celebrations to rites of passage and quasi-ceremonies. These events contribute to the thematic development of the plays while at the same time adding layers of performance to the works. The rituals in Pedrero's plays are generally unfulfilled due to interruptions and corrupt elements, and this underscores the author's social criticism. Anthropologists and critics generally agree that rituals establish order in a society, perpetuate traditions, and reflect the values of the people. In the words of Hornby (1986), "Ceremonies always convey meaning. They contain encoded signs by which their society understands both the external world around them, and the emotional world within. Since their purpose is always to provide an order, their pattern or form is always of the highest importance" (p. 51). By altering and subverting our rituals, Pedrero suggests that these models are no longer valid, or that they should be reinterpreted and revised in order to recover the real meaning and intensity of the acts. Regarding her subversion of ritual, Pedrero explains,

> En mi vida siempre me he inventado mis propios ritos. Nunca he seguido una fórmula hecha porque soy muy escéptica ... no soy escéptica para las cosas más

naturales, pero para lo que ya tiene orden soy bastante escéptica ... me parece que ese orden hace perder verdad, intensidad. No se puede hacer sentir una cosa que se repite siempre de la misma manera. Por lo menos yo siento que el ritual formal tiene algo de, que se ha perdido la verdad, la intensidad, y sin embargo, que inventándote un rito puedes volver a hacer verdad esa emoción. (All my life I have always invented my own rituals. I have never followed a fixed formula because I am very skeptical ... I'm not skeptical about the most natural things, but I'm pretty skeptical about what already has order ... it seems to me that that order causes truth and intensity to be lost. One cannot make felt something that is always repeated the same way. At least I feel that formal ritual has something of, that truth and intensity have been lost and, nevertheless, that by inventing your own ritual you can make that emotion true once again.)

(P. Pedrero, personal communication, October 2, 1997)

Rituals in Pedrero's theatre are modified according to the needs of the individual, and this reflects a growing tendency in today's society. According to Myerhoff (1982),

We have had to develop rituals and employ symbols in increasingly private contexts, living as we do in a diffuse, fragmented world with shattered or shallow consensual structures. This privacy leaves individuals nearly completely on their own when dealing with the subjects previously taken up by rituals ... (p. 126).

Myerhoff emphasizes that rituals continue to play a very important role in our social and psychological well-being because they orient us during crises. However, we must now invent the myths, rituals, and symbols necessary to interpret life. The individualization of rituals occurs in the works considered in this study. Carnival and St. John's Night are no longer collective celebrations but private rituals that facilitate the manifestation of personal identity. The ritualized meetings of Ana and Luciano serve the same function. Rituals constitute a means of communication for Pedrero's protagonists and are often vehicles of sexual, professional and/or emotional liberation. Finally, through her treatment of ritual Pedrero leads us to reflect on a number of problematic aspects of modern society, through such familiar traditions as a Carnival costume, a wake, and other customs that define and order our lives.

Notes

1 The portrayal of bullfighting in *Invierno de luna alegre* offers another excellent example of Pedrero's treatment of ritual. For a discussion of this topic, see my article "El toreo como vía de la identidad en *Invierno de luna alegre*" and my dissertation titled "El metateatro en las obras de Paloma Pedrero."
2 With the exception of textual quotes from *El color de agosto*, all translations are my own.
3 The wedding anniversary in itself constitutes an uncompleted ritual due to the corrupt nature in which it is carried out by Pedro and the resulting interruption. While the celebration is initiated in a traditional manner with roses and champagne, it is quickly marred by the perverse gift that Pedro offers his wife and his insistence that they use it to make love.

4 Additionally, Torres-Pou (1992) feels that *La llamada de Lauren* is developed along "unas coordinadas totalmente bajtinianas" due to the use of Carnival, the costume and the grotesque (p. 89).
5 *La noche dividida* was part of the original trilogy titled *Noches de amor efímero*.
6 The Spanish term "sanjuanada" refers to the series of festivities and traditions that correspond to "la Noche de San Juan"; that is, St. John's Night or Midsummer's Eve, which is celebrated on June 23 in Spain.
7 In her introduction to *Noches de amor* efimero, Virtudes Serrano (1991) describes Adolfo as "[O]tro ser mediocre que lucha por sobrevivir" ("[A]nother mediocre being that fights to survive") (p. 18).
8 In *The Ritual Process: Structure and Anti-Structure*, Victor Turner (1969) examines the emotional bond that is developed between those who participate in a ritual, and he refers to this phenomenon as "communitas."
9 Arnold Van Gennep (1969) divides rites of passage into three groups: rites of separation, rites of transition, and rites of incorporation. Wakes constitute a rite of transition for the deceased as well as the survivors, given that both find themselves between the world of the living and that of the dead.
10 Although not directly stated, it is obvious that Ana writes love letters to herself and pretends that they were sent by Raúl.
11 William Garcia (1993) also stresses the metaphorical value of the scene: "This particular scene is, if not the most important, extremely relevant due to its metaphoric value linked to the theme of women's creativity (body as text, painting)" (p. 156).
12 Makris (1995) notes that the metaphoric emptiness also suggests biological sterility:

> The images in many of María and Laura's visual texts focus on procreation and its absence: a sterile red womb, the fiery uterus containing a shell seeking an exit and the Venus with a caged bird near her reproductive organs. Such imagery is often accompanied by phallic euphemisms (a monolith, the fish, the paintbrush and the bird). Within this context, the sex act becomes a metaphor for creativity (p. 22).

References

Bakhtin, M. (1984). *Rabelais and his World*. Trans. Helene Iswolsky. Bloomington: Indiana University Press.
Bell, C. (1992). *Ritual Theory, Ritual Practice*. New York: Oxford University Press.
Berardini, S.P. (1996). El metateatro en las obras de Paloma Pedrero (Doctoral dissertation, State University of New York at Buffalo, 1996) *Dissertation Abstracts International*.
—— (1994). El toreo como vía de la identidad en *Invierno de luna alegre*. In J.P. Gabriele (Ed.), *De lo particular a lo universal: El teatro español del siglo XX y su contexto* (pp. 181–97). Madrid: Iberoamericana.
Bocock, R. (1974). *Ritual in Industrial Society: A Sociological Analysis of Ritualism in Modern England*. London: Allen.
Caro Baroja, J. (1979a). *El carnaval (análisis histórico-cultural)*. Madrid: Taurus.
—— (1979b). *La estación de amor (fiestas populares de mayo a San Juan)*. Madrid: Taurus.
Driver, T.F. (1991). *The Magic of Ritual: Our Need for Liberating Rites that Transform our Lives and our Communities*. San Francisco: Harper.
Garcia, W. (1993). Three One-Act Plays by Paloma Pedrero at the Pace Downtown Theatre, New York. *Gestos*, 15, 155–7.
Hare, A.P., and Blumberg, H.H. (1988). *Dramaturgical Analysis of Social Interaction*. New York: Praeger.

Harris, C. (1994). Juego y metateatro en la obra de Paloma Pedrero. In J.P. Gabriele (Ed.), *De lo particular a lo universal: El teatro español del siglo XX y su contexto* (pp. 170–80). Madrid: Iberoamericana.

Hornby, R. (1986). *Drama, Metadrama and Perception*. Lewisburg: Bucknell University Press.

Kristeva, J. (1969). *Semeiotike: Recherches pour une semanalyse*. Paris: Editions du Seuil.

Lamartina-Lens, I. (1990). An Insight to the Theatre of Paloma Pedrero. *Romance Languages Annual*, 2, 465–8.

Makris, M. (1995). Metadrama, Creation, Reception and Interpretation: The Role of Art in Paloma Pedrero's *El color de agosto. Estreno*, 21 (1), 19–23.

Moore, S.F., and Myerhoff, B.G. (1977). Introduction. In S.F. Moore and B.G. Myerhoff (Eds), *Secular Ritual* (pp. 3–24). Amsterdam: Van Gorcum.

Myerhoff, B.G. (1977). We Don't Wrap Herring in a Printed Page: Fusion, Fictions and Continuity in Secular Ritual. In S.F. Moore and B.G. Myerhoff (Eds), *Secular Ritual* (pp. 199–224). Amsterdam: Van Gorcum.

—— (1982). Rites of Passage: Process and Paradox. In V. Turner (Ed.), *Celebration: Studies in Festivity and Ritual* (pp. 109–35). Washington, DC: Smithsonian Institution.

Newberry, W. (1974). Three Examples of the Midsummer Theme in Modern Spanish Literature: *Gloria, La dama del alba*, and *El curandero de su honra. Kentucky Romance Quarterly*, 21 (2), 239–59.

—— (1975). The Baptist Betrayed: Juan Goytisolo's *La resaca* and *Fin de fiesta. Revista de estudios hispánicos*, 9, 47–63.

Pedrero, P. (1987a). *La llamada de Lauren*. Madrid: Antonio Machado.

—— (1987b). *Besos de lobo*. Madrid: Fundamentos.

—— (1989). *La noche dividida*. Madrid: Antonio Machado.

—— (1990). *Invierno de luna alegre*. Madrid: Antonio Machado.

—— (1994) *The Color of August*. In P. Zatlin (Trans.) *Parting Gestures: Three Plays* (pp. 1–27). University Park, PA: Estreno.

Rector, M. (1984). The Code and Message of Carnival: 'Escoplas-de-Sambal. In Thomas A. Sebeok (Ed.), *Carnival* (pp. 37–165). Berlin: Mouto.

Serrano, V. (1991). Introduction. *Noches de amor efímero* by Paloma Pedrero. Murcia: Universidad, Secretariado de Publicaciónes, 7–29.

Torres-Pou, J. (1992). Síntesis e inversión: Dos rasgos del teatro de Paloma Pedrero. *Alaluz*, 24 (1–2), 89–92.

Turner, V. (1969). *The Ritual Process: Structure and Anti-structure*. Chicago: Aldine.

Van Gennep, A. (1969). *Les rites de passage*. New York: Johnson Reprint.

Chapter 6

"And love thee after"
Necrophilia on the Jacobean stage

Richard W. Grinnell

Not until Ophelia is stretched out in her grave does Hamlet move to love her. Though the tides of sexuality wash around her during the play, her sexuality, and her role as a desirable object is frustrated until she is in her grave. Then, the young men are drawn to her. Laertes, after quarrelling with the priest who is burying her, declares: "Hold off the earth awhile, / Till I have caught her once more in mine arms," whereupon he leaps into the grave (5.1. 233–4).[1] Hamlet, watching covertly, responds likewise, leaping in beside Laertes and declaring: "I loved Ophelia: forty thousand brothers / Could not, with all their quantity of love, / Make up my sum" (5.1. 254–6). Lectured to and scorned throughout the play, Ophelia, it seems, becomes an object of desire once she is laid out in her grave.

Othello stands over Desdemona. "Be thus when thou art dead / And I shall kill thee and love thee after" he tells her as she sleeps (5.2. 18–19). Othello's sexual nausea, like Hamlet's, has been well documented by scholars, and it is not until Desdemona is asleep on her death bed, and then actually dead, that that nausea can be wiped away and Othello recognize her as the sexually desirable, chaste wife she has always been. "I kissed thee ere I killed thee. / No help but this, killing myself to die upon a kiss" (5.2. 368–9). Death is no final curtain for Desdemona. In fact, only after her death can the men in the play recognize her as a chaste, loyal, wife. Before that moment she is demonized as a whore, and at best, distrusted for her sexual power. "Look to her, Moor, if thou hast eyes to see. / She has deceived her father, and may thee" (1.3. 291–2).

In these plays, and in plays that follow, death fails to remove women from the circulation of erotic energy in Renaissance England. Instead, the English stage reinserts them into its system of desire, making necrophilia a tool by which it, and the culture that underlies it, struggles to understand and cope with the cultural upheaval of the early seventeenth century. How dramatists use stage necrophilia, and ultimately why it becomes an important dramatic sign at the beginning of the seventeenth century, is the subject of the following discussion.

Crossing boundaries

Human society is ordered. Social conventions, contracts, rules, taboos, serve to give human society shape and to set it apart from that which is not human. In her influential study, *Purity and Danger* (1966), the anthropologist Mary Douglas argues that our image of society "has form; it has external boundaries, margins, internal structure. Its outlines contain power to reward conformity and repulse attack. There is energy in its margins and unstructured areas" (p. 115). The social order, Douglas argues, flourishes within the cultural boundaries that mark its edges, and order is threatened whenever social boundaries are broken. To cross boundaries and interact with the energy that lies at the margins of society is to risk bringing danger back into the social system. "All margins are dangerous," Douglas writes (p. 122); to go into the margins "is to have been in contact with danger, to have been at a source of power" (p. 98).

In its general form, this anthropological construct was understood by early seventeenth-century dramatists, and served as the psychological underpinnings of much of the tragic action of the stage. Shakespeare demonstrates this clearly when, in his most famous soliloquy, Hamlet refers to death as "the undiscovered country, from whose bourn / No traveler returns" (3.1. 79–80). For Hamlet, death is a foreign country, charged with danger, because of its psychic distance from the "weary life" with which he is familiar. Crossing the boundary between life and death is a journey he is not willing to take.

For Shakespeare and his culture death is the realm of the other. William Engel (1995) writes in *Mapping Mortality* that "in the Renaissance the figure of Death connoted the alien par excellence and stood for what might be termed man's ultimate 'other'" (p. 72). In the Renaissance, as in most societies, taboos protect the boundary between the dead and the living, between that which is alien, and that which is human. The geographic movement from the social order of the living to the alien disorder of death gives the transitional nature of death its symbolic and representational power. As Douglas (1966) argues, "danger lies in transitional states, [sic] simply because transition is neither one state nor the next, it is undefinable" (p. 97). To cross that boundary, then, is to enter a dangerous realm and become charged with a dangerous power. Taboo acts to keep individuals from entering into those dangerous states, and protects society itself from the social repercussions of that danger. In times of cultural upheaval, however, the boundaries that have always defined a social system are challenged, the taboos are questioned, and the margins invaded.

The early seventeenth century in England was just such a cultural period. Tensions between the King and parliament (which finally result in civil war and the execution of Charles I) are simply one facet of a social structure that is being challenged in the economic, political, and social arenas. The drama of the period reflects that instability, and the necrophilia that we increasingly see on the stage in the early seventeenth century is a part of that reflection. As Jean Howard (1994) has convincingly argued in *The Stage and Social Struggle in Early Modern England*, "the drama enacted ideological contestation as much as it mirrored or reproduced anything that one could call the dominant ideology of a single class, class faction, or sex" (p. 7). The partial breakdown in the taboo against necrophilia that results in it becoming a popular stage device is symptomatic of larger breakdowns in early Jacobean culture, and leads us to a specific arena of social contestation: the ideology of sexuality, and of gender, that was being negotiated after the death of Elizabeth I, in the years prior to the civil war.

From 1601 until 1611, necrophilia appears in a surprisingly wide variety of plays, and it is quite overt and gender-specific necrophilia—powerful men taking possession of, and making love to, dead women. What we notice as we look at the use of this necrophilia is the direct relationship between it as a dramatic language (a language used for effect on the Renaissance stage), and the changing gender system of the time.[2] When in the drama of this period, powerful, if often corrupt, men retrieve dead women from the grave and reinsert them into the social system of desire, the drama is both presenting shocking and titillating scenes (there is an element of one-upmanship in the use of necrophilia during this period, an attempt to see who can provide the most shocking scene on stage), and reflecting the cultural anxiety about gender roles and power that attends James I's coming to the throne. That necrophilia would become a method by which dramatists would simultaneously shock and register the culture's dis-ease is not as surprising as it might seem.

In a literary and cultural sense, the connection between sex and death in the early seventeenth century is already well established. Peter Metcalf and Richard Huntington (1991) tell us in *Celebrations of Death: the Anthropology of Mortuary Ritual* that "some association of sex with death occurs in nearly every culture in the world" (p. 25). In early modern England that connection is explicit and understood. Sexual intercourse was colloquially (and in many cases scientifically) believed to shorten men's lives. As a consequence, even in the best of encounters sex was connected to death, and to engage in sexual intercourse was to partake, metaphorically if not literally, in the grave. Examples of this belief are easy to find. The poet John Donne writes in "Farewell to Love": "each such act, they say, / Diminisheth the length of life a day" (1983, p. 148). Claudio and Don Pedro pun on the colloquial double meaning of die and death as they discuss Benedick's apparent love sickness in Shakespeare's *Much Ado About Nothing*.

Claudio: Nay, but I know who loves him.
Don Pedro: That would I know too. I warrant, one that knows him not.
Claudio: Yes, and his ill conditions, and in despite of all, dies for him.
Don Pedro: She shall be buried with her face upwards. (3.2. 53–8)

Sophonirus in *The Second Maiden's Tragedy* (1611) can congratulate himself for his wife having taken a lover.

> Marry, his lodging he pays dearly for;
> He gets me all my children; there I save by't.
> Beside, I draw my life out by the bargain
> Some twelve years longer than the times appointed,
> When my young prodigal gallant kicks up's heels
> At one and thirty, and lies dead and rotten
> Some five and forty years before I'm coffined. (I. i. 42–8)

Because he engages in no sex, Sophonirus believes he has added twelve years to his life, and will live for forty-five years longer than his wife's young lover. There is a powerful relationship between sex and death.

For the Renaissance, the physiological connection between sex and death becomes a semiotic one as well in the conflation of death and chastity. In an interesting twist, death is, for Renaissance literature, one of the true ways of preserving a woman's chastity, and the iconography of chastity preserves that assumption. Death and chastity share semantic associations. Both are represented in the drama as cold and pale. When Othello begins to recognize that he has wrongly killed Desdemona, he says to her corpse: "Cold, cold, my girl? / Even like thy chastity" (5.2. 275–6). In *The Revenger's Tragedy*, chastity "lies a-cold," as Vindice says. In *The Second Maiden's Tragedy*, paleness and coldness mark the dead Lady. As Valerie Traub (1992) has noted: "for women in Shakespearean drama, 'chastity' requires being still, cold, and closed; to be 'unchaste' is to be mobile, hot, open" (p. 28). This pale, cold, chastity is much praised in the tragedy of the early seventeenth century.

Therefore, at the beginning of the seventeenth century in England, death is associated with both chastity *and* with sexuality. Though men see sexual encounters with women as leading to their *own* deaths (to have sex is to risk death, to engage in death), and as threatening to the patriarchal world that is premised on masculine power, the culture also sees death as chaste, as iconographically asexual, as a place where women can escape from the masculine desires that threaten them. These two cultural assumptions come together in the desire that results in necrophilia.

Another part of this interesting equation is that on stage, death often acts as a sexual transformer. Metcalf and Huntington (1991) note that transition dominates funeral symbolism (p. 32), and we can see that clearly in Jacobean drama. For example, as we have seen at the beginning of this discussion, Desdemona, demonized by Othello and Iago in life, is transformed into a chaste wife in death and is recognized by the men of the last scene as an ideal woman. Ophelia is transformed by death from a child into a sexualized adult, from being chastised for receiving Hamlet's advances, to being mourned by Hamlet's mother as the ideal mate for her son. In John Marston's *Tragedy of Sophonisba* (1606) death transforms Sophonisba into a wonder of chastity, the "wonder of women," as does the death of Antonio's wife in *The Revenger's Tragedy*.

Antonio:	Violent rape
	Has played a glorious act: behold, my lords,
	A sight that strikes man out of me.
Piero:	That virtuous lady!
Antonio:	Precedent for wives!
Hippolito:	The blush of many women, whose chaste presence
	Would e'en call shame up to their cheeks, and make
	Pale wanton sinners have good colours—
Antonio:	Dead! (I. iv. 3–11)

In early seventeenth century drama, death rewrites characters into their culturally imagined ideal. Even a character like Polonius undergoes a transformation in death (though not a sexual one), as Hamlet says: "Indeed this counselor / Is now most still, most secret, and most grave / Who was in life a foolish prating knave" (3.4. 187–9). Death is a powerful transformative power in the drama of this period.

The sexual transformation catalyzed by death reestablishes characters in the system of desire that circulates through the drama and the culture of the time. In the process of idealization, the dead woman becomes, not only a desirable sexual object, but one whose chastity has been confirmed. She becomes a fit mate for the men of the plays. Necrophilia occurs when, increasingly, men pursue those mates across the boundary of death and reinsert them into the sexual dynamic of the living world. The result, as we can imagine from Douglas' description of taboo, is disastrous. To cross the boundary that separates the living from the dead introduces dangerous energy and destructive power into society. The necrophilic lover and often the culture within which this happens is demonized, and ultimately the masculine forces that drive these plots are corrupted and destroyed.

The Tragedy of Sophonisba

John Marston's 1606 *The Wonder of Women* or *The Tragedy of Sophonisba* demonstrates two types of necrophilia, both apparently subordinated to a larger concern for defining gender. The first important reference to necrophilia comes from King Syphax in response to Sophonisba's threat to kill herself rather than have sex with him: "do, strike thy breast; know, being dead, I'll use / With highest lust of sense thy senseless flesh" (IV. 1. 57–8).[3] He reminds her, and the audience, that death is no escape from sexuality, that she can easily be inserted into Syphax's erotic world whether she is living or dead. Driven by lust, and influenced by the instability of the Jacobean historical moment, Syphax is willing to violate taboo and cross the boundary that prohibits the living from having sexual relations with the dead.

This threatened necrophilia, however, is just the beginning of Marston's interest in the relationship between sex and death. His interest, and the play's necrophilia, come together even more profoundly in the witch Erictho.

Erictho is simultaneously monster, woman, sexuality, and death, and when she enters the play, she transforms it into a critique of the patriarchally controlled gender system. The scene that introduces Erictho is so striking in its sensual, dramatic, language that it prompted one twentieth century critic to declare it "a scene of gratuitous horror, introduced merely to make our flesh creep" (Eliot, 1950, p. 230). Erictho's appearance *is* a surprise, not only because the language that describes her places her in an important and marginal position relative to Renaissance culture, but also because Marston introduces Erictho in the middle of what seems a traditional conflict between male armies defining honor and dishonor; a conflict in which Sophonisba, the title woman, is little more than a commodity of exchange between competing men. When Erictho "from naked graves stalks out, [and] heaves proud her head" (IV.1.108), she disrupts the masculine movement of the plot and refocuses the play on issues of gender, issues of sexuality, and specifically on Erictho and Sophonisba themselves.

Erictho is a conglomerate of terrors, of illegitimate powers, of marginal characteristics. Her appearance, her abilities, her actions, and her location all mark her as a creature from the margin, the dangerous and powerful place that Mary Douglas describes (p. 97). Syphax describes Erictho for us in terms that resonate with the horror of the female other.

> Here in this desert the great soul of charms,
> Dreadful Erictho lives, whose dismal brow
> Contemns all roofs or civil coverture.
> Forsaken graves and tombs, the ghosts forced out,
> She joys to inhabit.
> A loathsome yellow leanness spreads her face,
> A heavy hell-like paleness loads her cheeks,
> Unknown to a clear heaven; but if dark winds
> Or thick black clouds drive back the blinded stars,
> When her deep magic makes forced heaven quake
> And thunder spite of Jove, Erictho then
> From naked graves stalks out, heaves proud her head
> With long unkempt hair loaden, and strives to snatch
> The night's quick sulphur; then she bursts up tombs;
> From half-rot cerecloths then she scrapes dry gums
> For her black rites; but when she finds a corpse
> New graved, whose entrails yet not turn
> To slimy filth, with greedy havoc then
> She makes spoil, and swells with wicked triumph
> To bury her lean knuckles in his eyes;
> Then doth she gnaw the pale and o'ergrown nails
> From his dry hand; but if she find some life
> Yet lurking close, she bites his gelid lips,
> And, sticking her black tongue in his dry throat,
> She breathes dire murmurs, which enforce him bear
> Her baneful secrets to the spirits of horror. (IV.1.97–122)

Erictho is a cultural monster, made up of traits that reverse accepted cultural conventions.[4] Her power is greater than any wielded by the kings and male warriors of the masculine plot. Her magic shakes the earth, catches the lightening, and terrifies the gods themselves. She is connected to the storms that she controls, uncontrollable herself by any physical, social, legal, or cultural convention. She "contemns all roofs or civil coverture," her hair is long, unbound, and to emphasize her position outside of the rules ordering society, she is located finally in the desert graveyard, where she indulges in illegal, illegitimate, and necrophilic practices upon corpses.[5]

Erictho's graveyard home is a particularly powerful location for Marston. It is the place where the boundary between the living and the dead is most dramatically evident and Erictho moves across that boundary with impunity. Erictho's own interaction with the dead is presented in terms of cannibalism and necrophilia. She scrapes gums, gnaws fingernails, and bites lips; and in pointedly sexual language, "swells with wicked triumph / ... And stick[s] her black tongue in his [the corpse's] dry throat' (IV.1.115, 120). Her body adopts the male position in relation to the corpses that she thrusts herself into, inverting gender roles, transforming the corpses into symbolic feminine bodies. In this liminal space, Erictho's body blends with the corpses upon which she preys: they are taken into her, and become a part of her, and she thrusts herself into them, becoming a part of the dead herself. She is, in many ways, the grotesque described by Mikhail Bakhtin (1984) in *Rabelais and his World*: "unfinished and open—not separated from the world by clearly defined boundaries" (pp. 26–7), but in this case, Erictho's body is not mixed with the world, but with the liminal objects of the dead: with corpses and decay. When Erictho leaves the graveyard to interact with Syphax, she brings with her these powerful connections to the dead with which her character is mixed.

Syphax's interaction with Erictho is sexual. He hires her to use her magic to bring Sophonisba to his bed. This she does, and it is not until after he has consummated his lust that he realizes that Erictho has simply taken Sophonisba's shape and it is Erictho with whom he has copulated. This conflation of death and the figure of the chaste woman symbolically conflates Sophonisba's chastity with the love that Erictho herself brings from the graveyard, giving Syphax what he had earlier threatened to take from Sophonisba by force—physical consummation with the dead.

Elisabeth Bronfen (1992) argues in her monumental study of the aesthetics of death, *Over Her Dead Body*, that

> death and femininity are culturally positioned as the two central enigmas of western discourse. They are used to represent that which is inexpressible, inscrutable, unmanageable, horrible; that which cannot be faced directly but must be controlled by virtue of social laws and art. (p. 255)

Erictho makes explicit the implied connection between feminine sexuality and death, and makes explicit a recurring necrophilic theme in the play—that the only chaste woman, and the only chaste sex, is the dead woman and necrophilia.

Marston's necrophilia, then, occurs on a number of different levels. On one level is Syphax's willingness to "use / With highest lust of sense thy senseless flesh," a necrophilic impulse that sets the stage for a radical revision of the sexual dynamic in the play (a shift from masculine heroism to feminine sexuality). On another is Erictho's liminal sexuality that practices necrophilia on engraved corpses, but also represents, in more ways than one, the dead woman upon which Syphax practices his lust. The resolution of the play reaffirms the necrophilia that has taken over the last half of the play. Sophonisba kills herself for the honor of her husband Massanissa. The men who occupy the stage with her dead body find themselves unequivocally drawn to her, and she is hailed as "woman's right wonder" (V.i.59).

But whereas Marston reaffirms cultural order at the end of the play by reinserting his characters into their proper patriarchal positions (Sophonisba is good, chaste, unthreatening, dead; Massanissa is returned to the throne in an alliance with the Romans and their general Scipio; Syphax is imprisoned and subject to Scipio and Massanissa; Carthage has paid for its treachery against Massanissa with destruction), Erictho disappears. Erictho is not controlled, punished, or rehabilitated; she remains free, her power undiminished. She remains the female other, and she retreats back to the powerful margin, where her danger to society and the boundaries that contain it remains. Though Marston imagines both the patriarchal world of his resolution and the alien otherness of Erictho, by allowing her freedom at the end of the play he acknowledges the uncontrollability and the danger of the power she calls her own. Her power, as we've seen, is characterized in the most horrible terms imaginable for Marston and his culture, but nonetheless, it exists as an alternative to the patriarchal power that dominates Marston's play. Marston leaves the possibility of an alternative alive in the resolution of *The Tragedy of Sophonisba*.[6] The gendered forces that run through *The Tragedy of Sophonisba* remind us that though Jacobean society has a clear understanding of where women belong (Sophonisba makes that position clear), the society is also in the grip of forces that are reimagining the power available to women and men, and using theater to attempt to define that power.

The Revenger's Tragedy

We should not be surprised to find necrophilia as a central and controlling image in *The Revenger's Tragedy* (1606–7), a play that opens with Vindice praising the skull of his dead lover; in which the living duke is described as a desiccated corpse; in which Vindice can say "My life's unnaturally to me, e'en compelled; / As if I lived now, when I should be dead" (1.1.120–1); in which Spurio, the duke's bastard, can exclaim "And if a bastard's wish might stand in force, / Would all the court were turned into a corse! (1.2.35–6); in which the youngest son of the duchess rapes the wife of a gentleman and in which the wife subsequently commits suicide to the praise of all the men; in which Lussurioso, the duke's son, hiring the disguised Vindice, transforms him into a symbolic woman by paying him and saying "And thus I enter thee" (1.3.85) whereby Vindice, some lines later, can say, describing his sister, "That woman is all male, whom none can enter" (2.1.110); in which chastity is described in the same terms as death (as Antonio says, his dead wife is "as cold in lust as she is now in death" [1.4.35]); and in which the central revenge is effected by the bones of Gloriana, a woman who has been dead since the opening of the play.[7] Clearly necrophilia is but one particular sign in *Revenger's*, part of a larger group of images emphasizing the corruption, the moral, social and cultural breakdown, occurring in the world of the play. But if images of sex and death are prevalent, the necrophilic moment is central to unifying those images and making sense of them.

Like *The Tragedy of Sophonisba* before it, *Revenger's* is founded on constructions of sexuality and its plot gets its energy from the number and variety of characters who push at the boundaries of sexual behavior. At the beginning of the play, as the duke with his royal train passes over the stage, Vindice introduces them to us.

> Duke! royal lecher! go, grey-haired adultery!
> And thou his son, as impious steeped as he:
> And thou his bastard, true begot in evil:
> And thou his duchess, that will do with devil:
> Four excellent characters! (1.1.1–5)

From the first lines of the play, the court is defined in terms of improper sexual behavior, and the main plot—Vindice's revenge against the duke and his family for the killing of his lover—is a reaction to it. The duke and his son, the duchess and her sons, are sexual predators. All sub-plots lead to the bed-chamber and to the violation of cultural standards of sexual behavior.

The early part of the play focuses on Gloriana, the dead mistress of Vindice, the primary revenger, and Vindice opens the play with the skull of his dead lover in his hand:

> Thou sallow picture of my poisoned love,
> My study's ornament, thou shell of death,
> Once the bright face of my betrothed lady,
> When life and beauty naturally filled out
> These ragged imperfections. (1.1.14–18)

For Vindice, love is transformed into the death's head. Love has now become death. As Vindice tells us,

> Thee, when thou wert apparelled in thy flesh,
> The old duke poisoned,
> Because thy purer part would not consent
> Unto his palsied lust. (1.1.31–4)

For Gloriana, chastity both causes and is confirmed by death. But whereas Sophonisba's poisoning marks the climax of Marston's play (relegating Sophonisba's sexuality to the graveyard) and comes as Marston is resolving plot lines, Gloriana's poisoning occurs before the play begins. For *The Revenger's Tragedy*, the chaste woman's sexuality begins where Marston leaves it: in the grave. The difference is that in this play, the chaste woman, like Erictho but without the horror attached to her, returns to haunt the corrupt male society that has relegated her to that liminal position.[8]

To revenge himself on the man who has killed the woman he loves, Vindice lures the duke to a location markedly outside of the realm of the court with promises of an illicit sexual encounter with a "grave" young woman. The place of this rendezvous is, as Vindice describes it, a "darkened, blushless angle," a "fit place, veiled from the eyes o' the court" "wherein 'tis night at noon." On the margin of the court, through the application of appropriate clothing, he enables Gloriana's skull to pass as an amorous young woman. Gloriana becomes again a sexual object whose sexuality, tinged as it is with the corruption of the grave, is central to destroying the debauched old duke. As Vindice tells his brother Hippolito,

This very skull,
Whose mistress the duke poisoned, with this drug,
The mortal curse of the earth, shall be revenged
In the like strain, and kiss his lips to death. (3.4.102–5)

The duke begins his sexual liaison with the dead mistress, and the poison that Vindice has spread on her mouth eats into the duke's lips, teeth, and tongue. After Vindice and his brother beat him, and he is forced to watch his wife and his bastard son in an illicit, sexual meeting, he dies, a victim of the necrophilic relationship that he initiates.

Necrophilia makes obvious the sexual disorder that dominates *The Revenger's Tragedy*. As the duke steps over the line that separates the living from the dead, the nature of the disorder that has infected the world of *The Revenger's Tragedy* and threatens the existence of the social world of the play is thrown into stark relief. The boundaries that contain the disorder of sexuality have broken down, and the energies that should be controlled by society have been unleashed. Both male and female sexuality are held up as dangerous forces which lead to disorder and disaster and finally the destruction of the court itself, when they escape from the social boundaries that should contain them. Male sexual disorder sets the stage for the release of female sexuality which, with Vindice's help, becomes a revenant preying upon the corrupt patriarchal court. Simultaneous with the return of Gloriana as a revenger is the sexual incontinence of the duchess, who not only cuckolds her husband, the duke, but does so with Spurio, the duke's bastard son. The author of *Revenger's* makes clear that sexual disorder is what causes the social and political destruction we see. When the duke crosses the boundary between the living and the dead and kisses the grave young woman, he moves into a realm dominated by the other, and releases a power that quickly destroys him and his court. His own sexual corruption leads to his death, and the corruption of the rest of the court lead just as surely to their destruction as well. By the end of *The Revenger's Tragedy*, the entire court has been punished. The duke is dead, the duchess banished, the duke's and duchess' sons have been killed or have killed each other. Vindice and Hippolyto have been arrested for the killing of the duke and his son, and most of the nobles of the court have perished in the concluding melee. Only the virtuous Antonio remains, and he takes over the dukedom. The destruction of the court is a result of its sexual disorder, and the duke's liaison with the dead mistress of Vindice is the visible catalyst for this social meltdown.

The Revenger's Tragedy dramatizes the danger of uncontrolled sexuality. For the author of *Revenger's*, the play becomes a space within which the energy of the margins can be investigated and critiqued and then rendered non-threatening. The duke's necrophilic encounter with the dead Gloriana is a semiotic marker of the sexual violation that runs through the play. It marks the margin for us, and enables us to identify the destructive energy that is being released by the violation of sexual mores in the culture of the play. That we are intended to carry that insight beyond the confines of the playhouse, and make connections between the world of the play and the increasingly unstable society in which the play is written, is indicated in the self-consciousness with which the relationship between the behavior of the characters, and the historical moment is handled. The author gives the nod to what Molly Smith (1991) has called "the darker world" of Jacobean culture, and predicates it on sexual behavior. As Hippolyto describes the villain he has obtained for Lussurioso's use: "This our age swims within him: and if Time / Has so much hair, I should take him for Time, / He is so near kin to this present minute" (1.3.24–6). Throughout, *Revenger's* emphasizes the corruption of the historical moment, and that insistence marks a concern for the state of present day Jacobean culture. As Lussurioso, the duke's son, tells Vindice: "I'll trust thee with the business of my heart / Because I see thee well-experienced / In this luxurious day wherein we breathe" (13.107–9). Villainousness characterizes the historical moment chronicled in *Revenger's*, and illicit sexuality characterizes that villainousness. As the characters continually remind us, *The Revenger's Tragedy* is very much of its time, and the sexual corruption and necrophilia that interests and ultimately drives it is a sign of those times.

The Second Maiden's Tragedy

In *The Second Maiden's Tragedy* (1611), necrophilia has come to the center of the court. It is no longer necessary to go into the graveyards to look for the witch Erictho, or even to search out the "darkened blushless angle" of *Revenger's*. Instead, when the Lady kills herself to avoid the embrace of the usurping Tyrant, the Tyrant exhumes her corpse and brings it to his throne-room and addressing it openly in his court, says: "How pleasing art thou to us even in death! / I love thee yet, above all women living, / And shall do sev'n year hence. / I can see nothing to be mended in thee / But the too constant paleness of thy cheek" (V.ii.24–8). *The Second Maiden's Tragedy* makes necrophilia conventional, drawing upon traditional linkages between sexuality and death, while at the same time deflecting the destructive nature of the forces released. *The Second Maiden's Tragedy* grapples with the dangerousness and the allure of female sexuality, but posits finally the possibility of adopting or absorbing those forces harmlessly into the culture of the play by redefining necrophilia and containing it in the spiritual realm.

"I can see nothing to be mended in thee / But the too constant paleness of thy cheek." The Lady's chastity is confirmed by her death, in a transformation we noted at the beginning of this discussion, and that chastity both draws and repels the Tyrant. Her paleness, semiotically linked to chastity, causes him distress, and his first move after bringing the lady into the court is to find a face-painter to give her some color. Color is sexuality, and when the rightful king, Govianus, disguised as a face painter, has given the Lady color (and with it poison), the Tyrant expostulates: "O, she lives again! ... . / Does she not feel warm to thee? / Our arms and lips / Shall labour life into her" (V.ii.114, 117–19), whereby he embraces and kisses her, bringing his own death upon him.

On the surface, the Tyrant's necrophilia is a sign of his unlawful and excessive appetite, a sign apparent to other characters in the play. The Tyrant's obsession with the Lady is taken by her father as a dangerous sign that lust will dominate the court culture for the foreseeable future. As her father Helvetius says to the Tyrant:

If your lust keep but hot some twenty winters,
We are like to have a virtuous world of wives,
Daughters, and sisters, besides kinswomen
And cousin-germans removed up and down
Where'er thou please to have 'em! (II.iii.41–5)

This appetite leads ultimately to the distrust of his subjects and to his own downfall, and again, necrophilia becomes the sign that makes the impropriety of the Tyrant's appetite clear to his courtiers and the audience. As Memphonius, one of the Tyrant's courtiers, says when the Tyrant heads for the church to disinter the body of the Lady:

What should he make in the cathedral now,
The hour so deep in night? All his intents
Are contrary to man, in spirit or blood. (IV.ii.63–5)

That contrariness marks him, and by this point we recognize the markings well.

As a consequence, when Govianus paints the face of the lady with poison, and the Tyrant kisses her and brings on his own death, the nobles move to embrace Govianus as the new king, allowing the Tyrant to die without aid. Unlike *The Revenger's Tragedy*, the court in *Second Maiden's* is not inherently corrupt. The necrophilia of which the Tyrant is guilty marks him with corruption, and both the court and the audience recognize it. Necrophilia in this play is one more element defining the Tyrant as a political, as well as a sexual, monster. The court eventually sees the signs and after reading them correctly, supports Govianus, the true King. On one level, with the Tyrant's courtiers we read the Tyrant's necrophilia as a sign of *his* corruption and *his* unfitness. By 1611, when this play is believed to have been written and produced, the only thing surprising about the necrophilia is that the Tyrant so blatantly and forcefully entertains the dead Lady in his court. Necrophilia has become a mark of personal and cultural corruption in the drama, a release of dangerous disorder that marks both the Tyrant's court, and Jacobean society, for destruction. But necrophilia appears in another guise in this play as well, slipping into the play much more ambivalently than the Tyrant's grave-robbing, and providing a cultural antidote to the Tyrant's necrophilia that is intended to reconcile Jacobean culture to its necrophilic impulses as well.

After the suicide of the Lady Govianus praises her in conventional terms.

Eternal maid of honour, whose chaste body
Lies here like virtue's close and hidden seed,
To spring forth glorious to eternity. (IV.iv.37–9)

But when her ghost appears to him to exhort him to save her body from defilement, he immediately falls in love with the ghost, and in language that echoes the Tyrant's address of her body, Govianus addresses her spirit.

> O, never came astonishment and fear
> So pleasing to mankind! I take delight
> To have my breast shake and my hair stand stiff.
> If this be horror, let it never die!
> Came all the pains of hell in that shape to me,
> I should endure 'em smiling. Keep me still
> In terror, I beseech thee. I'd not change
> This fever for felicity of man
> Or all the pleasures of ten thousand ages. (IV.iv.45–53)

Govianus, indeed, finds himself so enamoured of having the ghost visit him that he delays the revenge that will lay it finally to rest.

> The poor spirit
> Was with me once again about it, troth;
> And I can put it off no more, for shame,
> Though I desire to have it haunt me still
> And never to give over, 'tis so pleasing. (V.i.194–8)

Govianus' love for his dead Lady is given a final necrophilic turn when he is crowned king at the end of the play. Govianus lifts up the corpse of his dead lady and declares:

> Here place her in this throne; crown her our queen,
> The first and last that ever we make ours,
> Her constancy strikes so much firmness in us. (V.ii.200–2)

In a move reminiscent of the Tyrant's necrophilia, Govianus cannot resist making an object of desire out of the dead lady, and here he crowns her his mate before sending her back to the tomb from whence she came.

We end *The Second Maiden's Tragedy* in a world in which necrophilia has been acknowledged and transformed. The play argues that necrophilia is only damnable when it is physical. Spiritual necrophilia, the loving of the ghost of the dead woman, is acceptable because it maintains the physical chastity conferred upon the corpse by death. It enables female sexuality to be disarmed in the grave, while maintaining the woman as a sexual object. *The Second Maiden's Tragedy* attempts to transform the horror of graveyard necrophilia into authorized chaste love. The move takes sexuality out of the physical world and places it in the spiritual. Govianus sends the Lady's corpse back to her tomb, and consummates his relationship only with her ghost, who brings felicities more powerful than "all the pleasures of ten thousand ages."

We have noted that death is transformative. We have noted too, that in the culture of the late Renaissance, death confirms chastity for women. Desdemona, Ophelia, Sophonisba, Gloriana, and the Lady of *Second Maiden's Tragedy*, all are lauded by their plays' resolutions as representatives of ideal womanhood. When the illusion of asexuality is broken by a predatory male who penetrates the boundary that separates these ideal figures from the sexual world and reinserts them into it, or by the woman-as-revenant, driven by a revenging lover or the supernatural power of a witch, the powerful and destructive asocial energies which lie beyond the culture's boundaries are released. Female sexuality is relegated to the grave in early Jacobean culture. When it returns from the grave in physical form, it comes as a revenger, as a destroyer. It comes as Erictho, from her graveyard home, to sexually master Syphax the king and take possession of his seed; it comes as Gloriana, kissing the lecherous old duke to death; it comes as the Lady, whose painted face destroys her necrophilic lover. The necrophilic revenger is the sexual lover, the result when the spiritual love of woman becomes physical, and the boundaries of control fall away. In Govianus and the Tyrant we see the two Jacobean alternatives for love of woman: in one, a spiritual love that is ultimately asexual, and in the other the physical love that is necrophilic and destructive.

And love thee after

Necrophilia is a valuable set of signs for Jacobean playwrights, and the transition from Elizabeth I to James I gives those signs their power and timeliness. As England moves from the culture of Elizabeth, in which the most powerful individual in the patriarchal state is a woman, to the culture of James, a profound shift in the way that women, and women's sexuality are interpreted occurs.

As many commentators have pointed out, Elizabeth deconstructed her own sexuality and positioned herself, in ideological terms, as simultaneously virginal, maternal, and paternal. Her own sexuality disappears in her roles as virgin queen and patriarchal monarch. As Theodora Jankowski (1992) notes, "She made her body natural serve her body politic by creating myths regarding the three major aspects of a woman's existence—virgin, wife, mother—and tying them to her political persona" (p. 71). What sexuality surrounds her as a woman is dissipated into the political realm and does not invest Elizabeth physically. As a consequence, Elizabeth manages to both represent woman, and distance herself from the frightening and alien power perceived by a patriarchal society to lie in women's sexuality. The anxieties attendant on the sexuality of women are, as a consequence, less pronounced and less apparent in the theater of the late Elizabethan period than they will be in the early Jacobean.

When he takes the throne in 1603, James I has no gender tight-rope to walk. Representationally he is able to insert himself immediately into a position of patriarchal leadership as King.[9] He is the country's father, husband, but most of all, its divinely ordained King. James lays down a strictly patriarchal line, and holds that line throughout his reign, strengthening it as he can with learning, rhetoric, and theater. The baggage that James brings with him to the English throne helps set the tone for much of the drama of his period.[10] Linda Woodbridge (1984) tells us that James I's "misogyny was legendary" and quotes a letter from the French Ambassador. "He [the king] piques himself on great contempt for women" (p. 144). The necrophilia that comes into the drama in the early years of James' reign is symptomatic of the social tension inherent in the movement from an Elizabethan to a Jacobean way of understanding the world. Representationally, the crown and the court labor to present women as other, and their sexuality as increasingly connected to death and to horror. All three of the plays we have looked at here wrestle with the insecurity of sexual representation in similar ways, all using necrophilia to help the playwright grapple with the tensions involved. All posit the dead woman as the culturally imagined ideal. Her sexuality is quiescent; she can no longer threaten the order of the patriarchal state with her sexual power. When women are sexually active in these plays, that sexuality is attended by images drawn from the graveyard and results, almost inevitably, in the death of the male figure who insists on physical consummation. The tension between these two ways of seeing femininity—as an ideal spiritual lover, or a revenging physical monster—can be seen in all three of the plays we have looked at, and underlies Shakespeare's more subtle references to necrophilia with which we opened this discussion.

Jacobean necrophilia looks forward to the social, economic, and political disorder of the civil war, and back to the stability of Elizabeth I and her modeling of the ideal woman—part mother, part father, all virginal chastity—and it is based specifically in gender and sexual confusion. The gender confusion that Linda Woodbridge (1984) has described in *Women and the English Renaissance*, which she claims is an essential element of Jacobean culture, and which Laura Levine (1994) and Stephen Orgel (1996) have helped to develop in their excellent books (*Men in Women's Clothing* and *Impersonations* respectively), among others, is the matrix within which we must place the necrophilia that is such a dramatic element of early Jacobean drama. Necrophilia is evidence that the playwrights, and the cultural forces that influence them, feel the boundaries that generally hold the geographic margins of a culture in place are beginning to break down. The sexual danger inherent in women who cannot be controlled is transformed into the signs of chastity, death, and necrophilia. In those signs, women are allowed representational power. The fears inherent in the culture are allowed free reign until a new form of order, or control, can be constructed to contain, or neutralize, the forces these female characters have released from the margin.

Notes

1   All references to Shakespeare's texts are from *The Norton Shakespeare* (1997), edited by Stephen Greenblatt.
2   By the term "gender system" I mean all of the various social and biological practices that served both to define subjective gender in the period, and to define the relationships between genders and sexes.
3   All references to *The Tragedy of Sophonisba* are from Peter Corbin and Douglas Sedge's edition, in *Three Jacobean Witchcraft Plays* (1986), pp. 33–84.
4   As many commentators have pointed out, the primary defining characteristic of English and European witchcraft during the 15th, 16th, and even 17th centuries is reversal. The historian Christina Larner (1981) writes in *Enemies of God* that it is an "anthropological truism that witch-beliefs represent a direct inversion of the values of the society in which they are held" (p. 134). Though Marston draws upon Lucan's *Pharsalia* (VI, 507ff) for his description of Erictho, the principles underlying that description underlie the definitions of witchcraft in Marston's time as well.

5   Body snatching, the unauthorized exhumation of corpses, and the practicing upon corpses with the intent to contact the dead (in this case "the spirits of horror") are all violations of Jacobean law.

6   The title of the play also asks us to see the play through these two lenses. It is both *The Wonder of Women* and *The Tragedy of Sophonisba*. From a patriarchal point of view the play is the story of the former: a woman whose dedication to the patriarchal power structure is so pure that she kills herself to maintain it. From the alternative, however, it is Sophonisba's tragedy, the story of a woman killed by the tragic choices she makes, the unfortunate flaws she demonstrates, both of which are connected to her dedication to patriarchal principles. Sophonisba's tragic flaw is her willingness to be ruled by the men of her world.

7   All references to *The Revenger's Tragedy* are from the Oxford edition of *Four Revenge Tragedies* (1995) edited by Katherine Eisaman Maus.

8   It is interesting to note that "Gloriana" is a name often given to Queen Elizabeth I during her reign by poets who sought to praise her. Throughout the Jacobean period there is a longing for the dead Queen that underlies the necrophilia of the period.

9   James I certainly had his own representational and social forces to overcome, the most important being his nationality and the deep-seated suspicion with which the English held the Scottish. In the end, though, his gender made his acceptance as King relatively easy.

10 Even more than Elizabeth before him, James was a great patron of the theatre. The connection between the throne and the drama has been described in studies such as Louis Montrose's *The Purpose of Playing* (1996), Steven Mullaney's *The Place of the Stage* (1988), Leonard Tennenhouse's *Power on Display* (1986), Christopher Pye's *The Regal Phantasm* (1990), among many others.

References

Bakhtin, M. (1984). *Rabelais and His World* (Helene Iswolsky, Trans.). Bloomington, IN: Indiana University Press.

Bronfen, E. (1992). *Over Her Dead Body: Death, Femininity, and the Aesthetic*. New York: Routledge.

Donne, J. (1983). *The Songs and Sonnets of John Donne* (2nd edition. Theodore Redpath, Ed.). London: Methuen.

Douglas, M. (1966). *Purity and Danger: An Analysis of the Concepts of Pollution and Taboo*. New York: Routledge.

Eliot, T.S. (1950). *Selected Essays*. New York: Harcourt.

Engel, W.E. (1995). *Mapping Mortality: The Persistence of Memory and Melancholy in Early Modern England* (Massachusetts Studies in Early Modern Culture. Arthur E. Kinney, Ed.). Amherst: University of Massachusetts Press.

Howard, J.E. (1994). *The Stage and Social Struggle in Early Modern England*. New York: Routledge.

Jankowski, T.A. (1992). *Women in Power in the Early Modern Drama*. Chicago: University of Illinois Press.

Larner, C. (1981). *Enemies of God: The Witch-hunt in Scotland*. Baltimore: Johns Hopkins University Press.

Levine, L. (1994). *Men in Women's Clothing: Anti-theatricality and Effeminization, 1579–1642*. (Cambridge Studies in Renaissance Literature and Culture 5, Stephen Orgel, Ed.). New York: Cambridge University Press.

Marston, J. (1607 [1986]). *The Wonder of Women or The Tragedy of Sophonisba*. In Peter Corbin and Douglas Sedge (Eds), *Three Jacobean Witchcraft Plays*. (The Revels Plays Companion

Library, E.A.J. Honigman *et al.*, Eds). New York: Manchester University Press.

Metcalf, P. and R. Huntington. (1991). *Celebrations of Death: The Anthropology of Mortuary Ritual.* (2nd edition). Cambridge: Cambridge University Press.

Montrose, L.A. (1996). *The Purpose of Playing: Shakespeare and the Cultural Politics of the Elizabethan Theatre.* Chicago: University of Chicago Press.

Mullaney, S. (1988). *The Place of the Stage: License, Play, and Power in Renaissance England.* Chicago: University of Chicago Press.

Orgel, S. (1996). *Impersonations: The Performance of Gender in Shakespeare's England.* New York: Cambridge University Press.

Pye, C. (1990). *The Regal Phantasm: Shakespeare and the Politics of Spectacle.* New York: Routledge.

The Revenger's Tragedy (1606–07 [1995]). In K. Eisaman Maus (Ed.), *Four Revenge Tragedies.* (The World's Classics, Michael Cordner, Peter Holland and Martin Wiggins, General Eds). New York: Oxford University Press.

The Second Maiden's Tragedy (1611 [1978]). A. Lancashire, Ed.(The Revels Plays, F. David Heoniger, E.A.J. Honigmann and J.R. Mulryne, General Eds.). Baltimore: John Hopkins University Press.

Shakespeare, W. (1997). *The Norton Shakespeare.* Stephen Greenblatt *et al.*, Eds. New York: Norton.

Smith, M. (1991). *The Darker World Within: Evil in the Tragedies of Shakespeare and His Successors.* Newark: University of Delaware Press.

Tennenhouse, L. (1986). *Power on Display: the Politics of Shakespeare's Genres.* New York: Methuen.

Traub, V. (1992). *Desire and Anxiety: Circulations of Sexuality in Shakespearean Drama.* (Gender, Culture, Difference. Catherine Belsey, General Ed.). New York: Routledge.

Woodbridge, L. (1984). *Women and the English Renaissance: Literature and the Nature of Womankind, 1540–1620.* Chicago: University of Illinois Press.

Chapter 7

Staging the social drama of Maghrebi Women in the theatre of Fatima Gallaire

Jan Berkowitz Gross

> Cultural identity is, to a large extent, an ideational construction of the real and the imagined, and its edifice has an obvious purpose: it's a machine for survival which uses the past and the future to reinforce the present.
>
> (Albert Memmi)[1]

As a Franco-Algerian living in France, Fatima Gallaire, like other writers poised at the crossroads and in the crossfire of two cultures, turns to writing as a constructive means of filling the glaring void in her existence: Algeria (Déjeux, 1992, p. 6). In those plays that depict Maghrebi society, Gallaire's identity ink (*"l'encre de l'identité"*) is unmistakable as it joins the French *encre* as ink to its homophonic partner *ancre* as anchor (Begag and Chaouite, 1990, pp. 98–103). However, despite its provisional stability, the identity anchor is also felt as a burdensome weight:

> I've always felt it, present and weighing down on my shoulders, this Middle Ages that I've carried with me everywhere, carefully protecting it in France. It's a constant presence, terrifying and familiar, which forbids any desire to forget.
>
> (Gallaire, *Rimm*)

Similar to Rimm, Gallaire's other female characters experience themselves simultaneously as subject and object. With "a self split up the middle" (Turner, 1987, p. 25), they struggle to discover a middle ground between their individual subjectivity and their sociocultural identity, as each reflects the other from a different angle, projecting what Turner calls "the eye by which culture sees itself" (p. 24). And, as subjects learning to speak from a "split space of enunciation" (Bhabha, 1994, p. 14), they are more inclined to become agents for change as they discover and invent new "notions of solidarity and community … and new subjectivities" (Pile and Thrift, 1995, p. 18). As Gallaire's theatre illustrates, such voices are uniquely equipped to rethink and refigure traditional norms of Maghrebi identity, especially for women.

Although Gallaire came upon writing for theatre "inadvertently" (Déjeux, 1992, p. 6), more than twenty plays to date point to her theatre's capacity to speak simultaneously from multiple sites, reproducing and juxtaposing a "situatedness" of sociocultural experience. Such an aesthetic experience yields results not possible in writing for the page alone.[2] On the seismic fault line *entre deux rives* (between two shores of the Mediterranean), Gallaire confronts the insider's view of North Africa with the outsider's more distant gaze. Penetrating the veiled intimacy of Arab culture and Muslim practices, her most recognized plays enable viewers and stage practitioners, Maghrebi and non-Maghrebi alike, to encounter and to participate in "structures of lived experience" which present "cumulative knowledge" about real world sociocultural realities through the performance genre (Turner, 1987, p. 84).[3] In this sense, Gallaire's theater provides a public form of "cultural mirroring" which represents the individual engaged in the process of "working meaning out" for him or herself (Turner, 1986, pp. 36–7).

With the skills of an ethnodramaturg, Gallaire enables bodies and voices oppressed by and embedded in silence to speak, to be heard, and, ultimately, to be seen on stage. Drawing from the explicitness of the physical body and the intimacy of interpersonal exchange, Gallaire affirms, "I must not be ashamed to telling tell all" (Surel-Turpin, 1995, p. 35), even to the point of confessing shock at seeing the power of her written words unleashed on stage.[4] Exploring the intimacy of unspoken topics, such as marriage to a non-Muslim, the ceremony of male circumcision, polygamy, repudiation, father–daughter relations, or the procreation of sons and their overvalued status within society, Gallaire's drama appears to reproduce what Turner defined as the "processual" stages of real-life "social drama" (1986, p. 39).

While anthropologists have often turned to the "drama analogy," theatre director Richard Schechner notes that "only a little anthropology touches a little of theatre," and that no anthropologist has done more to link the two than Victor Turner (1985, p. 3). Similar to Aristotle's model of linear movement from exposition to denouement in tragedy, Turner devised the four-stage "social drama" (breach—crisis—redress—reintegration or schism) to illustrate how all societies and societal groups confront moments of crisis and resolve conflicts in a developmental fashion. The Turnerian social drama proceeds as follows:

1   a breach of a norm or value causes tensions to erupt, creating a situation of disagreement;
2   a mounting crisis ensues as opposing groups take shape;
3   mode/s of redress seek to put an end to the crisis, at which point some interpretive efforts may be made to assess the crisis, resulting in social or "plural reflexivity"; and
4   an outcome resolves the crisis either through reconciliation and reintegration of the disturbed group or through irreparable schism and spatial separation, and may involve proposed paradigms for societal change (1982, pp. 9–12, 69–79, 108–11).

Looking beyond "normal social science" work, Turner found his best "evidence" of the processual social drama in genres such as art, literature, philosophy, etc., that, by nature, must do more than "recapitulate"; they must also "scrutinize and evaluate" (1984, p. 26). While acknowledging wide variation among different cultures, Turner views the social drama in modern industrialized societies as a replacement for tribal ritual, providing the "raw stuff out of which theatre comes to be created" and, as such, a "universal" form (p. 24). Since many of Gallaire's plays are grounded in specific sociocultural processes, the paradigm of Turner's "social drama" is an especially valuable tool for examining her plays about North Africa, particularly as they expose the third redressive phase of reflexivity and retributive action in which individuals and groups pause to contemplate from a "liminal" space. Based on van Gennep's notion of the *limen* or "a no-man's land betwixt and between the structural past and the structural future" (1986, p. 41), Turner associates liminality with performance (i.e., rituals, carnivals, festivals, theatre) which pulls viewers out of the flow of their lived reality into a suspended transitional space. As in the threshold phase during rites of passage, liminality invites viewers to "think about how they think ... or to feel about how they feel in daily life" (1984, p. 22). As a "gestation process," it may lead to plural reflexivity and "a striving after new forms and structures" (Turner, 1986, p. 42). Consequently, as Jean Duvignaud observes, societies confronting crises or painful transitions often produce an increased rate of theatrical activity as individuals and groups perceive a more acute need to represent themselves (Helbo, 1991, p. 59). Gallaire's plays use the reflective surface of theatre to afford both fictional characters and real-life viewers an opportunity to confront the tensions that afflict individuals and societies at a given point in time.

Turner also distinguishes between two different yet intrinsically related ways of experiencing the social, between "communitas" and "structure." In the former, society is viewed as a "homogeneous undifferentiated *whole*" (1974, p. 237) marked by spontaneous expressions of common purpose and shared experience which favor egalitarian bonds that unite "over and above" defined social structures (1974, p. 46). By contrast, "structure" as "all that holds people apart" reinforces differences of rank or status and strictly prescribes norms and behaviors (1974, p. 47). As a result, societies based largely on patrilineal kinship, such as the Muslim model in Gallaire's plays, will predictably display the dominant authority of what Turner calls a hard "line" of descent in contrast to the soft, affectional "side" of a sometimes mystical, less visible influence of what, in this case, is the "complementary filiation" of female kinship (1974, p. 235). Such distinctions are especially relevant in Gallaire's plays which illustrate the critical interplay between the hard "line" of official patriarchy and the soft "side" of daily lived experience. While these terms are normally associated with traditional male and female roles, Gallaire's male characters may align with the soft side while females may uphold patriarchal rigidity. Of primary interest to Gallaire, however, are the marginal characters who evade or challenge traditional status-states. As liminal figures in the Turnerian scheme, they are often outsiders, renegades, or of lowermost social status (1974, p. 237).

Seen as a "form of liberation" (Préface, 1993, p. 4), Gallaire's theatre often proposes new responses to societal impasses in what Turner calls "explanation and explication of life itself" (1982, pp. 12–19). Similar to Turner's rejection of functionalist anthropology's emphasis on the "indicative" mood of observable culture in favor of the "subjunctive" mood of telling and performing culture, Gallaire's "aesthetic" or stage drama enacts a newly configured rendition of Maghrebi cultural life—where the reality-driven "as is" of society is rescripted to produce an evocative "as if" or "what if?" In the "restored behavior" of theatre where the "self can act in/as another" (Schechner, 1985, p. 36), unique liberating effects are possible; for the stage drama not only "reflects" the social drama, it may also "affect" it through an "oscillatory" and reciprocal flow. Illustrated in a figure-eight infinity loop, the social drama "in the world" (both visible and hidden) continually intersects with the stage drama which works "on consciousness" (actual and virtual) (Schechner, 1988, p. 190). Given that neurological effects of effectively performed drama may also result in a "very high state of participatory arousal" among both performers and spectators, Schechner (1986, p. 349) helps to explain why live drama was for Turner the source of "the deepest experience" because of its ability to get people "bodily as well as mentally involved in another (not physically present) culture" (Turner, 1982, pp. 92–3).[5] Similarly, the vital link between the implicit social drama and the explicit aesthetic dramas in Gallaire's plays may lead to liberation for the author in the act of *poeisis* and for the observer in the receptive act of *aesthesis* and *catharsis* (Jauss, 1982, p. 35). As when the spectator moves from the identification and emotional upheaval of catharsis to a state of critical reflection, plays such as Gallaire's might well provide what Jauss considered "liberation from" and "liberation for" something (1974, p. 286). For this reason, performance genres are often considered breeding grounds for new ways of thinking about culture (Carlson, 1996, pp. 22–5; Ashley, 1990, pp. xviii), giving rise to both new models for change or confirmation of old ones (MacAloon, 1984, pp. 24–5).

Not unlike Turner's definition of liminality, cultural theorists (Bhabha; Pile and Thrift) rely on spatial metaphors of movement in the "beyond," in a "third space," or in a "space of intervention" to describe how persons of split identities seek shelter in a cultural "in-between" free from confining labels and arbitrary dividing lines. If the liminal state is by nature transitional, inviting separation, reflection and even invention, then the spatial endpoint of that process might well be the hybrid "interstitial space" as a stable location, mapped differently than the familiar tracings and dictates of the past (Deleuze and Guattari, 1987). Gallaire's theatre participates in both processes, as characters cross forbidden boundaries in an "insurgent act of cultural translation" (Bhabha, p. 7), where the "personal" drama of the "I" intersects and collides with the ever-evolving and crushing force of the "social" drama of the collective "we." At this precarious juncture many of Gallaire's plays attend to the wound of what Edouard Glissant defined as the contemporary sense of the (Tragic) when he spoke of Kateb Yacine's theatre as a place where personal destiny meets collective destiny head on.[6] However, with the notion of personal agency come individuals like those in Gallaire's theatre who may be "capable … of reconstituting or even transforming that structure" (Pile and Thrift, 1995, p. 1).

Given theatre's ability to speak in multiple voices beyond the self, Gallaire's characters embody different ages, genders, social classes, and educational levels. The following analysis will use the Turnerian social drama as a road map for the journeys of different women in their quest for self-definition within the context of contemporary North Africa: *Princesses, ou, Ah! vous êtes venus … là où il y a quelques tombes* (1988; 1991) [*Princesses, or, Ah, You've Come … There Where There Are Several Graves*], *Les Co-Epouses* (1990) [*The Co-Wives*], and *Rimm, la gazelle* (1993) [*Rimm, the gazelle*].[7] In *Princesses* and *Les Co-épouses*, the social drama unfolds within groups of female characters living in cloistered settings: an ancestral village in *Princesses* and a polygamous household in *Les Co-épouses*. By contrast, the solitary character of *Rimm*, an adult daughter alone in her Parisian apartment, travels mentally "beyond" the flow of daily life into a fully liminal space where her cultural identity is performed in the act of being "gropingly discovered" (Turner on Sapir, 1981, p. 140). Viewed in chronological order, each play takes a discursive step closer to mapping a successful path between self and community for the North African woman.

Breaking ground

> – But what is our crime, your Majesty?
> – Your offense is to be what you are: girls and women …
> – Just a minute, we may be condemned, but we have the right to speak.
> (Gallaire, *Le Secret des Vieilles*, p. 56)

In Gallaire's first, darkest, and most controversial play, *Princesses, ou, Ah! vous êtes venus … là où il y a quelques tombes*,[8] the tragic story of a liberated woman's decision to revisit her ancestral village follows the rhetorical path of the classic Greek tragedy: to the graveyard.[9] When a prodigal adult daughter "Princesse" or "Lella"[10] arrives unannounced from France to her native land after twenty years of exile, her surprise return sets into action the four-phase process of Turner's "social drama": breach—crisis—redress—outcome. Following her "breach," a forbidden marriage to a French non-Muslim, Princess was disowned by her father. Only with his recent death does she dare to retrace her steps home. To the elderly guardians of tradition, however, her return is a blasphemous affront to patriarchal authority. Unbeknownst to the daughter, her omnipotent father, the *hadj*, has entrusted his vengeance "beyond the grave" to the obedient village elders who agree to judge and punish the daughter in exchange for a generous inheritance.

Blind to the perils so evident to everyone else, Princess arrives loaded down with cultural "otherness," bringing from France weighty baggage filled with gifts for all, and with her precious books which she manages to get past wary custom officials always suspicious of revolutionaries. Her hybrid self reveals a glaring split between belonging to another life in France and longing to reunite, albeit fleetingly, with a much altered communal past. With great emotion and expectation, Princess returns to the soil that holds precious memories both of the living (her dear great grandmother-nursemaid Nounou, anchor of generations) and the dead (the tomb of her beloved mother).

The young woman who arrives "home" to horrific privation in "this land of the unbelievable" is the antithesis of her traditional Muslim analogue: a happy and fulfilled wife, mother of twins, intelligent, financially secure, well-educated, and hopeful for the future. Her joy is immediately tempered when her old devoted friend from the past whom she lovingly calls "*vieux père*" (also known as "the Renegade" for his drunkenness) alerts her to the threat that awaits her: "I was born a rebel … but in their eyes you have become one" (p. 19). Nevertheless, when Princess and her Nounou embrace amid an explosive burst of French and Arabic, it is as if the young woman's past emanates from the very pores of Nounou's 103-year old flesh, still "eternal and solid as a rock" (p. 25). The maternal lineage of the soft affectional side of kinship is revitalized, joining Princess' own twins in an unbroken line to Nounou who thrills to the thought of "the child of the child of my child" (p. 26). But when Princess proposes taking Nounou back to France with her, the old woman reminds her dear Princess of the hard and unyielding line of societal structure that governs time and space: "Bury me this very day and leave! … You've taken the wrong road" (p. 27).

Princess' false sense of belonging resurfaces when the chorus of young women welcome her and plead for stories of present happiness while Princess longs only for precious memories of the past. In a village "changed into bad and then worse," her female peers' lives and bodies have become a repository for pain, privation, repudiation, and physical brutality. They delight to hear of Princess' conjugal joy as they heap praise on her foreign husband "Erromi" for having the "heart of a good Muslim." As a great lover, he managed to erase even the most painful wounds Princess once thought "indelible" (p. 33). Set apart from her peers and steeped in Western privilege, habits and lifestyle, Princess' difference is again evident when her decreased appetite leaves her unable to indulge in the sumptuous feast: "I'll watch you eat and that pleasure will be worth more than any meal" (p. 54). However, the surface contrasts of lifestyle and experience are quickly erased as their jubilant reunion unfolds, set in an atmosphere of renewed "communitas" and marked by traditional song and dance. In the presence of their "Princess," all are momentarily uplifted as they recover the memory of what once was abundant, good, and pure in a village now mired in deprivation, fear, and corruption.

A single anguished voice punctuates the celebratory mood: Maboula or the Madwoman, a neighbor born in the same year as Princess, who claims that when Princess left her sanity left too. Now, her uncontrollable body expels "inhuman cries, half whimpers, half moans, enough to give goose flesh" (p. 43), only to be silenced by periodic blows dealt by the other women. In contrast to the complete erasure of past pain for the fortunate Princess, the Madwoman's body bears the indelible scars of inescapable despair, as if to embody woman's unspeakable collective destiny in the persistent refrain of her woeful lullaby: "Rock-a-bye, Rock-a-bye, your pain, you have only your pain, Rock-it gently" (p. 50). In a setting where bodies speak as loudly as words, the trunk of a "half-man," the legless Cripple (Cul-de-jatte), arrives as the next intruder on the celebration and urges his Princess to flee. His benevolent and diminished male presence marks the transition between the soft, affectional "side" of female exchange and the menacing shadow of patrilineal wrath looming ever larger in the background. In the repressive atmosphere where only social outcasts or inferiors dare to speak the truth (i.e., Nounou, the Renegade, the Cripple, the Madwoman), the other young women, although admiring of Princess, fade obediently into the background, leaving the imposing and confident Princess to fend for herself. As a dead end of the "hard" patriline, the young woman must stand alone in her challenge to a society that rules in accordance with ancient laws of senior male corporate domination (Combs-Schilling, 1989, p. 68).

Part II of the play ushers in the "crisis" phase of the social drama when a chorus of old women arrive imperiously wielding the hard "line" of patrilineal rights, as they refuse all forms of traditional hospitality offered by their compatriot Nounou. In the wholly separate worlds of males and females, the old women do the bidding of their male superiors in the commissioned act of judging Princess for her breach. The ensuing semi-juridical trial leads to phase three of the social drama: "redress" as "a time in which an interpretation is put upon the events leading up to and constituting the crisis ... whereby the whole, the total sociocultural phenomenon becomes intelligible" (Turner, 1987, p. 97). Assailed by the old women's blunt accusations of blasphemy and infamy, Princess is forced into reflexivity. When her cherished personal values are mercilessly pitted against the hateful intolerance of the reigning social order, Princess is aroused to act in a spontaneous cultural performance, forced into "mobilized attention" (MacAloon, 1984, p. 10). Devising her own "redressive" path, she calls upon a God who has created a diversity of human beings all "equal in the face of our creator" (p. 72). By indicting societal hypocrisy, ignorance, and the oppression of women, the self-righteous Princess stands firm against her accusers, as she explains to the illiterate women the politics of the double standard for mixed marriages and conversions, and the Semitic origin of circumcision for both Jews and Muslims. In "that mouth that says it all," she defiantly and eloquently rejects the distorted Islam of the elders. Regrettably, her reasoned defense falls upon deaf ears and her voice is fated to remain buried in the desert sand.

Yet, in her role as outsider in a liminal state, Princess sees what her society stands to lose when the natural bonds of "communitas" are strangled by a devious power structure (Turner, 1974, p. 232). And, even if her word is not heeded in the present, she heralds a new form of resistance, more pregnant with change than that of society's marginalized outcasts and inferiors. If other Princesses come forward (as the plural noun in the title may suggest), new types of redressive action are possible. When asked if she has a last wish, Princess replies cryptically that she will not divulge it, but that "it will come about" (p. 86), as a prophesy of an unknown order. With dignity and dry eyes, she defies her attackers' triumphant appropriation of Allah ("Allah is with us!") in her own final reclamation of Allah, "Farewell my loved ones! Allah is with me!"[11]

In the final phase of the social drama, the old women first strike down Princess' physically frail defenders (Nounou, the Cripple, the Renegade and the Madwoman), before unleashing the full force of their frenzy on Princess in a merciless clubbing carried out in a stylized ritual dance. In this phase of violent "schism," there appears no possibility of negotiated social change as "structure is maximized to full rigidity" (Turner, 1974, p. 268), drowning out all opposition and stripping away the humanity of communitas so resonant in the first half of the play. With the stage cleared of slain bodies, the male elders appear for the first time in collective unanimity. Dismissing the old women for their "kind mission," they take their rightful place next to the body of Princess prepared for burial as they "perform their duty as good Muslims" (p. 86). In contrast to Lella's non-Muslim husband with his heart of "a good Muslim," the male elders embody the intractable dictate of structure. Despite a cessation of conflict, the sacrificial restorative action taken appears devoid of societal consensus with no chance of reintegration, as only the old men remain on stage to go through the motions of an empty ritual. Behind the scenes, however, may be a silent younger generation deemed untrustworthy and selfish by their elders because they find religion too "confining" (p. 77).[12] Whether the young will find the collective strength to oppose the social order remains to be seen, but the exemplary, though untimely, model of Princess remains as a reminder of society's need to admit new spaces and subjectivities.

With Princess' body re-appropriated by the patriarchal order, her desire to be reunited with the collective is achieved only structurally through her murder. Her defeat, however, is more spatial than moral. Although her personal resistance failed, her words were silenced only in death. In an ironic twist of absent presence, the body of Princess resides with her enemies as their only means of suppressing her revolt in the only location available to her: the cemetery. Given the controversial nature of the ending and the striking similarity between real-life social drama and stage drama, some observers worried about inflaming fundamentalist fervor when the play was produced in Paris by activist director Jean-Pierre Vincent in 1991 (Leiblein, 1991, pp. 71–2). Other directors felt the need to make modifications for their audiences: at the Ubu Theatre in New York, the murder scene was presented as a dream sequence; and in Tashkent, male assassins replaced the old women in the final scene (Surel-Turpin, 1995, p. 34).[13] Whether the ending was conceived of as a nightmare in the unconscious of an author seeking personal expiation for her life in exile (Fernández-Sánchez 1996, p. 165) or a chillingly realistic reproduction of ritualistic executions carried out by forces of order, Gallaire insists on the social reality of a physical rather than a symbolic death. As such, the disbelief and shock experienced in Paris at the sight of blood-chilling executions on stage most likely produced that "shudder" of catharsis: a "disturbing oscillation between seeing and feeling" (Diamond, 1995, p. 153) when observers "see and feel ... the otherness of the other" (p. 161). Although Gallaire had never imagined that the tragic denouement of this 1988 play would come to prefigure later atrocities, it may now be seen to "induce" or "heighten" awareness about the mechanisms of real-life social forces, recalling what Turner considered theatre's ability to "heat up" preserved social experiences (1990, p. 13).

Compared to Gallaire's subsequent plays, the tragic ending of *Princesses* is decidedly an anomaly, though, perhaps, a necessary stepping stone in forcing submissive women to think "through" female identity in a hostile context. In retrospect, Gallaire admits that, if she were writing *Princesses* today, she would find a way to spare her ill-fated heroine (J.B. Gross, personal communication, June 8,

1998). In subsequent plays, Gallaire allows her female characters to achieve greater proficiency as wayfarers in their search for reconciliation between personal liberation and communal values. All of Gallaire's later plays depict social dramas which result in more hopeful and constructive redressive actions, allowing the subjunctive mood of culture to overcome impasses imposed by the indicative mood.

Breaking tradition

> But I know, and you know, that women are never lacking in resourcefulness. Inferiors? Superiors? What does it matter? For the moment, it's just a question of surviving.
>
> (Gallaire, *Le Secret des Vieilles*, p. 57)

In the "democracy of absurdity" of a polygamous household in *Les Co-Epouses*, Gallaire traces the identity paths of four generations of women living under the same roof within a strictly delineated patriarchal framework ruled by an entitled matriarch. The impassive great-grandmother (the Ancestor), the imperious mother (Nahnouha), the submissive wife and daughter-in-law (Taos), and the rebellious eldest daughter (Chems) all struggle to affirm their rightful place in relation to the sole male (grandson, son, husband, and father), Driss. Unlike the stylized female choruses of old and young in *Princesses*, *Les Co-Epouses* blurs the sharp dividing line between generations and introduces the "outside" voice of a young neighbor and family friend, Siréna, similar to Princess in her "worldliness," though considerably more savvy in negotiating patriarchal society's stranglehold on women. The uncompromising voice of patriarchy heard from beyond the grave in *Princesses* is humanized in the meek, vulnerable, sometimes sympathetic figure of *pater familias*, Driss. The exalted tone of tragedy shrinks to the mundane level of everyday life in a bourgeois *drame* as Princess' high-minded revolt and subsequent slaughter is refigured in the more commonplace, though no less heroic and dignified, death of co-wife Mimia coerced into an eighth childbirth by the patrilineal demand for sons.

Two stage presences rest in the background of the private interior space: the human presence of the blind and silent Ancestor and the material presence of first wife Taos' loom (later joined by a second loom for co-wife Mimia). Both objects (human and inanimate) define traditional family life and will acquire new life and significance in the course of the drama. Both *Princesses* and *Les Co-Epouses* highlight the plight of women embedded in the hard "line" of patriarchy. While each play posits male privilege and female submission, *Les Co-Epouses* unleashes an ever more potent form of female "communitas," along with a cunning interpretive stance in the face of confining societal structures. Most strikingly, the social drama of solitary resistance in embryonic form so brutally aborted during early gestation in *Princesses* is allowed to come to full term in the pregnant social drama of *Les Co-Epouses*.[14]

The male voice of an exhausted Driss opens the play as he enters, axe in hand, complaining of his mother's demands to the omnipresent ear of the passive Ancestor fingering prayer beads in the background. Her wise and sympathetic response brings her grandson to remark on her surprising capacity to "understand" his troubles, especially for a woman who never had any "rights." The old woman modestly explains that despite limited rights she never refrained from thinking, observing, and above all, listening (p. 13). Resigned, however, to her lowered social status removed from "the light," she is forced to defer to Driss' mother, Nahnouha, who now alone has the "right" to speak. And speak Nahnouha does, throughout most of the play, triggering in the process the "social drama" and trauma within the household.

In contrast to Princess' deliberate breach through marriage to a non-Muslim, the breach in this play is brought on by Nahnouha's expectation that the wife of her sole remaining son produce offspring, most particularly males. When her daughter-in-law Taos is unable to conceive in short order, Nahnouha demands that a fertile second wife be found. Her announcement of Taos' perceived "breach" sets in motion the ensuing social drama. When the soft "side" of Driss dares to express concern for Taos' feelings, Nahnouha crassly reminds him that a woman is merely "a piece of furniture." Relying upon the hard "line" structure of patrilineal kinship, the mother appropriates male authority to "put the world back in order" (p. 25). Taking issue with the husband's legal "rights," this play unleashes a critical questioning of the legitimacy of such rights, as it scrutinizes underlying societal behaviors governing the subjugation of young women both by male entitlement and matriarchal tyranny. The social drama inherent in the stage drama invites a re-examination of the practice of polygamy and the overall undervaluation of women within Muslim society.

In phase two of the brewing crisis, the infertile Taos privately confronts her degraded social status. In contrast to Princess' privileged social status and successful conjugal and professional life, Taos has only insecurity, material dependence, an infertile womb, and, most of all, social inferiority (with her absent father and brothers living in exile). Lacking in self-esteem and social rank, Taos as self-declared victim internalizes her subservient role within the patriarchal order (Brahimi, 1995, p. 128). An indefatigable worker wedded to her ever-present loom, Taos defines herself as an object of production, her best insurance against rejection or repudiation. However, as a woman in love with her husband, the thought of a co-spouse so enrages her that she releases her unspeakable thoughts in a monologue of revolt. Excusing herself before God for unbridled blasphemy, she articulates an eloquent indictment of God's ultimate "curse" on women: the fate of having been born with a "flower" instead of a "rifle" between her legs, because "with that first rifle he [man] goes on to win all the battles against the flowers" (p. 33). Taos' private outburst triggers the second phase of crisis which, like the young woman herself, awaits further elaboration within a larger familial and societal framework.

Taos' most influential ally is the young, literate and attractive outsider, their neighbor Siréna. An unmarried working woman who does not wear the veil, Siréna befriends Taos, bringing books and new ideas into the secluded household, and urges Taos to "revolt" against the injustice of her situation. As her namesake suggests, Siréna is vocal, seductive, and wily, in every way a worthy mentor and confidante to the illiterate and self-effacing Taos. A motherless daughter devoted to her aging father, Siréna vows never to marry unless he insists (an unlikely request given their mutual affection).[15] As such, Siréna's social experience enables Taos to imagine a woman's life beyond the confines of her personal domesticity. Urging uninhibited conversation, Siréna also gives the repressed Taos new insight into the power and influence of her sexuality and the beauty of her youthful figure unmarred by childbearing. When Siréna takes leave of Taos for a new job in a neighboring city, she takes care to infuse their parting embrace with a transmission of her instinctive "revolt and courage" (p. 49), firmly planting a potent seed of rebellion on fertile ground. While Princess was merely a lofty exemplar of female liberation to her subjugated and ill-fated peers, Siréna is a real-life guide to Taos' quest for self-realization.

Putting aside her pain and humiliation, Taos welcomes her co-wife Mimia as a sister, nursing her through an unending string of births of "their" seven daughters. In naming Mimia's first female child "Chems" ("the sun to light up my life") after her own mother, Taos initiates the "complementary filiation" of female kinship based on affective ties and genuine communitas. Conjoining Mimia's physical bounty to Siréna's mental prowess, Taos realizes the fullness of woman's potential. As the house proliferates with females, crisis escalates when Mimia, forced by her mother-in-law Nahnouha to try again for a male offspring, dies in childbirth. Tragically, Mimia's undying obedience to procreate led to the only form of personal liberation available to her: death. In contrast to the futility of Princess' death, however, the shameful loss of Mimia will not remain just another meaningless sacrifice of woman; it will be avenged. Except for Nahnouha, each woman in the household privately experiences "the gestation process" of liminality (Turner, 1990, p. 12) where social isolation and private reflection lead each female "liminar" to an ultimate transformation. In the palpable presence of their nascent collective strength, each emerges ready to seek collective justice in the redressive stage of action.

As the least likely agent of change, the Ancestor, similar to the ancient figures poised at the threshold between life and death, proves indispensable to the unfolding of the social drama. Exerting a supernatural influence as a kind of pre-Oedipal force that draws the younger women to her, she extends her protective aura in times of need. The healing power of her touch is felt in a variety of ways: her moving ritual performed with an amulet over the pregnant body of Mimia to assure a successful first delivery, or her comforting embrace and soothing therapy extended to Siréna when the young woman fears for the declining health of her father. And when the young woman collapses into restful sleep on the lap of the Ancestor, her comely thigh is seductively exposed to the passing gaze of a lustful Driss. However, the Ancestor's somnolent eye seems to freeze the desirous reach of the impertinent male's hand as it moves lasciviously toward the young woman's irresistible thigh. In this "unreal" moment, the stage is magically set for the final scene of redress against unbridled male desire.

In addition to the silent but potent role of the Ancestor, the eldest daughter Chems also learns to assert her will in the social drama. When the dutiful Chems finds Taos reduced to tears by her father's stinging rebukes, she threatens future revenge: "I know that I'm not the boy you had long hoped for and never had. And I also know that I am no stupider than a boy and that soon I will have my say in this house" (p. 81). When Nahnouha resolves to replace the newly deceased Mimia, three generations of women join forces. In response to Chems' call for outright defiance, her female elders demur, but when Taos dejectedly concedes that only a man's desire "counts," her words of resignation ignite the last lingering ember of revolt in the Ancestor who counters with: "Not so! *I* count!" As the Silent One speaks, the women know they are now "saved" (p. 88). Clutching Siréna's forgotten book to her breast as a newfound amulet of strength, the frail, blind woman rises to her feet to take her last moral and mortal stand against injustice toward women.

Speaking in veiled terms, the Ancestor hatches a plan based on pretending to "play the game." Each woman, helpless in her own right with no rights of her own, discovers the strength of collaborative action. By recruiting the willing accomplice Siréna to serve as the new co-wife, the Ancestor finds a way to use Siréna's irresistible body as a lethal weapon for their cause and, in the process, to disabuse Driss of further illusions of omnipotence in conjugal matters. True to the letter of oral law regarding marriage rites and rights, the women disable the system at its phallic core. Confident that her female protegees are in command of the situation, the Ancestor gratefully embraces death and bequeaths her "silent" role to her natural successor, the bigmouthed Nahnouha—now rendered mute and powerless for the remainder of the drama. Free from Nahnouha's doctrinaire "line" of patriarchal structure, the soft, affectional "side" of women now thrives.

Driss' initial flush quickly turns from pleasure to shame when his new union with Siréna fails to produce the obligatory stain on the sheet. When after seven days in a row Driss is unable to fulfill his duty, oral law prescribes that his bride be returned certifiably "intact" to her father.[16] While Siréna mysteriously manages to suppress Driss' masculinity by night, she busily bolsters Taos' femininity by day in seven explicit lessons on how to use her body to become "a seductive woman for her husband" so that Driss can "finally become a man." Though infertile, Taos' retrained body will serve and satisfy both male and female desire equally. When the official Matron verifies the bride's virginity, Siréna returns to her father, and Driss is struck down by the same public humiliation that earlier reduced Taos. In a playful diversion from worry over her father's impending death, the departing Siréna, like the Ancestor at her death, is proud to have played a role in putting "the world back in order" (p. 99), in an ironic echo of Nahnouha's hubris at the beginning of the play. In their roles betwixt and between, an outsider like Siréna, a diminished figure like the Ancestor or a "social" non-entity such as the girl-child Chems emerge as the most likely instruments of societal change.

The opening male voice of Driss is replaced by that of his daughter Chems who has the play's final "word." When her father insists on his "right" to take a new wife, Chems asserts her "right" to speak, as she reminds him of his "duties" as father and husband. When he dismisses her, she resorts to violence, picks up an axe, and strikes the final blow to male authority, bringing down the symbolic object of the second loom (that of Mimia, her deceased biological mother). Woman as object has been dismantled. In deed and now in word, Chems invents a new order of female identity accompanied by a ritual initiation of her father into his rank as equal:

> From this day forward, under this roof, mothers will be like daughters, they will all count. ... And God, who is also our God, will help us in this just enterprise. I now declare you descended from your pedestal, Father. From now on you will be satisfied to be just an ordinary man. (p. 102)

Along with the genuinely cathartic effects of ritual, both Chem's and the Ancestor's "inventions" illustrate how the frame of "play" can be used to bring about "transformed structure" (Turner, 1987, p. 128). As with the latent power of the carnivalesque in Bakhtinian terms, the playful "subjunctive" mood of carnival can force behaviors of the indicative mood to undergo change and even reversal (p. 102), so that "people are induced to want to do what they must do" (1974, p. 56). The successful revolt staged in this social drama predicts the emergence of a new societal framework where young women such as Siréna and Chems will take their place in growing numbers.

Despite the definitive dislocation of male patriarchy and privilege in the household, the social drama succeeds in preserving order within the familial structure, for the women take care not to destroy the man they care for in the process. As the Ancestor wisely remarked to Driss in the opening scene, "Our tradition is equally hard on women as on men" (p. 13). In the outcome phase of this social drama, Driss is successfully reintegrated into a new social order respectful of the rights of women as Chems takes the helm as the legitimate next-generation Muslim woman, successor to the self-proclaimed "wacky misfit" Siréna, and to the tragically defeated Princess. By deftly interweaving the threads of "communitas" from the female "side" with the seemingly inflexible hard "line" of structure, the females in this play construct a sturdy and serviceable framework which supports both freedom and tradition—as in Chems' selective gesture of breaking one loom while leaving the other intact.

Breaking through tradition

> I brought back this traditional Algerian clothing because I thought I would miss it, but it is the whole country that I miss!
>
> (Gallaire, *Rimm, la gazelle*)

Unlike the social dramas of Maghrebi life *in situ* of the first two plays, the private, monologic world of *Rimm, la gazelle* suspends the flow of everyday life and privileges the liminal mode of pure reflexivity. Alone in her Parisian apartment a year after the funeral of her mother in Algeria, Rimm sorts through clothes, trying to decide what to do with her traditional garb, "these old things" now far "too large" for her slender Parisian-style figure (p. 49). Stung by the pain of loss and longing and struck by the unexpected beauty of a stunning "gandoura," Rimm sets out to "perform" an imaginary conversation with her deceased mother as she describes in every detail the events of the funeral. Her performance recalls the Old English etymon "parfournir" or "to furnish completely" (Turner, 1982, p. 79) in the sense that her imaginary exchange "wholly furnishes" the tiny space of her studio apartment with the fullness of memory. Picturing herself carrying out filial duties on that eventful day in Algeria, Rimm in Paris re-enacts her simultaneous roles as "actress and spectator," subject and object, self and other, as she maps and remaps her experience, both in mind and in body. In fact, Rimm as created by Fatima Gallaire and played by actress Françoise Tixier embodies a doubled female gaze in triplicate: 1) in the character of Rimm her past self in Algeria and her present self in Paris; 2) in the author's reflections on her own mother's death; and 3) in the actress' representation of the double reflection of author-character in the text that she commissioned for her own one-woman performance.

As estranged daughters returning home to grieve the death of a parent, Princess' and Rimm's return visits are strikingly dissimilar. Whereas the orphaned Princess merely retraces familiar steps through a dimly lit past toward a broken lineage, Rimm's mentally reconstructed return to a loving father and family constitutes a genuine remapping (as in Deleuze and Guattari, 1987, p. 12) and re-framing of the present as a vital intersection between past and future. More importantly, through the process of retelling, Rimm relives her own primary experience with even fuller consciousness in this second(ary) rendering. Motherless and homeless, Rimm realizes the double loss of mother and motherland in a single blow. As a kind of "liminar" in a ritual gestation process, Rimm alone in her secluded Parisian apartment enters into spiritual communion with the living spirit of her mother in a struggle to discover a passageway for her journey between past and future. The initiand Rimm is poised on the threshold of "becoming" as her performance achieves the ritual enactment of that transitional moment.

Based on Rimm's recounting of her past, an implicit social drama emerges. Beginning with her original "breach" or decision to leave Algeria for France, Rimm chooses personal freedom, intellectual pursuits and social autonomy. Only after her mother's death does she encounter the crisis phase as she questions the "insignificance" of her independence in France. A self in turmoil "split up the middle," she arrives at the redressive phase where she engages in reflexivity about her self and her place in society. In the mental recovery of her homeland, Rimm "sees" herself in control of the situation (as she was during her mother's funeral), she sees the helpless servants and her lonely father, and she "hears" the desperate plea of the servant girl Dawia and the departing admonition of the old farmer: "You abandoned her when she was alive, you cannot abandon her now. You must come back" (p. 62). Thinking of the contribution she might make to the plight of so many miserable, uneducated, and desperate women who find in the act of mourning their sole outlet for the unhappiness in their daily lives (p. 61), Rimm realizes that she must face her guilt not only for abandoning her mother, but for letting down her country. In the company of such thoughts, Rimm projects herself freely and knowingly into the

"the future on its hither side" (Bhabha, p. 7) where she designs a new pattern for her life cut out of the fabric of her past.

Just as Princess longed to "bring back" the best of her new self in order to renew and strengthen the organic bonds of "communitas," Rimm, like Siréna, feels the same need to become a "qualitative individual" for others (Turner, 1974, p. 200). She reasons that "a single determined woman" in Algeria will "count" for much more than that same woman in France. In contrast to Princess' untimely and ill-advised return, Rimm's performed ritual of purification mentally prepares her for "reinduction" (p. 200).[17] In a kind of life-crisis ritual, Rimm's realization comes about as a "fairly late product of social reflexivity" with "the experiential under-standing that social life is a series of movements" (Turner, 1981, pp. 154–5). Unlike Princess, Taos, or Chems, Rimm's discovery of meaning is wholly self-induced and free of external social pressure; it reproduces the unique process of "feelingly thinking" (Turner, 1982, p. 14).[18]

At the end of the process of sorting through both her wardrobe and her thoughts, Rimm discovers a magnificent burnoose which she proudly tosses over her shoulders. Admiring herself transformed and "majestic," she decides in a dramatic reversal to pack only the clothes that her mother had made for her along with her books, placing the two halves of her divided self, finally reconciled, into the same suitcase. Rimm achieves a full reintegration of place and personhood, healing the gaping split up the middle that plagued Princess. Rimm's fully reconstructed Algerian self will return to take its rightful place on the road to helping others become "women who count and will count." While Princess, Taos, Chems, and Siréna reveal an ability to be "reflective in the sense of showing themselves to themselves," Rimm's performance illustrates "true reflexivity" born of an ability to be "conscious of her consciousness" (Turner, 1981, p. 132). Suspended in true liminality between two worlds, Rimm emerges confident that she has selected the items of lasting value, in her wardrobe as in her life. Imbued with the power of enduring "communitas," Rimm achieves the fourth stage of social reintegration in her personal drama. Projecting her return to her homeland, she is renewed and ready to lead others through the subsequent social dramas that await her there.

Remapping tradition

> … any society that hopes to be imperishable must carve out for itself a piece of space and a period of time in which it can look honestly at itself. This honesty is not that of the scientist, … It is rather, akin to the supreme honesty of the creative artist, who … reserves … the privilege of seeing straight what all cultures build crooked.
>
> (Victor Turner)

As an interstitial traveler, Gallaire journeys deep into the crevasses of female Maghrebi identity. Through her "supreme honesty" in striving to set "straight what all cultures build crooked" (Turner, 1984, p. 40), she takes pains to carve out new intervening spaces. At a time when new solutions for bridging gaping cultural clashes between individual and collective destinies are in short supply, Gallaire's theater is unique in its courageous reach toward reconciling self and community. As Servin remarks, "Situated between Algeria and France, Gallaire's 'word' should be listened to today, for it is born out of the History/Story for a tomorrow" (p. 247). As such, Gallaire's theatre extends hope for discovery of Bhabha's Third Space of enunciation where we "may elude the politics of polarity and emerge as the others of our selves" (p. 39).

Notes

1 All translations from French sources are my own.
2 For Gallaire, live theater's immediacy with the text provides "the inexplicable emotion that overcomes any writer when s/he suddenly sees words, sentences and expressions come alive in the mouths and bodies of living actors" (Laurent, 148). In addition, the author's ability to transmit the essence of Arab language and cultural experience in French is further conveyed on stage (Servin, 1991: 244; Déjeux, 1992: 8).
3 Based on Wilhelm Dilthey's explanation of how we discover meaning, Turner emphasizes the importance of the performance genres as sites for contact with experiences that would otherwise be unknown to us with the same immediacy, noting: "We acquire this [cumulative] wisdom not by abstract solitary thought, but by participation immediately or vicariously through the performance genres in sociocultural dramas" (1987: 84).
4 "When I see what I have written performed on stage I am often surprised and sometimes even terrified" (Discussion, 1993: 25).
5 In an attempt to realize "bodily" engagement, Turner experimented with theatrical representation by asking his anthropology students to "perform" ethnographies (1982: pp. 92–3).
6 "... le Tragique de notre époque, ... celui de l'Homme en face des peuples, celui du destin personnel confronté à un destin collectif." (11) ("... the sense of the Tragic in our times, ... is that of Man in the face of nations or peoples, that of personal destiny coming face to face with collective destiny")
7 All references to Gallaire's plays are based on the original French using my own English translations. *Princesses* was translated and performed in English as *You Have Come Back* (Jill Mac Dougall, Trans.) in 1988, and is currently available in *Plays By Women III* (New York: Ubu Repertory Theatre, 1996.) Due to major differences between the original French and the translation, however, all references in the present analysis will be to the original French version of the play.
8 The original French title *Ah, vous êtes venus là où il y a quelques tombes* was changed to *Princesses* at the prompting of Parisian director Jean-Pierre Vincent and printed under both titles in the 1991 publication by Editions des Quatre Vents. The 1988 American translation by Jill Mac Dougall shortens the original title to *You Have Come Back*. Both Vincent and Mac Dougall chose to omit the reference to death.
9 The similarities between *Princesses* and Greek tragedy are discussed by Brahimi (1994), Harbi in *Princesses* (préface, pp. 7–8), and Fernández-Sánchez (pp. 157–66).
10 "Princesse" is used in most exchanges among characters; "Lella" is used only by the chorus of young women, meaning "Mistress" in Arabic (p. 29). The symbolic power of Princess' status within the community as daughter of a revered *hadj* makes her breach with the patrilineal bloodline all the more egregious.
11 Princess' noble stance of resistance is absent in the English translation which omits her allusion to the future as well as her final invocation of Allah. Instead, an embittered Lella coarsely rebukes her attackers: "Get your hands off me ... filthy, greedy slaves." (*Plays*, p. 427)

12 In Jean-Pierre Vincent's 1991 production of the play at Nanterre, the chorus of old women was played by the same actresses as the young women (Leiblein), which may suggest a rather pessimistic view of the prospects for generational change.

13 Given the important and positive role of women in the local Muslim society in Uzbekistan, the author and director felt it would be ill advised to carry out the final scene using women as Princess' executioners.

14 Gallaire's allegorical play *Le Secret des Vieilles* stretches the demands of procreation to its ultimate limit when a kingdom decides to test the powers of its women by banishing 500 female subjects of all ages to the "Ile Stérile" or the uninhabited Sterile Island only to spare them death if they can return 1000 strong in a year's time.

15 The close father–daughter relationship is not unusual in Muslim families, and is often "one of unusual affection" (Combs-Schilling, p. 70), as Gallaire's plays illustrate. In *Au cœur, la brûlure* [*In My Heart … A Burning*] an elderly father confesses regret and pain at having let societal pressure inhibit him from expressing the love and admiration he felt for his now absent and estranged daughter.

16 Siréna impertinently offers an explanation for Driss' impotence to her mother-in-law Nahnouha: "As soon as he sees me, he freezes. He can't do a thing … He'll never possess me. I'm too high of an ideal for him" (94). A similar "miraculous" solution to a *bona fide* physical predicament occurs during the circumcision ritual performed on the adult non-Muslim fiancé in Gallaire's *La Fête virile* [*On Becoming a Man*].

17 Common in the structure of a hero's return to his homeland in Western literature is the process of reinduction which in ancient Greek myth was to be preceded by a purification ritual for the "impure" returning exile (Sessa, p. 210).

18 Based on Dilthey's process of discovering meaning, "past events remain inert unless the feelings originally bound up with them can be fully revived; meaning is generated by 'feelingly' thinking about the interconnections between past and present events" (Turner, 1982: p. 14).

References

Ashley, K.M. (Ed.). (1990). *Victor Turner and the Construction of Cultural Criticism*. Bloomington: Indiana University Press.

Begag, A., and Chaouite, A. (1990). *Ecarts d'identité*. [*Identity Splits*]. Paris: Seuil.

Bhabha, H.K. (1994). *The Location of Culture*. London and New York: Routledge.

Brahimi, D. (1994). Les Tragédies algériennes de Fatima Gallaire. [*The Algerian Tragedies of Fatima Gallaire*]. *Notre librairie*, 118, 53–6.

Brahimi, D. (1995). *Maghrébines: portraits littéraires*. [*Maghrebi Women: Literary Portraits*]. Paris: L'Harmattan.

Carlson, M. (1996). *Performance: A Critical Introduction*. London and New York: Routledge.

Combs-Schilling, M.E. (1989). *Sacred Performances (Islam, Sexuality, and Sacrifice)*. NY: Columbia University Press.

Déjeux, J. (1992). Avant-Propos. In Gallaire, F., *La Fête virile* [*On Becoming a Man*] (pp. 5–8). Paris: Editions des Quatre-Vents.

Deleuze, G., and Guattari, F. (1987). *A Thousand Plateaus* (B. Massumi, Trans.). Minneapolis: University of Minnesota Press. (Original work published 1980).

Diamond, E. (1995). The Shudder of Catharsis in Twentieth-Century Performance. In A. Parker and E. Kosofsky Sedgwick (Eds), *Performativity and Performance* (pp 152–72). New York: Routledge.

Fernández-Sánchez, C. (1996). Le Théâtre de Fatima Gallaire: Témoignage contre "le désir d'oubli" [The Theatre of Fatima Gallaire: Witness against "the desire to forget"]. In L.

Leguin and M. Verthuy (Eds), *Multi-Culture, Multi-Ecriture* (pp. 157–66). Paris-Montréal: L'Harmattan.

Gallaire, F. (1988). *Ah! vous êtes venus … là où il y a quelques tombes* [*Ah! You've Come … There. Where There Are Several Graves*]. Paris: Editions des Quatre-Vents.

—— (1988). *You Have Come Back*. (Jill Mac Dougall, Trans.). In F. Kourilsky, and C. Temerson (Eds), *Plays By Women III* 1996 (pp. 365–428). New York: Ubu Repertory Theatre.

—— (1990). *Les Co-épouses*. Paris: Editions des Quatre-Vents.

—— (1991). *Princesses, ou, Ah! vous êtes venus … là où il y a quelques tombes* [*Princesses or Ah! You've Come …There Where There Are Several Graves*]. Paris: Editions des Quatre-Vents.

—— (1992). *La Fête virile* [*On Becoming a Man*]. Paris: Editions des Quatre-Vents.

—— (1993). *Au loin, les Caroubiers suivi de Rimm, la gazelle.* [*Far from the Carob Trees followed by Rimm, the Gazelle*]. Paris: Editions des Quatre-Vents.

—— (1994). Discussion: Paroles de Femmes au théâtre [*Women in Theatre Speak Out*]. *Les Cahiers des Lundis* (pp. 21–30). Paris: Association THEATRALES.

—— (1994). *Au Coeur, la Brulure* [*In My Heart … A Burning*]. *L'Avant-Scène*, 954, 17–28.

—— (1996). *Le Secret des vieilles* [*The Secret of the Old Women*]. *L'Avant-Scène* 999–1000, 54–60.

Glissant, E. (1959). Le Chant profond de Kateb Yacine [The Deep Song of Kateb Yacine]. In Kateb, Y. *Le Cercle des représailles* (pp. 9–13). Paris: Seuil.

Harbi, M. (1991). Réflexions sur la pièce de Fatima Gallaire *Princesses* [Reflections on the play *Princesses* by Fatima Gallaire]. In F. Gallaire, *Princesses* (pp. 7–8). Paris: Editions des Quatre-Vents.

Helbo, A., Johansen, J.D., Pavis, P., and Ubersfeld, A. (Eds). (1991). *Approaching Theatre* (Rev. trans.). Bloomington: Indiana University Press. (Original work published in 1987).

Jauss, H.R. (1974). Levels of Identification of Hero and Audience (B. and H. Bennett, Trans.), *New Literary History*, 5, 283–317.

—— (1982). *Aesthetic Experience and Literary Hermeneutics* (M. Shaw, Trans.). Minneapolis: University of Minnesota Press. (Original work published in 1977.)

Laurent, A. (1991). Fatima Gallaire à Nanterre [Review of the play *Princesses* directed by J-P.Vincent]. *Esprit*, 7–8, 148–9.

Leiblein, L. (1991, fall). *Princesses* at Nanterre. *Western European Stages*, 3 (2), 67–72.

—— (1991, fall). Interview with Jean-Pierre Vincent. *Western European Stages*, 3, (2), 69–72.

MacAloon, J.J. (Ed.). (1984). *Rite, Drama, Festival, Spectacle*. Philadelphia: ISHI.

Memmi, A. (1997). Les Fluctuations de l'identité culturelle [Fluctuations in Cultural Identity]. *Espirit* 228, 94–106.

Pile, S. and Thrift, N. (Eds) (1995). *Mapping the Subject*. London and New York: Routledge.

Schechner, R. (1985). *Between Theatre and Anthropology*. Phildadelphia: University of Pennsylvania Press.

—— (1986). Magnitudes of Performance. In V. Turner and E. Bruner (Eds), *The Anthropology of Experience* (pp. 344–69). Urbana and Chicago: University of Illinois Press.

—— (1988). *Performance Theory*. (Rev. edn). New York: Routledge.

Servin, M. (1991). Question de texte ou de théâtre. [Review of *Les Co-Epouses* directed by M. Attias]. *Les Temps modernes* 536–7, 244–7.

Sessa, J. (1986). L'Exil au théâtre: du tragique à l'absurde [Exile in Theatre: from the tragic to the absurd]. In J. Mounier (Ed.), *Exil et littérature* (pp. 205–16). Grenoble: ELLUG.

Shaffer, E. (1993). The Hermeneutic Approach to Theatre and Drama. In J. Hilton (Ed.), *New Directions in Theatre* (pp. 120–44). New York: St. Martin's Press.

Surel-Turpin, M. (1995). Les dénonciations de Fatima Gallaire. *Etudes Théâtrales* 8, 34–5, 40.

Turner, V. (1974). *Dramas, Fields, and Metaphors*. Ithaca: Cornell University Press.

—— (1981). Social Dramas and Stories About Them. In W.J.T. Mitchell (Ed.), *On Narrative* (pp. 137–64). Chicago: University of Chicago Press.

—— (1982). *From Ritual to Theatre*. New York: PAJ Publications.

—— (1984). Liminality and the Performative Genres. In J.J. MacAloon (Ed.), *Rite, Drama, Festival, Spectacle* (pp. 10–41). Philadelphia: ISHI.

—— (1986). Dewey, Dilthey, and Drama: An Essay in the Anthropology of Experience. In V. Turner and E. Bruner (Eds), *The Anthropology of Experience* (pp. 33–44). Urbana and Chicago: University of Illinois Press.

—— (1987–88). *The Anthropology of Performance*. NY: PAJ Publications.

—— (1990). Are there universals of performance in myth, ritual and drama? In R. Schechner, and W. Appel (Eds), *By Means of Performance* (pp. 8–18). Cambridge: Cambridge University Press.

Part III

Anthropology and literature as travelogue

Chapter 8

Oriental imprisonments

Habaneras as seen by nineteenth-century women travel writers

Lizabeth Paravisini-Gebert

Upon her arrival in Havana on an extended visit to the Spanish colony of Cuba in 1869, Louisa Mathilde Woodruff, a sentimental "authoress" from the village of Hudson, New York, whose novel *Shiloh* had enjoyed moderate success a few years before, declares herself "unprepared to find Havana so thoroughly Oriental," so "Moorish" in its aspect. She describes it thus: "The same narrow streets, roofed with awnings—the same one-storied houses, built around a court—the same shallow shops, on a level with the pavement, and all open in front, exposing their entire contents to the view—the same long files of cumbrously laden mules, tied together, and with a gaily-dressed muleteer in charge—and the same bright-turbaned, stately-stepping negresses, with heavy burdens poised on their heads" (1871, pp. 20–21). The reader may well wonder if Miss Woodruff, "the most harmless and insignificant little woman in the world!," as she introduces herself, had ever ventured into that part of the world then known as "the Orient" in her travels, or whether the striking orientalism that meets her at every turn in Havana is but a rather conventional writer's strategy to make sense out of Havana's foreignness, its otherness, the disharmony between her familiar surroundings in the Hudson Valley and a region that had come to epitomize the exotic. Having placed Havana closer to her experience by equating it with a land more often read about—that of the *Arabian Nights* as she constantly reminds us—the comparison will permeate her description of the city, becoming the metaphoric translator of exotic and foreign reality onto familiar discourse. On seeing the *volantes*, a sort of barouche that was the most common mode of transportation in Havana at the time, she will wish that one could be transported to Central Park, where she was sure this conveyance of "barbaric splendor" would create "a greater sensation" than "Cleopatra's chariot, with the beautiful Egyptian Queen therein" (p. 27). Cleopatra, we can safely assume, she had never met.

I do not mean to deride the guileless Miss Woodruff, who pours into her occasionally giddy account of her six months in Cuba, *My Winter in Cuba*, all her wide-eyed astonishment before a country where, as she puts it, "[l]ife becomes continuous picture and poem, through which you drift so inevitably into dreamland" (p. 296). Her orientalist strategy is but an example of the ways in which women travelers to the Caribbean in the nineteenth century—confronted with the unfamiliarity of a region whose landscapes and cultures appear in their eyes as alien as those of Africa and Asia—attempt to bring them into the realm of their, and their readers', experience. Her orientalism, it is fair to point out, is neither rare nor perhaps very original: it will be one of the most common textual strategies when approaching the Spanish Caribbean in English and American women's travel narratives. Eliza McHatton-Ripley, arriving in Havana to become a sugar planter after her cotton plantation near Baton Rouge had been invaded by the Union Army during the Civil War, found Havana to be a city of Oriental opulence, Moorish in design, a city "fairly drunk with the excess of wealth and abundance" crowned with "Oriental quintas and pleasure gardens" (1889, p. 126). Julia Ward Howe, the well-known American feminist and author of the "Battle Hymn of the Republic," on first visiting the famous Dominica café in Havana, describes it as "deeply Moorish" in aspect: "I see the fountain," she writes, "the golden light, the dark faces, and intense black eyes, a little softened by the comforting distance" (1860, p. 110). It will be extraordinarily easy for these travelers to see themselves, as Miss Woodruff does, "walking under the vast tent of Peri-Benon, of Arabian Night's fame, if there were only a few turbans and caftans about to help the illusion"; there will be, to many of them, "an almost ridiculous incongruity between the quaint, Oriental aspect of Cuban architecture and manners, and the [then] modern French fashions—stove-pipe hats and close-fitting pants" (p. 72). There is in Woodruff's assessment of Havana's exoticism a distinct consciousness of the cultural and architectural syncretism that typifies colonial societies and which becomes—for lack of a better term—"oriental." Many of these writers—amateurs for whom descriptions of travel provide an excuse for an incursion into professional writing—cannot escape the colonial imperative. Like Miss Woodruff, who marvels at the perceived incongruity of the juxtaposition of an exotic urban landscape and French fashions, they will be unable to transcend their perception of themselves as belonging to the imperial center and therefore authorized to interpret the periphery.

There is an extraordinary richness and variety in the extant accounts of travel to the Caribbean region by men and women in the second half of the nineteenth century, a time of interest particularly because it represented both the apogee of the British empire and the period of American apprenticeship in imperial ways that followed the Monroe Doctrine of 1823 with its declared opposition to European interference in the Americas. Their importance to our understanding of the stresses and clashes of that process are just beginning to be explored.

My focus here is on a handful of English and American visitors to Cuba in the second half of the nineteenth century and then again very narrowly on some of the ways in which they seek to "understand" Havana, its customs, and more tellingly, its women, ways that often result in misunderstandings at once amusing and disturbing for what they reveal about the tensions between imperial centrality and colonial marginality. The more than thirty such accounts published by women I have come across in my research include texts by Julia Ward Howe, Fredrika Bremer, Julia Newell Jackson, Rachel Wilson Moore, Jenny Tallenay, and the Countess of Merlin. I am particularly interested in English and American women because they constitute the largest and most homogeneous group, similar enough in outlook and approach to be seen as a group. The well-known accounts of non-English European travelers like Fredrika Bremer (the Swedish Jane Austen as she came to be known) and the Countess of Merlin, on the other hand, defy easy classification. Miss Bremer's *The Homes of the New World*, for example, rich in domestic detail gathered from close observation, anthropological in its careful reconstruction of folk celebration, religion, and dance, proto-feminist in its nuanced discussion of women's relationships across race and class, belongs to a category apart.

English and American women travelers, unlike the *sui generis* Miss Bremer, seem to fit a classic profile. They will be educated Protestant women of the middle and upper-middle classes, democratically or parliamentarily scornful of Spanish tyranny, secure in the solid power of their burgeoning empires, rarely speaking more than the most rudimentary Spanish, and above all, white; their representations of *las habaneras* will be truly "oriental," cast often in the mold of the pre-conceived, dependent on missed encounters, resting frequently on language misunderstood, habitually overshadowed by Anglo-American notions of race. Anglo-American women's assessment of Cuban society and its women will often rest on a transference of English and American notions of relationships between ruler and ruled in the context of empire. Spanish women (particularly those of the nobility), for example, will appear as individualized, speaking, often named subjects; while Creole women of the middle and upper-middle (but still colonized) classes will appear in groups, as generic *cubanas* or *habaneras*, the words appearing in Spanish, signaling their subordination by their group appearance and establishing their distance from empire-bound observers through their generic name in Spanish. It will be on the *habaneras* or *cubanas* that the burden of orientalism will fall.

Julia Newell Jackson, in *A Winter Holiday in Summer Lands*, the account of her travels in Cuba and Mexico circa 1890, offers a characteristic description of upper-middle-class Cuban women as:

> Ladies evidently belonging to the most low-necked, therefore the highest, circle of society, powdered until their olive skins had turned to ivory, with great shadowy black eyes and wavy, dusky tresses—there are enough drops of African blood flowing through Cuban veins to add a wave to the tresses pretty generally, suggestive of Cleopatra and the Orient. (pp. 33–4)

In their particular version of orientalism, these visitors will struggle with ways to approach the question of race, exposing their discomfort with a society in which race is not perceived as falling on one or the other side of a black/white divide but covers a wide spectrum that cuts across classes. Lacking a language adequate to address their astonishment at the racial continuum they encounter in Havana, they will conflate Africa and the Orient, seeking examples (Cleopatra being a particularly popular one) that can help them approach the unfamiliarity of the racial classifications prevalent in Cuba. One can glimpse in their fixation with the degree to which they are willing to acknowledge any beauty in Cuban women the specter of racial prejudice—the *habaneras's* beauty and taste in clothing becomes the gauge through which we can measure the degree of opening to different perspectives on race on the part of the visitors. Woodruff, for example, alludes to *habaneras'* being called "white, by courtesy ... for there are really only degrees of dark in Cuba" (p. 94). The famed "extraordinary beauty" of Cuban women, however—their resplendent and brilliantly dressed hair, "their eyes!, their figures!, their manner of walking!," usually described as something so exquisite that no woman of more northerly climes would venture to compete with them—rarely succeeds in pleasing the foreign female visitor. Upon first meeting them, Mathilde Houston confessed herself "terribly disappointed," finding them too pale for her taste, not doubting that the pronounced yellow tint of the skin was due to the excessive heat, their particularly graceful walk a mythical trait since they were too indolent to move (Araújo, 1983, p. 168).[1] Houston, meeting several young English beauties when invited to a dinner at the British consulate, is gratified to find that their rosy coloring had not paled under the influence of the tropical sun and contrasted pleasantly with the sallow beauties of the island (1884, p. 176).[2] Louisa Woodruff, almost invariably delighted by everything she sees, is particularly severe on the subject of the famed beauty of Cuban women:

> The ladies, according to their wont, are bareheaded and decollettés, with their long, showy skirts hanging out of their *volantes*; and one look at the combinations of colors in their toilets would go far to make a French *modiste* a candidate for the mad house. Yellow and scarlet, blue and purple, green and orange, seemed to be the favorite combinations; and though the dark eyes and complexions of the Cubanas carry off these astonishing contrasts with a far better grace than their fairer sisters to the north could do, still they give them a look undeniably "dowdy"—not to say vulgar—to those unaccustomed to such gaudiness of attire. Perhaps this was the reason why so very few of them seemed anywise pretty to me. After a little, I came unwillingly to the decision that my cherished ideal of Cuban beauty could never stoop to incarnate itself in any of those fat, fussy, overdressed matrons, nor those thin, sallow, lifeless, and likewise overdressed maidens. (p. 47)[3]

Much emphasis was placed by visitors on the richness of apparel of upper-class Cuban women, particularly when describing the "most animated and bewitching sight imaginable in those affluent days of Cuba," the *paseo*. In the cool of the evening, ladies would sally forth in their *volantes* and victorias, with coachmen in full livery, to take the prescribed fashionable drive and be seen in their full regalia. Magnificently dressed in full evening costume,

> their trailing robes, of brilliant colors and light, gauzy material, arranged to float outside the open vehicles, with shoulders and arms bare, and raven locks crowned with flowers, among which were tiny birds mounted on quivering wires, made a display of striking and unusual elegance. (McHatton-Ripley, p. 136)

The visitors' isolation of the *paseo*, which centers primarily on an open display of women's beauty and goods, as a cultural oddity of somewhat questionable taste, underscores their lack of awareness of its function as a source of relief from the unrelenting heat of the Cuban climate. This inability to connect cultural practices to what is appropriate to the location and climate emerges with particular irony in their discussions of clothing. The *habaneras'* colorful, gay, and luxurious apparel contrasted sharply with demure Anglo-American Victorian fashion, of which the bonnet—"so important a part of a lady's costume in Europe and America," an item rarely worn by Creoles—was a centerpiece. Cuban women rarely donned hats and were content to venture out with a lace mantilla or gauzy veil over their faces, thrown back on their shoulders, if absolutely necessary (Moore, 1867, p. 56). Bonneted foreign visitors hazarding a walk on the streets of Havana "with the latest fashion of this ever varying article" were regarded with the deepest curiosity and subjected to mocking stares (Woodruff, p. 27). One British visitor felt intimidated enough by the gawking to stop wearing hers, substituting it with a cap and black veil. Julia Ward Howe saw them as "audacious bonnets" which, together with "more assertive stares and louder laughs attracted stares in the few public places that tolerated the presence of foreign women."[4] When it comes to bonnets—the priority of which is taken as a matter of fact by the visitors—the item's inappropriateness to the climate does not enter the discussion.

In nineteenth-century Havana, historian Luis Martínez-Fernández has argued, "clearly established social rules designed to both 'protect' and subdue women contributed to keep white Habaneras under seclusion"; they were the object of society's apparent obsession with female virginity and chastity, which had led to "legislation obstructing interracial marriages [in an effort to protect] white women and their race—and by extension their class—from what was perceived as 'racial pollution.'" The prevailing Cuban etiquette forbade Cuban ladies from walking on the streets. In Cuba, Julia Howe discovered, "[t]hey of the lovely sex ... undergo, with what patience they may, an Oriental imprisonment"; a few days' acquaintance in Havana with "the little rabble who could not be trusted in the presence of the [other] sex," make clear to her "the seclusion of women in the East, and its causes" (p. 43). Of all Cuban social habits, none will be so irksome to foreign female visitors than this social edict which confined them within doors, forbidding them to drive or ride about with any male other than a husband, father, or brother, and debarred them from walking, except to church, and then only if chaperoned. Miss Woodruff, impatient with her confinement in a stifling hotel room, able to walk only up and down the hotel corridors, throws care to the wind and decides to go shopping "after the American fashion" in "a daring breach of universal custom" that attracted many disconcerting stares (pp. 69, 70).

Much will be made of female "imprisonment" in travelers' descriptions of Havana, particularly by male writers seemingly titillated by the thought of these beautiful caged women. Woodruff described *habaneras* as forever standing behind the iron grates protecting them from the outside world: "If you are passing outside, you often see [them] … gazing at the outer world through the iron bars; with so much the aspect of prisoners, that, at first, it makes you melancholy to look at them" (Woodruff, p. 125). She imagined them forever suffering from "the tyrannous restraints of their social customs," but deeper acquaintance disabused her of such notions, leading her to conclude that the desire to "get out," except in a *volante*, "[n]ever enters the Cuban feminine mind" (Woodruff, p. 125). The iron grille, an apparent prison gate, however, did not succeed in isolating women from the world beyond their homes. Windows were always kept wide open, allowing women to chat freely with passersby and receive the attention of admirers and suitors. Eliza McHatton-Ripley described how at night, door and windows of houses were flung wide open, "showing a vista of rooms, from the brilliantly lighted salon through bedroom after bedroom, until the line of view vanished at the kitchen." In long rows of rocking chairs, in neverceasing motion, "the señoras gayly chatted and sipped ices; while idle strollers in the streets paused to admire and audibly comment upon the elegant ladies or listen to the light nothings that were being uttered with so much spirit and gesture" (McHatton-Ripley, p. 136). One visitor recalls attending a music entertainment where the daughter of the house played exquisitely, her audience not confined to those in the *sala* but encompassing the appreciative group that had gathered outside the grille, listening attentively to the end.

Despite the impression of female vivacity implicit in these architectural and domestic arrangements, the *cubanas* or *habaneras* of these texts will be primarily silent. Accounts of conversations between travelers and Cuban women are most infrequent; the absence of a shared language being the greatest barrier to communication. Throughout these accounts, the burden of knowing the other's language is placed consistently on the native woman, who is then chastised for the inappropriateness of her knowledge of English. British abolitionist Mathilde Houston tells of watching a group of Cuban ladies sitting in a semicircle, "never uttering a word," opening and closing their fans "with great perseverance." (She does not stop to consider that their silence may be the result of a polite reluctance to hold an animated conversation in Spanish that would perforce exclude their guest.) Discovering by accident that her neighbor spoke a bit of French, they entered upon a conversation which, "with the aid of her incessant questions and my patient responses," they managed to sustain desultorily for a few minutes, thus killing time. Only Miss Woodruff's account and that of Eliza McHatton Ripley, both of them women who spent extended periods in Cuba, report extensive dialogues between visiting and Cuban women. In contrast to the typically silent *habanera* of most travelogues, Miss Woodruff will describe Creole women's conversation as "a storehouse of vivid imagery, an inexhaustible fount of graphic and animated narrative of home incident and daily routine," self-deprecatingly referring to her Spanish, "having chiefly been used for book intercourse hitherto," as "not sufficiently at [her] tongue's end to carry [her] through a sustained conversation with a roomful of strange people" (p. 91). Her book, *My Winter in Cuba*, contains the only report of a substantial, meaningful dialogue between a foreign visitor and a Cuban woman. Woodruff, prefacing her brief description of this exceptional conversation, frankly confesses that prior to meeting Doña Angela, her gracious hostess during a visit to the provinces, she had not found "the Cuban ladies and myself entirely in harmony." Their education, religion, habits of life, and thought were "so dissimilar that the maintenance of a certain degree of reserve had seemed a wise precaution against uncomfortable jarring of sentiment." Doña Angela openly avowed "all manner of Spanish prejudice and misconception," to which Miss Woodruff parried with "many rude Americanisms."

> She was very severe on our civil war, had a holy horror of "filibusteros," and could be especially eloquent about the length of our tax-list. I predicted the speedy adoption of republican institutions in Spain, the ultimate absorption of Cuba by the United States ... She ridiculed the squeamishness of American women, alleging that it was currently reported in Cuba that they never confessed to a pain in any organ lower than the throat, even to their family physician. I retorted that it was universally believed in the United States that all Cuban ladies smoked. She animadverted upon the flippancy, free manners and flirtations of our young ladies; and I commented on the vacuity and inefficiency of her countrywomen. Privately, however, I more than half concurred with Doña Angela in her last stricture. (pp. 260–2)

This account—suggestive of a well-informed, self-assertive, intelligent, thinking Cuban woman—sharply contrasts with the image of the mute upper-middle-class *habanera* of most English and American women's travel narratives; a *cubana* cloistered behind the bars of her Moorish abode, kneeling in fervent prayer with fingers clasping a rosary in church, objectified in self-display as she is driven through the Paseo in her *volante*, furiously fluttering her eyelashes (her only organ of communication) behind the faster flutter of her *abanico*. The unreal, silenced middle-class Cuban woman of most travel narratives seems to be the product of a silence imposed on the traveler herself by her inability to communicate, an inability that emerges in these texts as a source of protection against the intrusion of the Cuban otherness into the sheltered sphere of white American and British middle-class womanhood.

Julia Howe, restricted upon her arrival in Cuba to communication through the reading of facial expression, sees "all the hatred of race [in the Spanish officials'] rayless eyes."

> Is it a crime, we are disposed to ask, to have a fair Saxon skin, blue eyes, and red blood? ... the first glance at this historical race makes clear to [her] the Inquisition, the Conquest of Granada, and the ancient butcheries of Alva and Pizarro. (p. 43)

The eyes—those behind the fluttering fans as well as the insolent ones of Cuban *caballeros*—will be silenced in turn, muted, by the traveler's refuge in the cocoon of her Spanishlessness. Sitting at the Dominica on one of several visits described in *A Trip to Cuba*, Julia Howe will caution, the foreign woman will feel every black eye directing "its full, tiresome stare at [her] face, no matter how plain that face may be." And she continues: "But you have learned before this to consider those eyes as so many black dots, so many marks of wonder with no sentence attached; and so you coolly pursue your philosophizing in the corner …" (p. 106). An American woman's propriety is safely defended by her ability to silence the Cuban male's impropriety through her incomprehension of any possible offending language. Her ability to look at Cuban men's eyes "as so many marks of wonder with no sentence attached" restores the imperial balance: Cuban men of doubtful racial origin cannot and will not penetrate the sphere of white American womanhood, since she cannot be made to understand his words. Rachel Wilson Moore, a preacher for the Society of Friends visiting Cuba for health reasons, similarly describes how, despite the interdictions against ladies walking in the street, she ventures out with some friends, "her republican habits could not be circumscribed by such arbitrary rules" (1867, p. 37). "The people looked at us in astonishment," she reports, "and made their remarks as we passed along; but not understanding them, we took no notice of them." Julia Newell Jackson will go as far as to deride her companions' efforts at learning some colloquial Spanish as counterproductive and unnecessary. A companion she calls Herr Professor, having made "rapid strides in its acquisition," is portrayed as beginning to understand it "too well."

> "We fail to find the market," she writes: though we have been there more than once. Herr Professor goes into a bookstore to inquire. When he has asked in his colloquial Spanish and pantomime, a map of Cuba is offered him by way of answer. He next tries a drug-store, and in reply to his question receives a sticking plaster. We find it at last, but it is not done by inquiring.
>
> (Jackson, 1890, p. 125)

Another visitor confesses that sometimes she is

> fain to pass off my knowledge of Spanish for something less than it is, in order to escape from the weariness of being civil and sociable in a foreign tongue, and to be free to use my eyes and ears to the best advantage.
>
> (Woodruff, pp. 126–7)

The latter's reluctance to communicate, coupled with Jackson's conviction that her objective could best be reached without inquiry, underscores the foreign subject's confidence in her ability to form opinions about Havana, its environs and citizens, without the benefit of the latter's input. It is more comfortable indeed to see the native other as incapable of the undesired communication.

Given the class- and race-bound assumptions that pervade these texts, the black and mulatto Cuban woman of the lower classes, when not entirely absent from the text, will more often than not be cast in the "blackest" light, either sharply contrasted against the brilliant sunlight in all her idleness and sauciness or fading into the walls of the dark corridors, lazy, stupid, sullen, unwashed—the Other's Other, triply separated from the traveler by virtue of her race, class, and language. They will never be referred to as *habaneras* or *cubanas*; as slaves and servants they will have no claim to nationality.[5] The black housekeeper that Eliza McHatton Ripley meets upon her arrival at her freshly purchased plantation, *Desengaño* (Dissapointment—only someone unfamiliar with Spanish would have ventured to purchase such an inauspiciously-named plantation), is characteristic of the portrayal of the black Cuban servant in these travel narratives:

> When the black woman, in a dirty, low-necked, sleeveless, trailing dress, a cigar in her mouth, and a naked, sick and whining child on one arm, went about spreading the table, scrupulously wiping Royo's plates with an exceedingly suspicious-looking ghost of a towel the prospect for dinner was not inviting. (p. 151)

Miss Woodruff describes a servant "belonging to the African tribe of the Lucumís" with almost ferocious scorn. "I am sorely puzzled to decide what nice degree of upward or downward gradation would place her on a level with the baboon," she writes (p. 104). If called, Woodruff asserts, she answers "with the harshest, most guttural, most unintelligible jargon conceivable, resembling more the cry of a bird of prey than the human voice" (p. 104). If the upper-class *habanera* is reduced to silence, the lower class, unmistakably black Cuban woman is reduced to animal-like grunts and comparisons with baboons—her humanity vanished.

Women of color enjoyed, on the other hand, greater liberties than those of higher social status. Unlike white or light-skinned ladies, they walked about as they pleased, sold goods from house to house, "and frequented places like cockpits which were completely barred to white women."[6] This freedom seems to have attracted to them an even greater degree of disdain. The Countess of Merlin, in her account of her visit to the homeland she had left many years before, scorned the jauntiness with which *habaneras* of color walked the street, "cigar in mouth, almost naked with their round shining bare shoulders" (p. 107). One visitor was struck by the figure of a "massive negress" planted solidly upon a street corner, "with a gigantic cigar in her mouth, and a broad, unctuous aspect of the serenest satisfaction" (p. 192).

In foreigners' accounts we catch only glimpses of the subtle intricacies of the relationships between upper class Cuban women and women of the lower classes— servants and peddlers in the city, field hands and house servants in the countryside. Servants were numerous, and were often seen moving leisurely about, "but there was no running to do one's bidding." Female servants lived in very close intimacy with their mistresses and were charged often with the most delicate of tasks, from selecting items of clothing and jewelry to serving as their most trusted messengers. They were in constant attendance on their ladies, always ready to pick up a dropped handkerchief or rearrange a stray ribbon. A lady's maid did not serve more than one lady, a nurse cared for only one child, an arrangement that fostered intimacy. Mistress and servant were often to be seen through their iron grilles toiling and spinning together. Servants would occasionally work as sellers of sweetmeats in the streets, by the preparation and sale of which many decayed families supported themselves. Eliza McHatton Ripley was struck on first arriving in Cuba, by the complete dependence of upper-class women on their servants, and by the latter's apparent devotion and unceremonious relationship to their mistresses, which she reports unquestioningly. Invited to a dinner at the home of their country neighbors, she tells of being waited upon by "a score of darkies, in various stages of inexperience":

> There was no attempt at style or ceremony, no whispering of orders or sly hints as to duties, no gestures or winks; everything was free and open, every order given in an unmistakable key; so that there was an abandon at one of these country festivals absolutely bewitching. (p. 231)

Amelia Murray, a British aristocrat and lady-in-waiting to Queen Victoria, in her *Letters from the United States, Cuba, and Canada*, is oblivious to the subtleties of these relationships, and sees only the idleness of Cuban female servants:

> While I am writing, I see two mulatto women with cups in their hands, standing at the great, wide, coach-house looking door opposite; they are sharing their breakfast with a negro; and now two or three more come to gossip with them.... for three hours this morning these women have been lolloping and gossiping in my sight, and there they will be until they find the heat too great for this kind of enjoyment. (1856, 2:176)

Her letters from Cuba provide one of the most bizarre examples in these texts of the projection of otherness onto the black Cuban woman—in a narration of an incident in which no black woman had an actual role. Having returned from an outing, the botanist and naturalist Miss Murray sees something in a little basket on her dressing table which she mistakes for a fossil.

> I touched it with an exclamation, when a maid (fortunately not black) saw what it was, caught up the basket, and carried it at once to a man a few yards from my door, who killed the creature instantly. A negro woman would have laughed and stared, and have allowed it to sting me, before she would have remembered that a scorpion is an ugly customer.
>
> (Murray, 2:237)

The gratuitousness of the narration, where the Negro woman is found guilty *in absentia* of an imagined crime, guilty by comparison with a maid "fortunately not black," emphasizes the recurrence in these texts of pre-conceived, pre-determined, pre-judged accounts, forcing us to remember that travel narrative as a genre, despite its ostensibly objective, factual, descriptive nature, is at heart ideologically biased, and in these cases, imperially bound. Even the kindly Miss Woodruff, in her rose-colored account of her Cuban dreamland, tinted with her devoutly Christian naiveté, will distort the vision to fit her aims. She will portray black and mulatto women as devoted shadows to their mistress, describing them at the Havana railway station as "gloriously turbaned" but dressed as a "broad caricature of their mistresses," or depicting a little black girl as so devoted to her young mistress that she follows her everywhere, sharing her playthings, candies, scrapes, and punishments, accepting her caresses and her blows with the same placid satisfaction, and never making any moan or murmur "till bedtime brings the one thing unendurable—namely, separation—whereupon, it sets up a howl that almost raises the roof" (p. 114). Underscoring these notions of blissful servitude is a tradition of imperial writing, chiefly produced by British writers, that underscores the colonial subject's gratitude and devotion to the colonizers, a fantasy of harmony that was one of the major "selling" points of imperial dogma. For the honorable Amelia Murray, she of the Victorian nation ruling over India, a nation brimming with pride at their never sun-less empire, this notion of servantly devotion would have been comfortingly familiar. Submission seen as voluntary and emerging from the deepest love, from a deep need in the Oriental subject's own character to be made into the image of the ruling Other, was an intrinsic part of the ideology of empire.

It is the American nation's embrace of this ideology of empire which allows the sweet Miss Woodruff—a believer in the ultimate absorption of Cuba by the United States—to stand on the airy, shaded balcony of her hotel, confidently surveying the city and suburbs or Havana, "gilded with noontide glory," as

> [s]weet snatches of rare old songs come fitfully to your lips—gorgeous bits of *Arabian Nights* imagery float hazily through your memory—air-castles rise, rose-hued and radiant, on the sapphire foundations of the cloudless sky—existence becomes a luxury, and life a dream! (pp. 78–9)

Many of these writers are, after all, writing barely a decade before the Spanish-American War and are acutely conscious of the raging debate over the United States' "natural" position of dominance vis-à-vis the Caribbean region, particularly the profitable and vulnerable possessions held by the waning Spanish empire. They are also alert to the possibility that their travelogues can open a space for them as women in the public debate from which their gender otherwise bans them. For the Puritan Miss Woodruff, as for the Julia Howe of "The Battle Hymn of the Republic," the Confederate Eliza McHatton-Ripley and others, writing with avowed awareness of American designs on Cuba, imbued with the conviction that their nation was poised on the brink of empire, the orientalist metaphor seemed to translate Havana into an exotic locale fit for imperial intervention, after which the society would be shorn of its Inquisitorial roots and thus be made more humane, where women would be liberated from their oriental imprisonment and allowed to walk the streets in Victorian conventionality, where Catholic mumbo-jumbo and a tyrannical government would give way to Protestant ritual simplicity and democracy, where Cuba would become an American land in which the Orient would have no dominion.

Notes

1   In sharp contrast, European travelers to Cuba (other than English), will exalt the ravishing beauty of the *habaneras* they came across. Doña Eulalia de Borbón, a Spanish princess on an official visit to Cuba, attested that she had "always heard the beauty, elegance, and

above all, sweetness, of the *habaneras* lauded, but the reality surpassed everything she could have imagined." (pp. 90–1)

2   Not all American or British beauties travel so felicitously to Cuban soil. Miss Woodruff tells of a fruit seller vainly tempting her with

> a string of small, withered, tough-looking, red apples from my native shores. Vainly—though I really cannot tell whether it was disgust at their uninviting aspect, or mortification at the sorry figure they made beside the fresh and luscious tropical fruits, or a rush of homesick memories, that forced me to turn my eyes away from them as quickly as possible." (Woodruff, p. 196)

3   Interestingly enough, just ten pages later, Woodruff will wax poetic about the beauty of Cuban women she observed in church, recanting the sharpness of the criticism she spewed above:

> The ladies were nearly all dressed in black—the prescribed costume for church-going—with the graceful Spanish mantilla of black lace covering their heads and falling around their shoulders. I was surprised to see how much prettier, more delicate and more womanly, they looked thus than as I had seen them on the *paseo*; and I remembered half-remorsefully the sweeping criticism on their personal appearance that I there registered against them. The young girl who had made room for me looked positively lovely, with her eyes cast down, her long lashes sweeping her cheek, and her face partly shaded by her mantilla; and just opposite was a lady of regal beauty, whose large, black, steadfast eyes, and statue-like grace and stillness of pose, held me spellbound with admiration. It was melancholy to think that such loveliness should be disguised, degraded, utterly lost, in those tawdry fineries of the *paseo*! (p. 57)

4   Luis Martínez-Fernández, quoting Howe's *A Trip to Cuba* (106), in "Life in 'A Male City': Native and Foreign Elite Women in Nineteenth-Century Havana."

5   Sympathetic commentary on the plight of black or mulatto *habaneras*, rare as it is, is to be found almost exclusively in the writings of self-avowed abolitionists like Mathilde Houston, who visited Cuba in 1842 and was horrified at her first sight of the marks of a lash on a woman's shoulders, a sight that filled her with dread and disgust at slave-owners, a caste of "miserable beasts" that "could punish a woman thus" (Houston, reprinted in Araújo, p. 154).

6   See Martínez-Fernández, "Life in 'A Male City.'"

References

Araújo, N. (1983). *Viajeras al Caribe*. Havana: Casa de las Américas.

Borbón, E. de. (1958). *Memorias de Doña Eulalia de Borbón, Infanta de España*. Barcelona: Editorial Juventud, S.A.

Houston, M. (1884). *Texas and the Gulf of Mexico or Yatching the New World*. London: John Murray.

Howe, J. (1860). *A Trip to Cuba*. Boston: Ticknor and Fields.

Jackson, J.N. (1890). *A Winter Holiday in Summer Lands*. Chicago: A.C. McClurg.

Martínez-Fernández, L. Life in "A Male City": Native and Foreign Elite Women in Nineteenth-Century Havana. Forthcoming in *Cuban Studies*.

McHatton-Ripley, E. (1889). *From Flag to Flag*. New York: D. Appleton and Company.

Merlin, Condesa de [Mercedes de Santa Cruz y Montalvo]. (1974). *Viaje a la Habana*. Havana: Editorial de Arte y Literatura.

Moore, R.W. (1867). *The Journal of Rachel Moore*. Philadelphia: T. Ellwood Zell.

Murray, A.M. (1856). *Letters from the United States, Cuba and Canada*. 2 vols. London: John W. Parker.

Woodruff, L.M. [pseud. W.M.L. Jay]. (1871). *My Winter in Cuba*. New York: E.P. Dutton.

Chapter 9

Travelers possessed
Generic hybrids and the Caribbean

Ivette Romero-Cesareo

"When the anthropologist arrives, the Gods depart."[1]
Haitian proverb.
"I have left possession until the end, for it is the center toward which all the roads
of Voudoun converge. It is the point toward which one travels by the most visible,
the most physical means, yet for the traveler, it is itself invisible."[2]

Maya Deren

Many studies dealing with Caribbean culture have been lost in the undefined spaces
of overlapping fields and genres. Texts by novelist/folklorist/anthropologist Zora
Neale Hurston (*Tell My Horse: Voodoo and Life in Haiti and Jamaica*, 1938; 1983; 1990;
1992; 1995) and choreographer/anthropologist Katherine Dunham (*Island Possessed*,
1969; 1994) fall somewhere between anthropology, ethnographic document, and
travelogue. *Tell My Horse* is a stylistic melange including anecdotes about Hurston's
travels and travails, astute portraiture, comprehensive historical accounts, keen
political analyses, detailed ethnographic descriptions of religious ceremonies, and
direct folkloric cataloguing. *Island Possessed* collects Dunham's observations on Haitian
life, ranging from elaboration on political events, portraits of well-known historical
figures, analyses of Haiti's "color" nomenclature, to highly personal descriptions of
her processes of initiation into *vodoun*.[3] Filmmaker Maya Deren's *Divine Horsemen:
The Living Gods of Haiti* (1953, 1970, 1990, 1991) has been recognized as a classic
ethnographic study of Haitian vodoun, although reviewers do not hesitate to point
out the "special" nature of this book. Inside the jacket of the 1991 edition, *Divine
Horsemen* is described as "a classic of its type—an anthropological investigation written
with the special insight of personal encounter." In other words, Deren wrote as
both an ethnographer *and* a vodoun initiate. While nurse/entrepreneur Mary Seacole's
Wonderful Adventures of Mrs. Seacole in Many Lands (1857; 1984; 1988) is suspended
not only between the genres of travelogue, autobiography, and historical account,
but also between fields, it is more often classified as Slavic history because of Seacole's
recording of events in the Crimean War, although a large part of it deals with her
travels in the Caribbean basin.

The books mentioned above have all shared an uneasy reception in the public eye
but are by no means similar to one another. The reader might wonder what could

bring these disparate works together. *Tell My Horse* and *Island Possessed* have many formal components in common, leading us to surmise on their authors' shared academic, ethnic, and social backgrounds—both institutionally backed African-American women traveling to the Caribbean in the 1930s,[4] both aware of the political situation preceding their visits (namely, the United States occupation of Haiti from 1915 to 1934, and their own uneasy status within the North American framework of race relations), and both imbued in the historical, ethnographic and anthropological writings of the founding fathers of their fields (ranging from Martinican historian Moreau de Saint-Méry to anthropologist Melville Herskovits and psychoanalyst/social philosopher Erich Fromm). In intention, Dunham's project to study dance and ritual in the Caribbean and Brazil resembles that of Maya Deren, who first traveled to Haiti in 1947 to film and photograph Haitian dance "as purely a dance form" (Deren, 1991, p. 5). Although Deren, backed by a John Simon Guggenheim fellowship like Dunham and Hurston, was not trained as an anthropologist, her text is the closest (in form and organization) to an anthropological text. It is only in her preface and, most particularly, in the last chapter, "The White Darkness," that the author offers a radically different discursive rendering of her Caribbean experience, framing six chapters of ethnographic data within the confines of personal motivations and authority as an "adopted" insider/participant. Of the four books studied here, *Wonderful Adventures of Mrs. Seacole in Many Lands* shares the fewest elements with the other three. Writing in the 1850s, Seacole is separated in terms of chronology and historical grounding, professional background, nationality, and intention. Her book would hardly be considered anthropology and has rarely been valued for its ethnographic content. However, her work—along with narratives such as *The History of Mary Prince, a West Indian Slave: Related by Herself* (1837; 1987)—allows us to trace back to the preceding century a similar manner of observing and interpreting the self and the Other from diverse standpoints. Mary Seacole, along with other nineteenth-century women writing from the margins, can be seen as a precursor of twentieth-century travelers who seem to constantly shift viewpoints, oscillating between "native other" and the "traveler/visitor."[5]

Despite their disparity of form and authorial intention, two elements these texts have in common are their stylistic shifting, making them difficult to categorize, and, to varying degrees, their candid discussions on the notion of hybridity. Racial hybridity as well as a consciousness of fluctuating class differences characterize these writers' observations and representations of the Caribbean "others" they encounter, regardless of whether they are themselves Caribbean—like Mary Seacole—or not—like Zora Neale Hurston and Katherine Dunham. Kiev-born Maya Deren, the only non-black woman in this selection of writers, explains her sensitivity to "otherness" by defining her own fluctuating status as "artist/native" (Deren, p. 8). This study focuses on how these women's recognition of a fluctuating status colors the perceptions of their own authority/authorship as researchers, observers, and/or witnesses of social phenomena. In most cases, their sense of objectivity alternates with feelings of solidarity with the people they study or come across (for example, of being "one of them" in terms of racial—or in Deren's case, spiritual—allegiance, or in being discriminated against as "colonized others" on the basis of color or gender) and that the instability produced by these alternating and sometimes conflicting viewpoints results in texts that are as difficult to classify as their authors.

The shifting viewpoints and apparent narrative instability in these texts have been perceived as severe literary flaws or even political betrayal by some critics. *Tell My Horse*, for example, has been considered Hurston's "poorest" book, a stylistically defective and flawed text. The book's author has been considered a shameless apologist for the United States occupation of Haiti and, although Hurston is herself a black woman, she has been especially condemned for her ostensibly racist views of Haitians and Jamaicans. The same has been said of Mary Seacole for voicing the British Empire's views on the North Americans, Greeks, Italians, Maltese, Turks, Spaniards, Native (Central) Americans, and the African diaspora. One such critic states that *Wonderful Adventures* ... "reflects an enthusiastic acceptance of colonialism in the aftermath of slavery" and that throughout her narrative, "Seacole celebrates her subject status in an empire that had systematically exploited and abused her native land and the majority of its inhabitants since the British captured Jamaica in 1655" (Pouchet Paquet, 1992, p. 651). Nevertheless, in the various readings of this book, Seacole is portrayed as much a victorious and sly critic of both North American and English societies as a self-serving profiteer who rejects her country of origin. Precisely because of their ambiguity, texts like these have received multiple and contradicting interpretations. Addressing the difficulties in reception and perception of *Tell My Horse*, Caribbeanist critic Kevin Meehan explains that the biggest challenge in reading these texts is difficulty in situating the writer's roving narrator and the comparative cultural commentary articulated in a first-person narrative voice:

> The problem is that the narrator is ambiguous about her position(s) within a social setting structured by imperialism. Like every anthropological voyage before and since, Zora Neale Hurston's Caribbean sojourn occurred against a backdrop of European and North American domination of the region.
> ("Decolonizing Ethnography: Zora Neale Hurston in the Caribbean," 2001, p. 248)[6]

Although Hurston and Seacole's books are separated by almost a century (*Tell My Horse* and *Wonderful Adventures* ... were published in 1938 and 1857 respectively) and are very different in terms of the authors' nationalities, affiliations, political alliances, intentions, professions, and narrative styles, Meehan's claims equally apply to Seacole's work. While the historical framing of Hurston's work is the United States' occupation of Haiti and British rule in Jamaica, Seacole's is the United States' political presence in Central America and control over the Isthmus of Panama, the Gold Rush (in 1855, North American financial interests joined to build the Panama Railroad across the isthmus to transport prospectors bound to the California gold fields; construction of the Canal was undertaken between 1902 and 1914, when it was opened), and that juncture in the nineteenth century when the United States had not yet managed to abolish slavery as England had in 1833. It is understandable, given the countries of origin of these travelers, that Hurston seems to be more critical of English than North American colonialism, racism, and patriarchy while it is the exact opposite in Seacole's writings.

Both writers, aware of their readership, are veiled in their criticism of their countries of residence (the United States for Hurston and England, where Seacole settled after her travels through Central America and Crimea) while mimicking these countries' biased outlooks on others. While Hurston responds to Caribbean society critically but with a certain amount of empathy, she often voices the feelings of superiority that go along with the empire-building enterprise. She admiringly describes the arrival of North American warships in the Port-au-Prince harbor as a propitious event marking the demise of the "revolution": "The smoke from the funnels of the U.S.S. Washington was a black plume with a white hope. [...] It was the end of the revolution and the beginning of peace" (Hurston, 1983, p. 93). This statement seems to echo endlessly repeated tropes of colonial discourse, where the white, "civilized" world's light was considered necessary to heal the black masses from the eternal darkness of ignorance and barbarism. Hurston follows this section by describing (at the beginning of the following chapter) the Haitian revolution as the moment when "the blacks began their savage lunge for freedom" (Hurston, p. 94). The concept of a "white hope" needed to heal the Haitian society's diseased souls is reflected throughout the text. She attributes certain character flaws to what she suggests is the inferior nature of Haitians; for instance, she announces that lying is "the most striking phenomenon of Haiti," prevalent at all levels of society: "The habit of lying! It is safe to say that this art, pastime, expedient or whatever one wishes to call it, is more than any other factor responsible for Haiti's tragic history" (Hurston, p. 101). She also refers to the Haitian people as "gentle and lovable except for their enormous and unconscious cruelty" (Hurston, p. 102). Although, in this section, she is referring to cruelty to animals, it follows the chapter "Rebirth of a Nation," which is profusely peppered with images of dismemberment, massacres, bodies chopped into parts, torsos dragged in the streets, bloody stumps, crushed skulls, clots of blood, and the image of a kneeling black peasant woman, arms outstretched like a crucifix, crying, "They say that the white man is coming to rule Haiti again. The black man is so cruel to his own, *let the white man come!*" (Hurston, p. 92; author's emphasis). The tendency to take the stance of the superior, "civilized," onlooker is not surprising, given Hurston's academic steeping in anthropological and ethnographic traditions that have barely changed since the chronicles of expansionism of the fifteenth and sixteenth centuries. Meehan evokes the description of anthropology as "the child of imperialism" (Meehan, p. 248) to elucidate how ethnography collaborates at a crucial moment in the history of empire by projecting indigenous cultures in a subordinate relationship to metropolitan powers:

> Within the specific framework of representations of Caribbean culture, what links ethnographic writing like Herskovits' and even Katherine Dunham's, with the history of European and North American travel culture from Columbus down to the present, is the production of a symptomatic vision of the Caribbean "natives" as dependent in some way on "first" world society. Sometimes childlike,

sometimes savage, always archetypically underdeveloped, Caribbean societies consistently appear in ethnographic travel documents as desperately needing, if not desperately seeking, outside intervention of some kind.

(Meehan, p. 259)

This projection of a subordinate and needy indigenous culture that necessitates the aid or intervention of metropolitan powers is best illustrated by Hurston's description of her visit to Accompong, a Maroon settlement in Jamaica. Struck by the under-development and lack of "amenities" in the settlement, Hurston tells the leader of the Maroons, Colonel Rowe, that he should buy a stove and teach the community how to use it rather than have the women cook and iron over an open fire. When the Colonel answers that he cannot afford this imported and expensive luxury, she decides to design one and have the men construct it. What is striking in her narration of the events at Accompong is the use of the "I" which punctuates her central role in directing the stove-building project and the unwavering determination to transform the community's lifestyle without asking questions:

> *I told* Rowe that he ought to buy a stove himself and teach the others what to do. […] *I recognized* that [he could not afford one] and *took* another tack. We would build one! *I designed* an affair to be made of rock and cement and Colonel Rowe and some men he gathered undertook to make it. […] *I measured* the bottoms of the pots and designed a hole to fit each of the three.
>
> (my emphasis, Hurston, p. 37)

There seems to be no modesty, restraint, or doubt in her determination of what is best for the community; she does not suggest "We *should* build one" but rather announces conclusively, "We *would* build one." While the decision-making, designing, and measuring is expressed in the first person singular, the actual work is all narrated in the third person (Colonel Rowe, his son, his grandchildren—the men of the community). We never find out what "they" are actually thinking about the process. Hurston switches back and forth from the first person singular to the plural several times, perhaps indicating a slight shortening of the ethnographic distance with which she initially approaches the settlement; the plural is mostly reserved to express the general approval of the project's success:

> We were really joyful when we fired it the next day and found out that it worked. Many of the Maroons came down to look at the miracle. There were pots boiling on the fire; no smoke in the room but a great column of black smoke shooting out of the stove pipe which stuck out of the side of the house.
>
> (Hurston, p. 24)

This time it is not the "black plume with a white hope" that the United States naval forces bring, but rather the "column" of black unity. Although this is one of the moments in which Hurston seems to make a gesture of solidarity with people with whom she might have something in common, it is couched in the language of difference from beginning to end. One could argue that Hurston's decision to undertake the construction of the stove is made as a feminist impulse: it is the scene of women squatting on their haunches as they cook over an open fire that strikes her as unacceptably primitive. But what she voices as distressing is that Jamaica seems to be so far "behind" in economic and technological development compared to Massachusetts.

Although Meehan includes Katherine Dunham in his description of a narrative representation of "the Caribbean 'natives' as dependent in some way on 'first' world society," her perception of her own role as observer seems very clear; the first paragraph of *Island Possessed* announces:

> It was with letters from Melville Herskovits, head of the Department of Anthropology at Northwestern University, that I *invaded* the Caribbean—Haiti, Jamaica, Martinique, Trinidad, passing lightly over the islands, then Haiti again for the last stand for the real study.
>
> (emphasis added, Dunham, 1994, p. 3)

She firmly (and repeatedly) places herself in the role of "invader" playing her opening paragraph against the second, where she offers the backdrop of the United States "Occupation" (the capital "O" cannot be ignored) and the exodus of the Marines a short time prior to her arrival on the island. This historical detail serves to explain her role as a "first" in the production of texts by outsiders about Haiti. She emphasizes her gender and racial placement from the beginning, stressing that

> it was not the policy of the first government after the Occupation to sponsor young women visitors in investigations that might verify to the world outside what has been a crucial problem to Haitian statesmen since the independence: the irreconcilable breach between the thin upper crust of the Haitian élite—who would have liked to be rulers of the land, participating in the revolution only to get rid of the French—and the bubbling, churning ferment of the black peasants, who really were by numbers and by historical content and character and humanness, I was to find, the true Haitian people.
>
> (Dunham, p. 3)

Although her description of the peasantry as a "bubbling, churning ferment" might echo the aesthetics of texts produced before her arrival, many details in her text, including her qualification of the "humanness" of the black population and her subsequent ridicule of the "thin upper crust," light-skinned élites, ever anxious to cover their complexions with white powder to intensify an "egg-shell" appearance, places this ferment within a positive light; she invariably concludes with images of the productivity, dignity, creativity, tolerance, will to survive, and "humanity" reflected in a black majority that has been oppressed in all aspects.

Her role as mediator or link to the "outside" world seems to confirm Meehan's view of writers like Hurston and Dunham as feeling superior to the "native" population that needs outside intervention, but, unlike Hurston, Dunham continually points out the detrimental influence of the United States on Haitian politics and national identity. This is seen not only in *Island Possessed*, but also in recent interviews (for example, in a 1994 article in the *New Yorker*, "Miss Dunham's Haitian Home") and her eloquent actions—for instance, her forty-seven-day hunger strike following the coup that deposed President Jean-Bertrand Aristide.[7] Joan Dayan, in "Haiti's Unquiet Past: Katherine Dunham, Modern Dancer, and Her Enchanted Island," states:

> An outspoken supporter of Aristide in exile, she exposed the cruelty of Clinton's forced deportation of Haitian refugees, as well as his empty rhetoric. Further, she brought this dehumanizing treatment to the attention of many who might have continued to ignore the plight of those the media called "the Haitian stampede," the Haitian "hordes," or "containers of contamination."
>
> (Dayan, 1995, p. 156)

While Hurston expresses pride in the United States intervention and is evidently eager to intervene in and provide correctives to Jamaican social life, Dunham (who describes herself as "the first lady anthropologist to camp out with the Maroon people in Jamaica") is painfully aware of her own presence as an "invasion" and of the mistrust with which she is received, especially in the aftermath of the occupation. Her observations of the conditions surrounding her arrival reveal, on the one hand, her awareness of how those preceding her have affected public perception of the "Americans" and, on the other, a sense of justification, of being, perhaps, a more appropriate witness by virtue of her gender and her indeterminate position in the Haitian color scheme. Although, as Dayan indicates, Dunham's references to Haiti as a "magic island" or a "possessed and obsessed island," draw directly from William Seabrook's *The Magic Island* (1929), which was "published for the delectation of readers in the United States who sought justification for the occupation of Haiti" (Dayan, p. 160), in the opening pages, she describes this type of text as obstacle:

> Being a "first" on the scene helped. Seabrook and his *Magic Island* had been a great handicap because the élite were offended, not so much by the text, which, compared to much that has been written about Haiti, isn't so vilifying, but by the illustration—grotesque impressions not only of the peasants, which wouldn't have mattered, but of the élite. Officially, Seabrook was not to return to the island.
>
> (Dunham, pp. 3–4)

She considers herself a "first" even though other writers were seen in a more positive light: "Harold Courlander had been there and Melville Herskovits had just published the first serious and sympathetic study of the people and their social structure." But, there is an unspoken criticism of these writers latent in the single sentence, "They were white and male, these writers" (Dunham, p. 4). Having just received support and letters of introduction from Herskovits himself, she does not openly voice her reservations regarding these men's works. Although, like Hurston, she occasionally echoes "the signal tropes of a dominant—and dominating—line of commentary that stretches from Columbus down to Hurston's contemporary and fellow Boasian anthropologist Melville Herskovits" (Meehan, p. 246), more often Dunham assumes a rebellious stance, recounting with delight her transgressions of expected social comportment and crossing of the rigid class and color demarcations—not only in her host country, but also at home. Though she considers herself "a first," one cannot help but wonder how conscious she is of alternative precursors, what Meehan refers to as "a dissident tradition of African diasporan travel and cultural production" (Meehan, p. 246). It is difficult to ascertain whether she was aware of Hurston (or vice versa) or of her almost parallel traveling in the Caribbean, and it is oddly surprising that the two never crossed paths in Haiti.[8] She was certainly immersed in the oral tradition of the Accompong Maroons during her stay in Jamaica, and she must have been exposed to the works of Frederick Douglass and Langston Hughes, but she seems to be better versed in the historical figures from Haiti's past and present.[9] In contrast to Hurston's ambiguous analysis of a black nation (in the chapter "Politics and Personalities of Haiti") Dunham's recounting points to a personal relationship and extended interaction with some of these figures, intellectuals like Dr. Price-Mars and his wife (the leading feminist at the time), or political figures like Louis Borno, François Duvalier, and Dumarsais Estimée (the latter to whom she was romantically attached).[10] She studies these figures in their full complexity, taking into account the political upheavals in which they were immersed, class and race issues, and personal experiences.[11] Her approach to Haitian history is much more textured, complex, and analytical.

Dunham is acutely aware of the local population's understanding of the social context from which she has arrived:

> My authorizations were also unorthodox: (…) two universities, when everyone knew not only because of the atrocious behavior of the Americans during the Occupation, but since the showing of the film, *Imitation of Life*, already seen in Port-au-Prince, that blacks, even mulattoes, couldn't attend universities in the United States, much less be sponsored by them.
>
> (Dunham, pp. 10–11)

At another point, she adds that the

> State Department ... sent raw Southerners in as marines to put peace into the troubled little black island, going through one of its characteristic blood baths, and made hell out of purgatory. Haiti was good practice ground for what goes on now between black and white in the United States of America.
>
> (Dunham, pp. 72–3)

Upon her arrival, Dunham is aware of how she must appear to the immigration officer (whom she describes as having the same effect on her as an encounter with a Chicago traffic policeman),[12] "a lone female loose on shores rightfully his" (Dunham,

p. 10) because of the unorthodoxy of her mixed fields—anthropology and dance—and her non-American-sounding sponsors—Herskovits and Rosenwald—but it is precisely this unorthodoxy which helps her gain entrance into a hugely varying social circles. She chooses to shift the attention from the "white and male" writers to herself:

> Of my kind, I was a first—a lone young woman easy to place in the clean-cut American dichotomy of color, harder to place in the complexity of Caribbean color classifications; a mulatto when occasion called for, an in-between, or "griffon" actually, I suppose; most of the time an unplaceable, which I prefer to think of as "noir"—not exactly the color black, but the quality of belonging with or being at ease with black people when in the hills or plains or anywhere and scrambling through daily life along with them.
>
> (Dunham, p. 4)[13]

What separates her from her male precursors, besides her quality of being an unplaceable in-between, capable of crossing class/color boundaries, is her sense of solidarity and belonging to, working alongside, or "scrambling through daily life" with the black majority.[14] Despite her status as foreigner, Dunham explains her "authority" and justification for speaking in the name of a Haitian majority through her virtual adoption into that society.

We see a similar expression of solidarity with an "oppressed" other and justification for the recording of Haitian life in *Divine Horsemen*. When Deren returns to the United States after her first trip to Haiti, she realizes that

> in a modern industrial culture, the artists constitute, in fact, an "ethnic group," subject to the full "native" treatment. We too are exhibited as touristic curiosities on Monday, extolled as culture on Tuesday, denounced as immoral and unsanitary on Wednesday, reinstated for scientific study on Thursday, feasted for some obscurely stylish reason Friday, forgotten Saturday, revisited as picturesque Sunday. We too are misrepresented by professional appreciators and subjected to spiritual imperialism, our most sacred efforts are plagiarized for yard goods, our histories are traced, our psyches analyzed …
>
> (Deren, pp. 7–8)

In her view, it is precisely this uneasy standing as an "'artist/native' in an industrial culture" that make possible her total acceptance into Haitian communities (rural and urban). Much like Dunham, for Deren "racial" allegiance is much more determined by spiritual/psychological affinity than hue. When she claims that the Haitian peasants "early formed the conviction that I was not a foreigner at all, but a prodigal native daughter finally returned," she adds:

> This conviction was shared by much of the Haitian bourgeoisie who felt that only an element of Negro blood in me would account for the psychological

affinity with the peasants, since the city dwellers were only too proud to protest for themselves a psychological alienation.

(Deren, p. 8)

While savouring their unstable status in both the North American and Caribbean contexts, Dunham and Deren seem to find the axis of belonging when they are initiated into the mysteries of vodoun. As opposed to Hurston, who chooses to remain on the outside, these writers often speak as insiders.

Hurston's approach to the "mysteries" seems different, but in the end we find her siding with the "poor blacks" in spite of herself. When Hurston is not expressing her desire to intervene in Jamaican or Haitian community life, voicing her disgust with Caribbean gender relations, or displaying a scientific attempt to catalogue objectively, she is distancing herself by revealing the impossibility of her access into local knowledge, especially where the "magical" or undefinable are concerned, coolly expressing awe and, perhaps, admiration in the face of inexplicable events:

> What is the whole truth and nothing else but the truth about Zombies? I do not know, but I do know that I saw the broken remnant, the relic, or refuse of Felicia Felix-Mentor in a hospital-yard.
>
> (Hurston, p. 185)

In another instance, Hurston recounts, in great detail, two episodes where food had been cooked without fire. She concludes the anecdotes by saying that she and her friend Dr. Reser "tried bribery and everything in our power to learn the secret, but it belongs to that small group and nothing we could devise would do any good," and that the young girl (who had demonstrated how she could cook an egg by putting it in a cup of cold water and mumbling a prayer) had said that it was an inherited secret originally brought from Africa that she could not divulge under pain of death (Hurston, pp. 263–4). And again, speaking of the process of zombification, she seems triumphant, even defiant, when she pronounces, "The two doctors expressed their desire to gain this secret, but they realize the impossibility of doing so. These secret societies are secret. They will die before they will tell" (Hurston, p. 206). When elucidating Caribbean spiritual life, her text betrays great respect and, perhaps, delight that no ethnographer or anthropologist (including herself) is able to penetrate the guarded secrets of certain rituals. Embedded in her discourse of first-world superiority are the many moments of narrative "subversion" that Kevin Meehan refers to as a "decolonizing force:"

> Once we dethrone (so to speak) Hurston's roving narrator, we can then look for clues as to the narrative politics of this background drama, which, in my reading, has a strong counter-imperial message. In fact, Hurston adapts and adopts the language of vodou spirit possession as a strategy for staging scenes of social protest.
>
> (Meehan, p. 256)

Here Meehan is referring to Hurston's oblique criticism of United States policies in Haiti, as well as local oppression, through her description of spirit possession, especially by the loa Papa Guedé, in the chapter "Parlay Cheval Ou (Tell My Horse)."[15] Hurston explains, "Sometimes Guedé dictates the most caustic and belittling statements concerning some pompous person who is present. A prominent official is made ridiculous before a crowd of peasants. On several occasions it was observed that Guedé seemed to enjoy humbling his betters" (Hurston, p. 234). Noting that people "mounted" by Papa Guedé are suddenly free from class, race, and gender restrictions and can express anything at all, she claims,

> Gods always behave like the people who make them. One can see the hand of the Haitian peasant in that boisterous god, Papa Guedé, because he does and says the things that the peasant would like to do and say. You can see him in the market women, in the domestic servant who now and then appears before her employer "mounted" by this god who takes the occasion to say many stinging things to the boss. [...] This manifestation comes as close to social criticism as anything in all Haiti.
>
> (Hurston, p. 232)

In a sense, Hurston seems to dethrone herself—as the wry, distrusting American ethnographer—by pointing out the many gaps that she cannot and will not fill with intellectual speculation. She refuses "to serve up" the Caribbean "either in easily digested popular stereotypes or authoritative ethnographic pronouncements" (Meehan, p. 256). Just as Hurston considers the phrase "Parlay cheval ou" a blind for self expression, Meehan sees her as identifying with this loa of social protest to articulate what she cannot easily declare on her own, "tell my horse" becoming a blind for her own self-expression: "In Hurston's hands, then, ethnography becomes 'possessed': she makes it speak in a language of indigenous protest" (Meehan, p. 258). Hurston's ethnography indeed becomes a vehicle for protest, in some cases, very explicitly. When a well-known physician from Port-au-Prince refers to certain secret sects as "bad elements" that the undermanned police force has not been able to control, and who represent, in his eyes, obstacles to cultural and economic advancement, Hurston retorts, "But ... with all the wealth in the United States and all the policing, we still have gangsters and the Ku Klux Klan. Older European nations still have their problems of crime" (Hurston, p. 220). This riposte betrays more than meets the eye. She brings up the Ku Klux Klan as a parallel to the Sect Rouge— a feared group that allegedly eats human flesh—making the social criticism of her own country's ills explicitly chilling. Suddenly, her position in the civilized/barbaric dichotomy shifts dramatically. Although Hurston does not go through the process of initiation into vodoun, her pursuit of the secrets of Haitian spiritual life seems to expose a personal exploration that she does not allow herself to articulate in her anthropological study. Ultimately, she prefers to maintain the distance expected of her.

Katherine Dunham and Maya Deren deliver a more personal view of the decision-making involved in their plunge forward to explore vodoun as insiders, whether in the name of scientific research ("Melville Herskovits saw one side of me of which even I did not know at the time—the eternal chercheur, the eternal commentator on the flux of people in life." Dunham, pp. 66–7) or personal conviction and commitment ("'Each one serves in his own fashion.'" Deren, p. 14). As Deren describes in her final chapter,

> I have left possession until the end, for it is the center toward which all the roads of Voudoun converge. It is the point toward which one travels by the most visible, the most physical means, yet for the traveler, it is itself invisible. One might speak of it as the area of a circle whose circumference can be accurately described; yet this circumference is not, itself, the circle which it defines. To know this area, one must finally enter.
>
> (Deren, p. 247)

Regardless of their reasons for entering, both writers embark upon a journey to this center, and both seem to transit between worlds to which they feel they belong or do not belong. They punctuate their observations in terms of being outsiders and/ or insiders, or both simultaneously. Deren, like Dunham, credits her being able to access certain circles to her unconventionality:

> I had begun as an artist, as one who would manipulate the elements of a reality into a work of art in the image of my creative integrity; I end by recording, as humbly and accurately as I can, the logics of a reality which had forced me to recognize its integrity, and to abandon my manipulations.
>
> (Deren, p. 6)

When she began her investigation, she felt an outsider not only in the Haitian community, but also in scientific territory, "for I was well aware of the fact that it is unorthodox for a non-professional to speak of matters that are normally the province of trained anthropologists" (Deren, p. 6). In the same way that Dunham sets herself apart from the "white men," Deren finds that she has something unique to offer that, in some way, transcends the contributions of "those professionals who have been concerned with Haitian culture: Herskovits, Courlander, Simpson, and others." After reading their works, she discovers that

> my background as an artist and the initial approach to the culture which my film project induced, served to illuminate areas of Voudoun mythology with which the standard anthropological procedure had not concerned itself, or, if so, from a different position entirely.
>
> (Deren, pp. 6–7)

She goes on to explain that she had "no preparation or motivation, no anthropological background (and anticipation) from other ethnic cultures, no systematized approach to an established methodology for collecting data, no plan of questions to ask" which might have induced an artificial self-consciousness in the people observed, and that having no professional or intellectual urgency or commitment had permitted the culture to emerge on its own terms. She also stresses the impossibility of studying "Oriental or African" cultures from the grounding of Western thought and points to her advantageous position as an artist, because, in her view, artists do not "accept certain beliefs which have for so long been the premises of Occidental thought" (Deren, p. 9). What Deren concludes is that the "reality" of vodoun mythology reveals itself to her precisely because she does not have an anthropological agenda and because she is not rigidly rooted within a prescribed viewpoint. She explains her attitude as not one of complete passivity, but rather of,

> a deliberate discretion, reflecting a strong distaste for aggressive inquiry, staring or prying, and which both resulted from and was rewarded by a sense of human bond which I did not fully understand until my first return to the United States.
>
> (Deren, p. 7)

This human bond and the gradual process of becoming an insider are described in minute detail in "The White Darkness."

Similarly, Dunham emphasizes aspects of belonging in trying to describe her initiation process:

> Fred tried to discourage me from entertaining the idea of becoming a hounci, and, by consequence, I grew more determined than ever. I had to move very carefully, however, among the followers of Cécile's compound, because, while all of them were close friends to me, and we danced for hours under the same tonnelle, and ate from the same cook pot much of the time, and exchanged face powder and toilet water, still I continued to observe the strict regulation of vaudun, that it does not proselytize, and, by the same token, it does not accept petitions for entry. As a matter of fact, there is no such thing as strictly "belonging" to the vaudun. One is or one isn't; one practices or believes or one just stands on the fringes and watches and interprets as one chooses.
>
> (Dunham, p. 58)

While she is not an insider to vodoun, she is already an accepted member of the community, sharing in all facets of their lives. Although she claims that there is no such thing as *belonging* to the vodoun in terms of membership, and that there is no precise moment when access is granted, there are certainly unspoken rules and a specific protocol which must be respected. Disclaiming tourists' tales about becoming vodoun initiates overnight, for a fee, she states:

> It is conceivable that some Prête savant directly from 'Nan Guinée, still damp with sacrificial blood from his own temples and scarred with tribal markings and jangling gris-gris from neck to ankle, as is the custom in Africa, could so

impart his "belongingness" that taboos would fall, the way would be immediately opened, and centuries and oceans bridged in moments. But this would be a special and very rare case, and the stranger would have to come to evidence in some way his intention and willingness to submit to the protocol of the local vaudun, for the Haitians are proud of what they have conserved of the power of 'Nan Guinée from preslavery times, and rightly so.

(Dunham, p. 59)

Dunham's experience of initiation—first, the *lave-tête* (the first stage) and then the *canzo*, or trial by fire (the second stage)—which she calls "the Great Experience," is described in anything but romantic terms. She details the discomforts and deprivation to which she submits and the doubts that assail her as she lies on a dirt floor, "at four in the morning wearing a nightgown soaked by someone else's urine, chilled, disconsolate, feeling none of the promised ecstasy, and no signs of it, alien to gods, people, and land" (Dunham, p. 65). It is here that one sees that she is both an insider and outsider in all spheres:

With aching knees tucked under the buttocks of the woman in front of me I even wished I were back in Chicago or in Joliet, which indicated a state of total eclipse. Then I continued sorting out the situation, after all, I was there for the purpose of learning and experiencing the unusual, and my Fellowships were a trust more sacred than any vows yet taken.

(Dunham, p. 68)

Not betraying the trust placed in her by Melville Herskovits, Erich Fromm, Franz Boas, and others, and not wasting what she considered the fortune the Rosenwald and Guggenheim Foundations had spent on her seem to be her principal concern; her loyalties or feelings of belonging seem to be "back home" in the United States and she feels "alien" to everything, a "state of total eclipse."[16] As Dunham continues to explain her feelings of alienation, she characterizes herself in a dramatic scene depicting her role as sacrificial:

Here I lay aching and feeling a sore throat coming on, all in the cause of curiosity or science, and I, Iphigenia tied to the mast, as Erich Fromm had pointed out in friendly conversation, and all the while the black race broiling on hot coals below.

(Dunham, p. 69)

If she feels, like Iphigenia, sacrificed to the gods for a noble cause—in Dunham's case, the name of science, and in Iphigenia's, to allow Agamemnon's ships to sail—who is Agamemnon? Does he represent the group of father figures who supported her studies and research trip? Her "sacrifice" presents a provocative reversal of Caribbean and Hellenic mythologies: animal sacrifice is usually associated with Afro-Caribbean religions, and has been the characteristic mostly used to vilify vodoun; and in Greek mythology, Agamemnon must slit his daughter's throat for his ships to sail. In this scenario, Dunham is sacrificed by the anthropologists in the name of science. Her portrayal of the "black race broiling on the coals below" is more enigmatic. One could read this, on the one hand, as a Hurston-like impulse to see herself as an outside force necessary for the survival of the Haitian people. On the other hand, she seems to want to provide a corrective to what has previously been written about Haiti, to position herself as a link between different worlds, in an effort to heal some of the wounds inflicted by misconceptions—she sees herself, after all, on the same boat with the black race. When she speaks of her "in-between" status in terms of race and class, she considers herself an unplaceable mulatto in the Haitian color gradations, but prefers to think of herself as *noir*, which she defines as "the quality of belonging with or being at ease with black people when in the hills or plains or anywhere" (Dunham, p. 4). Later, when describing her initiation, she speaks of becoming a first-degree servitor of "the pantheon of vaudun gods brought back by *our* ancestors from Africa" (Dunham, p. 70, emphasis added). However, she stresses the uncertain state of belonging when she speaks of her sisterhood with the Haitian people through vodoun:

> Being an American meant to the Haitian peasants a whole complex of things at one end of the balance, just as being a "member," a term not used in those days, one of the "race," a "sister," tipped the scales into balance at the other.
>
> (Dunham, p. 72)

In terms of the Haitian élite, she feels accepted in spite of her "unpredictability, *deliberate clinging to the role of outsider*, crashing naïveté, ruthless trampling of customs or often sensibilities." Nevertheless, she continues to accent her cultural mobility and her ability to become a social chameleon: "As the situation presented itself, I seem to have wavered or catapulted from mulatto to black, élite to peasant, intellectual to bohemian, in to out, up to down." (Dunham, p. 13, emphasis added). Ultimately, she chooses to identify herself racially, as belonging to the black race, but emphasizes that color need not be a determining factor to this sense of belonging:

> Being a member of the race was a distinct advantage. Skin color, hair texture, facial measurements, yes, these are the external part of "race"; but, as Fay-Cooper Cole so often pointed out, race is psychology. [...] I am, however, sensitive to "kind," to blackness in the sense of spirit, a charismatic intangible, and this is what the Haitians and Brazilians and Malaysians and Chinese and those Africans with whom I have had time really to discuss things must have felt, must feel.
>
> (Dunham, p. 74)

Notwithstanding, Dunham refuses to choose sides and to remain "married" to one of them. As she stands at "the altar of decision with circumspection and belief each as strong as the other," ready to be married to Damballa (the serpent deity), she sees herself "being an observer with the skepticism of youth bound by intellectual obligations and trying to live up to a higher education of cold science; and, more important than any of these, as *Iphigenia ready for the supreme sacrifice*" (Dunham, p. 112, emphasis added). Towards the end of the text, Dunham speculates about surrendering herself totally to a single cause:

> I have often wondered whether my reluctance to attach myself solely the houngfor[17] which I had known best and which was responsible for my spiritual protection in the vaudun, was because of the never-ending quest for the novel, the statistics gathering of the researcher, or another reason ... [...] Could Herskovits tell me, could Erich Fromm, could Téoline or Dégrasse tell me what part of me lived on the floor of the houngfor, felt awareness seeping from the earth and people and things around me, and what part stood to one side taking notes? Each part lived in participation was real; still, without arranging this expressly, without conscious doing or planning or thinking *I stayed outside the experience while being totally immersed in it.* [...] I can still observe with some pity, even amusement, the newly traveled, ethnic-saturated, homesick-for-Chicago *Iphigenia* wondering what next to do to prove herself a scientist to her Alma Mater; the true scholar to her country; the selfless sacrificial maiden to her people.
>
> (Dunham, pp. 227–8)

As she compares herself to Iphigenia for the third time, it is evident that her sacrifice entails a threefold sense of obligation: to the academic sphere, to the United States, and to her people, namely, the black race. Although she speaks with apprehension and uneasiness of her being inside and outside crucial experiences simultaneously or of her inability to commit, she more often concludes—like Deren—that her multifarious personality, eclectic influences, and unorthodox approach are assets which enable her to go through the series of purification rites to become an *hounci* (spirit wife; in her case, wed to Damballa) and to endure life's trials:

> It was perseverance, many common interests apart from common ancestry, love for babies and old people, enough medical background to see my way through diagnosis and prognosis of minor cuts and burns and snake-bite and intestinal parasites and first-stage venereal disease, preferably guided, but working on my own if necessary, and intuition, and the flawless training in social anthropology field technique begun by my professors at the University of Chigago and polished off by Melville Herskovits, that tipped the scales in my favor.
>
> (Dunham, p. 74)

What first appears to be instability and unwillingness to commit, ultimately becomes her greatest strength.

While Dunham compares herself to Iphigenia, Mary Seacole prefers to see herself as a "female Ulysses," accentuating her freedom of movement and adventurous spirit. This choice of mythological identification places her in a more empowered position, investing her "character" with more decision-making and drive; she avoids any imagery alluding to sacrifice, although she claims heroic feats in the name of the British army. Even her title, *Wonderful Adventures of Mrs. Seacole in Many Lands,* downplays the obstacles she faced. Perhaps more than any of the modern travelers previously mentioned, this nineteenth century Jamaican woman relishes her lack of real ties and her inclination to wander. In contrast to Hurston, Dunham, and Deren, who all traveled from the "centers of discourse" to the lands that were being "explicated," Seacole decides to move away from her Caribbean home with the purpose of finding an adoptive home in England. She declares that, as she grew into womanhood, she began to indulge a longing to travel in stately ships and to "see the blue hills of Jamaica fade into the distance." This same inclination that drives her to leave Jamaica is what ultimately brings her to self-awareness as a Jamaican abroad.

Seacole is able to embark on her journey because she enjoys, to a certain extent, a social mobility which allows her, or perhaps forces her, to circulate in an ever-shifting spectrum of race and nationality. She justifies this mobility by stating early in the text that she is a widow and that her mother has died. Her choice of profession as hotel keeper and merchant reinforces her mobility. Although these professions were not rare for Creole women in the nineteenth century—both her mother and sister were hotel keepers—she was the only mulatto woman known at the time to have traveled to so many countries to set up shops and inns.

Seacole's reasons for traveling—through Haiti, the Bahamas, Cuba, Panama, Colombia, England, all the countries from there to Crimea, and finally, back to her "home" in England—are complex. She sometimes presents herself as an entrepreneur trying her luck as a hotel keeper, a gold prospector, and a sutler, selling provisions in war zones or other types of liminal areas, but she mostly stresses her role as a healer. Wherever she goes to sell goods, she doubles as a nurse or doctor in folk medicine. She also seems to travel as a self-appointed representative of the English empire and to help the English soldiers overseas, whom she insists on calling her "sons." In doing this, she alternates her role as an adventurer with that of a mother, using it as a tactic for safeguarding her reputation in her ambiguous role of a mobile subject.

Like Dunham, Seacole also specializes in shifting performances. She identifies herself as a Jamaican Creole, a female, and a widow, but race seems to be the major factor in her narration of self. When she states, "I am a Creole, and I have good Scotch blood coursing through my veins," or that she owes the "energy and activity which are not always found in the Creole race" to her Scottish blood, one is struck by her apparent acceptance of the standard prejudices of the English regarding the black and mulatto population. However, as we find her doing throughout her auto-biography, she usually follows this type of biased comment with veiled irony, implicit reproach, or contradiction: "I have often heard the term 'lazy Creole' applied to my country people; but I am sure I do not know what is it to be indolent" (Seacole, 1984, p. 56). She constantly attempts to dispel stereotypical images of creoles by stressing the qualities that have led her to travel far and wide, for example, the impulse to be active, her lack of idleness, and a powerful will.

Hurston, Dunham, and Deren travel to islands where there is a black majority and they are, like it or not, privileged in terms of race and class. Seacole's voyage is, if not more complex, more transgressive, taking into consideration her historical context: she was a black woman circulating within areas still uneasy with the abolition of slavery (it had been abolished in England in 1772, in the British West Indian colonies in 1833, and it had not yet been abolished in the United States). Of the four, Seacole is the only one who never embarks on the return trip "home." She moves through several countries where she is part of a very small mulatto minority— in many cases the only one—finding herself in perilous situations or becoming a target for jeers and insults. She carefully illustrates the reception she is often given because of her color. For instance, her most vivid recollections of her first trip to London were of the efforts of street-boys to poke fun at her and her companion's complexion:

> I am only a little brown—a few shades duskier than the brunettes whom you all admire so much; but my companion was very dark, and a fair (if I can apply the term to her) subject for their rude wit [...] our progress through the London streets was sometimes a rather chequered one.
>
> (Seacole, p. 58)

Judging by Seacole's witty prose, her use of the word "chequered" is hardly accidental.[18] While we can imagine the contrasting situations the travelers encounter in London, we are also presented with a world in black and white, with none of the complex cataloguing of Caribbean color nomenclature that Dunham presents in her work.

There are other instances where self-defense does not play a role; she offers numerous observations on the excellent qualities of African-Americans, especially those who have settled in Central America. One of the few positive characteristics the narrator sees in Panama is that it offers freed blacks from different countries and runaway slaves from the United States, the opportunity to prosper. She praises the industriousness of blacks in this new and free world and stresses their progress in obtaining important positions and becoming landowners. This is reminiscent of Dunham's comparison of the sense of history of black youth in Haiti and in the United States. Speaking of the reform of the educational system, she says:

> Haitian teachers gradually replaced French; the history of Haiti became a curriculum requirement in public schools, because without it the young of the proletariat would have no reason for pride in themselves, would be as deracinated as American negroes, who knew only the brilliant exploits of people whose skin color automatically made them superior in the social structure. This, I now realize, was the very beginning of the movement for black identity, become now a cry for revolution in North America.
>
> (Dunham, p. 46)

In both cases, these women present a North America that is arrested in its social development, lagging far behind other geographic areas considered backwards or barbaric.

Always aware of her shaky stature as a loved but not completely accepted English citizen, she does not adopt an entirely "official" voice, but, when speaking of other colonized groups, it is easy to see the acquired baggage that weighs down her encounters with non-English people, for example, the Greeks, Maltese, and Turks— portrayed as liars and thieves—and especially, Native Central Americans, whom she depicts as uncivilized, treacherous, and lazy compared to the industrious black population in Panama. She considers "the natives" to be "constitutionally cowardly" because they "made not the feeblest show of resistance" during the cholera epidemic and is disgusted by their religious fervor and superstitions as sole response to their suffering (Seacole, p. 78). Their passivity and acceptance of illness and death make them childlike, but not in the least endearing, in her eyes. Some of her judgments are reminiscent of Hurston's when she details the ills of Haitian history or the backwardness of Jamaica, and some are harsher. Seacole goes as far as to allude to cannibalism to suggest the barbarous nature of the indigenous population:

> The native fare was not tempting, and some of their delicacies were absolutely disgusting. With what pleasure, for instance, could one foreign to their tastes and habits dine off a roasted monkey, whose grilled head bore a strong resemblance to a negro baby's? … They were worse still stewed in soup, when it was positively frightful to dip your ladle in unsuspectingly, and bring up what closely resembles a brown baby's limb.
>
> (Seacole, p. 78)

She adopts the same language used in nineteenth century racist descriptions of African peoples to describe a group she deems inferior.

Seacole's shifting viewpoints are sometimes difficult to follow, especially where race and ethnicity are concerned. In many instances when she uses the word "nigger"—the accepted term in her time—she offers cartoonish depictions of her "black" servants with white teeth bared, or disdainfully portrays them as superstitious cowards. However, when she is shocked into the position of the discriminated Other, she shows a sense solidarity. Although she consistently speaks of the virtues of the English compared to the uncouth hostility and savagery of North Americans, there are moments when a direct accusation of the English finds its way into her critiques:

> My experience of travel had not failed to teach me that Americans (even from the Northern states) are always uncomfortable in the company of coloured people, and very often show this feeling in stronger ways than by sour looks and rude words. I think, if I have a little prejudice against our cousins across the Atlantic—and I do confess to a little—it is not unreasonable. I have a few shades deeper brown upon my skin which shows me related—and I am proud of the relationship—to those poor mortals whom *you once held enslaved*, and whose bodies America still owns. And having this bond, and knowing what slavery is; having seen with my eyes and heard with my ears proof positive of its horrors … is it surprising that I should be somewhat impatient of the airs of superiority which many Americans have endeavoured to assume over me?
>
> (Seacole, p. 67; emphasis added)

Here she purposely sides with all blacks, slaves and freed, from different continents, and the *other* becomes both the Americans and the English, whom she is addressing when she says, "*you* once held enslaved." She actually does not accuse the English of on-going prejudice instead, she cleverly diverts the attention from *them* by pointing to her own prejudices toward white North Americans. However, Seacole suspects she is the victim of English racism, and expresses it clearly, when she tries to volunteer to help Florence Nightingale's corps of nurses to tend to the wounded soldiers in Crimea. After suffering rebuffs and humiliation, she gingerly confesses:

> Doubts and suspicions arose in my heart for the first and the last time, thank Heaven. Was it possible that American prejudices against colour had some root *here*? Did these ladies shrink from my aid because my blood flowed beneath a somewhat duskier skin than theirs?
>
> (Seacole, p.126)

In spite of her caution, the message is clear enough.

Seacole's description of the "candid" racism demonstrated by an American makes the English pale in comparison. While offering a toast in Aunty Seacole's honor, for her role in fighting a cholera epidemic in Panama, the speaker expresses regret that she is not white. Seacole's fearless answer is:

> Gentlemen—, I return you the kindness in drinking my health. [...] But I must say that I don't altogether appreciate your friend's kind wishes with respect to my complexion. If it had been as dark as any nigger's, I should have been just as happy and as useful, and as much respected by those whose respect I value; and as to his kind offer of bleaching me, I should, even if it were practicable, decline it without many thanks. As to the society which the process might gain me admission into, all I can say is, that, judging from the specimens I have met with here and elsewhere, I don't think that I shall lose much by being excluded from it. So, gentlemen, I drink to you and to the general reformation of American manners.
>
> (Seacole, p. 98)

Although she seems to echo the expansionist views of the British, Seacole constantly subverts this discourse with contradictory tales. In her healing prowess, highlighting the way in which some doctors are mystified by her ability to heal where they have failed and the mysterious ways in which she single-handedly fights plagues, remaining unscathed by illness, she seems to parallel Hurston, Deren, and Dunham in proudly finding something undefinable, a secret, to which *they* (scientists, ethnologists, anthropologists, medical doctors) cannot have access. Focusing on her gift for healing is the closest Seacole comes to remotely alluding to "magico-religious" elements. She credits her Caribbean background for her knowledge of herbs—mostly transported from her land of origin to be used in emergencies—but she stresses the scientific approach rather than the popular beliefs in the healing properties of these plants. Her healing powers gain her a certain degree of temporary recognition and public acceptance, and she is acclaimed far and wide as Dame Seacole, Aunty Seacole, the Mother of the Regiment, La Madre, La Mère Noire, "the excellent lady," "the genial old lady," or, more often, as "the yellow woman from Jamaica with the cholera medicine" or "the yellow doctress from Jamaica." Hoping to take advantage of this renown, Seacole conceived *Wonderful Adventures* as a project to ensure her financial survival in England; paradoxically, she died impoverished and in virtual anonymity.

While Seacole was not able to profit—financially or socially—from her travel experiences and writing, the other travelers studied here did to a varying extent. Hurston became well known for her novels (much more so than for *Tell My Horse*); Dunham gained celebrity as a dancer and choreographer, using and incorporating her Caribbean and African lived experiences into her performances; Deren gained recognition for *Divine Horsemen* as well as her documentaries and other artistic ventures (recordings of vodoun music, photography). As evidenced by their texts, all of these writers share an awareness of their presence in the public arena, a sense of performance. All of them know that their survival and their ability to deflect blows—personal, economic, academic, artistic, etc.—make their unplaceability necessary. For this reason, they not only write texts that are difficult to place in terms of genre, but they choose to represent *themselves* as hybrid.

These women can be considered "hybrid" in the sense that they are difficult to categorize in all aspects, being able to slip in and out of identities with ease, and it is evident through their writing that all of them cultivate this "unplaceability."[19] In the case of Mary Seacole, Zora Neale Hurston, Maya Deren, and Katherine Dunham, this resistance to classification seems to be a chosen strategic stance. In their movements between different social classes, racial categories, and, in particular, their confrontation with discrimination in these areas, they are obliged to position themselves and to take a stand one moment, whether directly or obliquely, against the injustices they perceive, while the next moment they shield themselves by adopting an ambiguous pose. By the same token, "hybridity" seems to invest these women with the ability to shift their positioning, assume alternative standpoints, and comment on transcontinental problems.

As these writers have had to do in their travels, through their texts they are able to negotiate, and perhaps provide links, between cultural spaces, artistic production, social practices, spheres of knowledge, and historical perspectives. In the same way as these women expose themselves to the destabilizing effects of travel, they exert a similar destabilization on the reader by not providing a secure point of reference. In contrast to conventional, metropolitan travel writing—described as an "incantation zone" by Mario Cesareo in "When the Subaltern Travels: Slave Narrative and Testimonial Erasure in the Contact Zone"—the writing produced by these women as a result of their travels, does not perform an exorcism of the other, nor does it allow for the comfort of a familiar "home," as the conclusions of our four texts attest to. Seacole ends with her "return," not to Jamaica, but to England where she finds herself wounded and bankrupt, but still "ready to take any journey to any place where a stout heart and two experienced hands may be of use" (Seacole, p. 231).

Hurston ends her journey with a Haitian folk tale about how Shango, the god of thunder and lightning, sent music and dancing to Guinea. The last words of her text are: "So that is why music and dancing came from Guinea—God sent it there first," sending us back to metaphorical origins in a mythical Africa (Hurston, p. 275). Dunham speaks of her exorcism of the maledictions attached to the Habitation Leclerc, former home of Pauline Bonaparte (Napoleon's sister), and her intention to return to live there:

> Now that all the springs have been cleansed and all the hiding places of trouble-some souls forever sealed and the souls themselves sent back to sleep peacefully in 'Nan Guinée, I shall see what it feels like to be mistress of Leclerc and leave the maintaining of order to the master, my husband.
>
> (Dunham, p. 273)

the latter refers to Damballa (her spiritual husband in vodoun). She speaks of a return to her Haitian home from her African "home"—Dakar, Senegal. Deren's return seems to be based in Haiti and Africa (Dahomey), because hers is a "return" to her spiritual "home," vodoun, or rather, possession, "the center toward which all the roads of Voudoun converge" (Deren, p. 247). Her last words are: "As the souls of the dead did, so have I, too, come back. I have returned. But the journey around is long and hard, alike for the strong horse, alike for the great rider" (Deren, p. 262). We are left with a return to what will remain unknown unless we too embark on our own journey.

Notes

1 Quoted by Joseph Campbell in his foreword to Maya Deren's *Divine Horsemen: The Living Gods of Haiti*, Kingston: McPherson & Company (1991), p. xiv.
2 Campbell, p.247.
3 I have chosen *vodoun* out of the many possible spellings—voodoo, vodou, voudoun, vaudou, vaudoun, vaudoux, vôdou. The reader will notice that Zora Neale Hurston, Maya Deren, and Katherine Dunham all use different spellings. Etymologically, it derives from the Dahomeyan language, Fon, and means "spirit," "god," or "image." See Joan Dayan's Vodoun or the Voice of the Gods, in *Raritan* (1991). In vodoun, everything in the universe is interrelated—the living and the dead, the animate and the inanimate. Not only are humans beings considered to have a spirit—which retains each individual's personality traits after death—but the spirit is thought to be present within objects and natural elements, such as plants and bodies of water.
4 Katherine Dunham studied anthropology at the University of Chicago; her first trip to Haiti was funded by a fellowship from the Rosenwald and Guggenheim Foundations. Zora Neale Hurston was a doctoral candidate at Johns Hopkins University and was, likewise, financially backed by a Guggenheim Foundation Fellowship.
5 Seacole's work has been chosen here (rather than other nineteenth-century works such as slave narratives or European travelogues) because of her precarious position as a free, black woman circulating within circles still uneasy with the abolition of slavery. We must remember that slavery in the British West Indian colonies was abolished in 1833 (although it was prohibited in England as early as 1772) and it was not until 1865 that the United States managed to secure the abolition of slavery in all states.

6 In Lizabeth Paravisini-Gebert and Ivette Romero-Cesareo's *Women at Sea: Travel Writing and the Margins of Caribbean Discourse*. New York: Palgrave (2001).
7 See Joan Dayan's Haiti's Unquiet Past: Kathleen [sic] Dunham, Modern Dancer, and her Enchanted Island, in *Transition* 67, (1995) pp. 150–64.
8 Zora Neale Hurston and Katherine Dunham both traveled to Haiti in 1936. It is possible that they missed each other because it is believed Hurston stopped briefly in Haiti and then proceeded to Jamaica where she stayed from April to September of 1936, and then returned to Haiti. Joan Dayan claims Hurston arrived in Port-au-Prince sixteen months after Dunham. Whichever the case may be, it is still improbable that these two women had not heard of one another, either in the Caribbean or the United States. The fact that they never mention one another in their writings about the Caribbean seems peculiar.
9 Kevin Meehan refers to a tradition of African diasporan travel to and writing about the Caribbean that presented defiant alternatives to the accepted accounts:

> The representative figures in this tradition include maroons, enslaved Africans who were trans-shipped within the Americas, present-day migrant workers, and luminary African American travelers such as Frederick Douglass, James Weldon Johnson, and Langston Hughes, all of whom spent time living in and writing about the Caribbean. What unifies this dissident tradition, and its expressions both written and non-written, is a denunciation of impoverishment and imperialism, a celebration of the liberating potential of Caribbean civilization, and a commitment to advocating Caribbean sovereignty. (Meehan, p. 246)

Although it is probable that she was aware of Hughes, Douglass, and others from that tradition, Dunham seems to be more versed in prominent historical, and perhaps controversial, figures from Haiti's past and present, for example, Presidents François Duvalier, Dumarsais Estimée, Sténio Vincent, and Paul Magloire, and from Jamaica, for instance, the Manley family, among others.
10 Even in describing her romantic liaison with Estimée, she perceives the complexities of sociohistorical contexts and personal goals:

> In retrospect, I must have been, in my way, in love with the Deputy, and he, in his way, with me. I must qualify for both of us because now I see clearly the force of ambition, not for personal gain in either of us, but expressed in a drive for knowledge and experience and achievement through which to serve some cause, which cause would, if possible, encompass the black race. As I see it now, we were one with the avant garde of negritude. (Dunham, pp. 144–5)

11 In order to explain Dumarsais Estimée's anger when Dunham uses his car to pay a visit to former president Louis Borno, she clarifies,

> Dumarsais disliked white people, identifying most of them with Marines and functionaries of the Occupation. Another reason for his sentiments occurred much later, after he was President. I shall speak of that elsewhere. At this time, however, he carried as well as his feelings against people of the white race a smoldering resentment against the mulatto élite of Haiti and their multiple ways of preserving within the country a caste system based on color distinctions. He was particularly offended that his car had been seen in the driveway of the Bornos, because for him Louis Borno represented what a freed octoroon collaborator with the French must have represented to the first black leaders of the slave revolt. (Dunham, pp. 22–3)

> Though now I understand Haitian feelings of revulsion towards anyone even faintly suspected of collaboration with the members of the Occupation, having done some research in the control methods used by Marines and their chiefs, I nevertheless feel that the position of whoever had been President at the time would have been extremely

> delicate and his behavior not too divergent from that of Borno. The Americans occupied Haiti with very little consideration for the customs, desires, and habits of the people themselves, and with no wish, until the harm was done, to find out what the national character was like. (Dunham, pp. 23–4)

The latter quote reflects Dunham's refusal of simple answers and her attempt to see different, and sometimes contradictory, sides—Borno was perceived by many as a traitor for accepting United States intervention and mistreatment of the Haitian population. Although Dunham was emotionally tied to Dumarsais Estimée and credits him with her civic awakening, she studies each man in the light of their political contexts, their individual experiences, and their psychological and philosophical framework (we must not forget Dunham was Erich Fromm's student).

In the first quote, the incident to which Dunham refers as influencing Estimée's perception of white America is his experience with racial segregation in the United States:

> I knew that he had gone to Washington for a Pan American Union conference, been refused expected hotel accommodations because of color, stayed in a Negro hotel, I am told, separated from other chiefs of state—those classified as non-Negro—and had left vowing never to set foot on American soil, though in the end he did. (Dunham, p. 51)

12   According to Joan Dayan, "Dunham's own history in a racist United States no doubt gave her a deep awareness of the paradoxes of performance in a prejudiced society. She knew that, no matter how much the audiences appreciated her on stage in shows such as *Tropic*, *Le Jazz Hot*, and *Carib Song*, racial discrimination would affect her reception in hotels and even determine the complexion of her audiences. In her biography of Dunham, Ruth Beckford recalls that Dunham not only performed dances of liberation but consistently fought hotel authorities and the 'black-in-balcony-only' policy of segregated theaters in the South, as well as in New York City, in Chicago, and on the West Coast" (p. 158).

13   Dunham expresses the complex nuances in Haitian society's color scheme by citing an eighteenth-century precursor, Moreau de Saint-Méry, "the most descriptive and perhaps unbiased of the historians and chroniclers of Saint Domingue," who "notes the forty gradations and mixtures recognized at the time of his writing between black and white, sometimes with Arawak or Carib Indian blood thrown in. Haiti of today recognizes the following: mulatto, marabou, griffon, black" (Dunham, p. 8).

14   Dunham finds and "escape clause" in the caste-like social regulation which consisted in staying "closely knit to your own color or degree of black-white blood-mixture grouping," which she expresses with a Haitian proverb: "'Mulatre pauvre—neg'; neg' riche— mulatre!' or a poor mulatto becomes a black, a rich black a mulatto" (Dunham, p. 8). In her case, she is all the more unplaceable in terms of class—where does she stand as a North American/dancer/anthropologist/student from the wrong side of the tracks in Chicago?—and the company she keeps. The variety of her dubious (in the innkeepers' eyes) connections are a source of much speculation and wonder.

15   The loa are the gods of the vodoun pantheon; the loa manifest themselves by possessing someone. Speaking of Guédé, Hurston explains, "He manifests himself by 'mounting' a subject as a rider mounts a horse, then he speaks and acts through his mount. The person mounted does nothing of his own accord. He is the horse of the loa until the spirit departs. Under the whip of the spirit-rider, the "horse" does and says many things that he or she would have never uttered un-ridden" (Hurston, p. 234).

16   In the end, never she belonged totally to either world while maintaining ties with both— she made the decision to relinquish her graduate studies for a career as a dancer, and she lost the ring symbolizing her marriage to Damballa, the serpent deity, although she

continued to "serve" the loas. Her artistic career allowed her the flexibility to move from one sphere to another.

17 Also known as *hounfort* or *ounfò*, it refers to the temple, the surroundings, and ceremonial altar for Haitian vodoun, includes a central dwelling of one or more rooms, circumscribed by the *peristyle* (or tonnelle), in the middle of which is the *poteau-mitan* or center post, that images the traffic between heaven and earth. See Glossary in Olmos, M. F. and Paravisini-Gebert, L. (Eds). (1997). *Sacred Possessions: Vodou, Santería, Obeah, and the Caribbean*, New Brunswick: Rutgers University Press.

18 "Checker" is also an archaic form meaning "chessboard."

19 However, hybridity is a problematic term—as problematic as other labels—creolité, métissage, mestizaje, texto mestizo—critics have struggled with in an effort to define texts like the ones studied here. As one Caribbean writer stated simply, "When you say 'hybrid,' it makes me feel like an animal or a fruit." Hybridity can be seen as a deformation, a handicap, being neither grapefruit nor orange, being neither here nor there. In discussions about this "in-betweenness" of texts or writers, it has been compared to another term, "mulatto"—derived from mule, neither horse nor donkey, but rather a sterile in-between.

References

Cesareo, M. (2001). When the Subaltern Travels: Slave Narrative and Testimonial Erasure in the Contact Zone. In L. Paravisini-Gebert and I. Romero-Cesareo (Eds), *Women at Sea: Travel Writing and the Margins of Caribbean Discourse* (pp. 99–134). New York: Palgrave.

Dayan, J. (1995). Haiti's Unquiet Past: Kathleen [sic] Dunham, Modern Dancer, and her Enchanted Island. *Transition* 67, 150–64.

—— (1991) Vodoun or the Voice of the Gods. *Raritan* X (3), 32–57.

Deren, M. (1991). *Divine Horsemen: The Living Gods of Haiti*. Kingston, NY: McPherson and Company.

Dunham, K. (1994). *Island Possessed*. Chicago: The University of Chicago Press.

Hurston, Z.N. (1983). *Tell My Horse: Voodoo and Life in Haiti and Jamaica*. Berkeley, CA: Turtle Island.

Meehan, K. (2001). Decolonizing Ethnography: Zora Neale Hurston in the Caribbean. In L. Paravisini-Gebert and I. Romero-Cesareo (Eds), *Women at Sea: Travel Writing and the Margins of Caribbean Discourse*. New York: Palgrave.

Olmos, M.F., and Paravisini-Gebert, L. (1997). *Sacred Possessions: Vodou, Santería, Obeah, and the Caribbean*, New Brunswick: Rutgers University Press.

Paquet, Sandra Pouchet (1992). The Enigma of Arrival: The Wonderful Adventures of Mrs. Seacole in Many Lands. *African American Review* 26(4), 661–63.

Paravisini-Gebert, L., and Romero-Cesareo, I. (2001). *Women at Sea: Travel Writing and the Margins of Caribbean Discourse* (pp. 245-79). New York: Palgrave.

Prince, M. (1987). *The History of Mary Prince, a West Indian Slave: Related by Herself.* (M. Ferguson, Ed.). London: Pandora Press.

Seabrook, W. (1929). *The Magic Island*. New York: The Literary Guild of America.

Seacole, M. (1984). *Wonderful Adventures of Mrs. Seacole in Many Lands*. Bristol: Falling Wall Press.

Chapter 10

Anthropology and literature
Of bedfellows and illegitimate offspring

Mario Cesareo

After reading such a diverse collection, having accepted to embark upon so many ventures, having visited so many half-explored sites, the feeling is one of an over-abundance of riches, of worlds discovered, of precious objects yet to be unearthed. Things, worlds, words, practices ... and more words: or nothing but words? That is one of the questions the reading of these essays suggests to me, as I am myself asked to add a few more sentences: things, worlds, words, pactices. *Between Anthropology and Literature*: is(n't) there a difference? In this chapter I would like to explore the silences suggested by the ambiguous "and" of the collection's title, for in its every-dayness, in its uncomplicated openness and accumulative promise, as in most things desired, may lie concealed a greater good: an Other defiantly staring.

Writing as anthropology: interdisciplinarity and the weekend anthropologist

To the extent that the question of the relationship between literature and anthropology is posited, the main preoccupation of the essays in this collection falls upon:

1   functionalizing anthropological notions, themes, and metaphors, as tools that can deepen our understanding of literary texts—whereby the literary is rendered as a "text," while the anthropological is posited as a "concern"; and
2   highlighting anthropology's historical use of various literary texts as sources for its analysis.

The book, thus, implicitly constructs the relationship between literature and anthropology as one made up of shared concerns and a mutually beneficial difference. Both moves end up locating the problematic of the relationship between literature and anthropology at the level of interdisciplinarity, that is, as an hermeneutic, academic, and inter-departmental problem. In the following pages, I would like to meditate upon some of the problems implicit in this interdisciplinary, academicist model.

The use of anthropological notions to read literary texts and that of literary texts to perform ethnographic work is problematic, as the sets of analytic categories of each discipline have historically evolved in direct relation to the particular types of primary sources that have constituted their fields. Even though both literary criticism and anthropology are practices based on typification, the range of what constitutes their "materiality" differs in important ways: whereas anthropology deals with the semiotic of communally constructed objects and practices, literary studies has more often than not emphasized objects over practices—underplaying the generic and institutional dimensions of the production, circulation, and reception of the works it analyzes.[1] Thus, the incorporation of anthropological tools to examine literature becomes misleading: they are circulated strategically *within the structure* of a text, to aid in its interpretation, to unravel hidden structures within the narrative world, while the findings are then posited as anthropological insights made to function without that structure—a process that leads to the kind of textualization of historical experience so common to cultural studies production.[2]

In performing an "anthropological reading," analysis has to go beyond the application of ethnographic notions on to a text. In other words, there is no ethnographic reading without an ethnographic writing—without a complex reading of the multiplicity of objects and practices that constitute the semiotic and material universe of the text studied, of its production, consumption, and interrelationships, as well as of the institutional structures within which that multiplicity of objects and practices is produced, circulated, and apprehended. And more: to fully "anthropologize" a text into a material practice means going beyond a semiotic or hermeneutic of signs: it necessitates retaining the material excess that escapes the semiotic circuit: all its textually non-sensical, non-signifying elements[3]—an omission already, and symptomatically, performed by the volume with respect to anthropology itself: the textual indifference to the full range of practices and problematics that constitute physical anthropology, with the ensuing rendering of cultural anthropology into an anthropology *tout court*.

What allows for cultural studies' passing of a textual reading as an ethnographic enterprise? The answer seems to lie in its notion of text-as-vestige, whereby the object (text) is understood as a microcosm of the social relations that created it. The archeology of this artifact is seen as an unearthing of the traces of its making, and more: the discovery of the remnants of what it has eliminated. The task of the cultural critic here is one of unveiling the repressed dimensions of the text, making its silences speak, visibly articulating the otherwise fuzzy logic of its narrative universe. But, the notions of "anthropological methods-as-tool-box" for literary criticism, "literature-as-ethnography," and "literary text-as-vestige," all serve to question literature, not anthropology. It is then perhaps not surprising that anthropology, in the present volume, seems to survive critical reflection unscathed.

The academicist model framing the discussion about literature and anthropology, because of the interdisciplinary, multidepartmental imperatives that form its institutional unconscious, finds its logical resolution in hybridity—a construct that functions as a dispeller of the tensions and contradictions the academic fields, in their turf wars, have resiliently maintained. In her essay on the ethnographic novel, in the present volume, Janet Tallman mentions Dan Rose's vision of "the dissolution of boundaries between literature, sociology, anthropology, critical theory, philosophy, cinematography, computer science, and so on ... [calling for] a polyphonic, hetero-glossic, multigenre construction" that would replace the old ethnography. What is not brought into discussion here is the fact that what distinguishes these practices as such is not the distinctness (and interdisciplinary character) of their operational tools but the systematizing role of theory as constituting them into discrete fields. What appears as a hybrid form that bridges the distance between literature and anthropology—the "ethnographic novel"—is perhaps but a textual mirage. In Tallman's understanding, the ethnographic novel, "from either insider or outsider, is one that conveys significant information about the culture or cultures from which the novel originates." The ethnographic novel would seem to surpass the standard ethnography, as it "has a point of view unsullied by the culture-boundedness and the blind-spots that accompany any outsider, no matter how well-trained." She constructs the differences between ethnographer and novelist, ethnographic novel and standard ethnography, insider and outsider (the objectivity, textual and existential detachment, blind-spots, and partial knowledge of the former, versus the biased point of view, based on the class, gender, or age ascription of the latter) as a result of two kinds of restrictions: generic

> the novelist need not shun conflict, anger, hatred, or passion, and may often become a participant in the drama of the novel in a way denied the ethnographer, who has in the past been at pains to observe carefully and not to become too involved

and epistemological

> writers ... have access to cultural knowledge unavailable to the anthropologist, because they live fully in the culture that serves as the source of their writing ... On the other hand anthropologists must construct the understanding of norms and values from external data ...

But what allows Tallman to construct this difference between literature and ethnography as a better or worse mode of description is the imputation of an identical purpose to both practices: to produce insights into a culture, to understand its functioning, to uncover the cultural assumptions of a certain order of experience. This disembodied, formalistic understanding of the practices of fiction writing and ethnography masks what is properly the incommensurableness of their spheres. Only by looking at the "ethnographic" objects as "texts" can such a comparison be made. Once these artifacts are placed in the realm of their production, circulation, and appropriation—once they are seen as practices—what was understood as "better" or "worse" is now seen as proper to differing projects. It is, therefore, not a question of what quantity of knowledge, but of what kind: what matters is the purpose of such knowledge, not its mediations, proximity, or remoteness from the object studied, as typification always already implies an outside, a positioning that allows the segmentation and re-articulation of social phenomena that makes heteroglosia, and therefore the novel—including the ethnographic one—possible.

From this perspective, it would be in the discrete sphere of practice where the difference of anthropology and literature could be found, where the ethnographic novel "brings to the reader's awareness characters who, in their life stories, reveal possibilities open to the people of those times and places." In contrast to ethnography's retrospective, archeological move, literature could be seen as a prospective ethno-graphic practice: that is, as a writing and creation of social logic not already found in the world it describes and recreates by going beyond its given limits. But, isn't this already the case with all ethnography? Have not concepts such as "chain of being," "race," "civilization," and so forth, played a prospective role in the exploration, discovery, and colonization of the world according to the logic of capitalist accumulation and expansion throughout the past five centuries?

The lack of a clearly formulated understanding of ethnography's discreteness (the historicity of its institutional functioning) results in a flattened notion of the ethnographic that, by de-historicizing anthropology, reifies and disaggregates it into a set of tools, themes, or data. Once this operation has been achieved, the remnants of its practice are freely circulated within the hybrid forms of cultural studies. This is plainly registered in the reiterative search for ethnographic "riches" within the literary so many of these essays perform. But I would like to suggest that the fact that a novel contains a "wealth" of information regarding social rituals, food, and social institutions, does not make it ethnographic. After all, information is only "ethnographic" to the uninitiated in the ways and customs of the particular culture being described: for the one well-versed in it, the proliferation of that same information would, by itself, be seen as a folkloric depiction of manners and customs. The determining element that makes a text ethnographic is the particular articulation of those rituals and practices with meaning and social structure. Even where the novel might, in fact, be an ethnographic study, the text itself is a step removed from the materiality it depicts, essays on, elaborates. In other words, the novel might have performed an ethnographic feat, but not its reading (not even the cultural critic's).

Anthropology as travel writing: the weekend encounter

Following through the impetus of Paravisini's and Romero's essays dealing with travel narrative as narrative forms that blur the distinctions between literature and ethnography, I would like to momentarily reverse the direction of the collection's gaze from literature-as-anthropology to that of ethnography-as-travel writing, as it will allow us to problematize the key intervention of both literary and ethnographic analysis: their claims to a production of knowledge about the Other—the explicit subject of their archeology. For this purpose, I would like to posit the relationship of literature and anthropology in slightly modified terms from the academicist model:

anthropology does not *encounter* literature (as the interdisciplinary construct would lead us to believe[4]): it is engendered by it. To be more precise: ethnography is the result of writing under the particular conditions of travel.[5]

The very origins of anthropology are situated within, and are a result of, the practices of European transatlantic exploration, discovery, and colonization initiated in the late fifteenth century and later sustained by the more modern forms of the same colonizing impetus during the nineteenth and early twentieth century. The locatedness of ethnographic practice was more than a geographical grounding: its grounding was thematic and epistemic as well. The coupling ethnographer/subject coincided with that of traveler/travelee, which was to be crystallized as European/ Subaltern, Same/Other, European/African, and so forth. In these series of couplings are contained the principal junctures, intersections, frontiers, and (therefore) the liminality of anthropological discourse. As ethnography was only one of the forms adopted by writing during its nineteenth-century travels, a look at travel writing will perhaps suggest one alternative set of questions from which to think the relationship between literature and anthropology as practices of empire.

Travel implies the subject's removal from one institutional order into another. But what constitutes that other order into an other world is not a geographical matter but an institutional one: institutions form the bases for the existence of a world other than the Same's own. Institutions create both the inside and outside of legitim-ate(d) experience. This outside is both interior and exterior to the geography of the Same: its exterior is formed by what lies outside its political and temporal frontiers— the empire's periphery, the past, the uncharted world; its interior is constituted by the marginal(ized)—women, criminals, the repressed dimensions of everyday experi-ence. If the Same's world—the political, representative, and everyday economies of his "home"—is to be understood as the territory articulated by the institutional logic of its hegemonic order (its common sense), its other world, is what lies (patho-logically) beyond that articulation: the political unconscious of its desire. But one of the particular effects of writing is precisely its ability to "produce" this otherness: to "imaginarily" articulate the proliferation of voices, logic, and experience proper to this multiple outside as moments of the Same, as encounters, or as the apparition of the other.

Travel and writing, therefore, are forms of displacement through other worlds. As I have already argued elsewhere,[6] from the material encounter of territories, peoples, and the natural habitats of travel, to the imaginative and experimental rehearsal of new logic that discourse makes possible, both travel and writing are practices that locate themselves in, and produce, an other world. In this sense, travel and writing confront their primary materiality (a foreign world and the semiotic universe of a particular culture, respectively) as a referential. This "stuff" of travel and writing bring about the possibility of a playful passage (an entering and exiting) into the (un)known world. The dialectic of this nomadism of traveler and writer, this temporary (geographical, fictional, or theoretical) habitation in the realms of another world also constitutes the space of home, in the same manner as the apparition of the Other (the one who inhabits that Other geography) and that of the other logic (the possible worlds lying dormant or repressed within the very world the Same inhabits) posits anew the subject of home. In this respect, travel and writing are similar practices structurally situated between self, other, and discovery, the last of these constructs understood as the production of a certain knowledge, the opening up of a practical and/or theoretical space in which the self is recreated and repositioned in a new configuration. These similarities, plus the fact that European travel has been historically linked to the practice of travel writing, has recently led to a critical erasure of their differences. Let me elaborate.

Travel implies the removal of the subject from a known institutional order into new territories and political orders that make necessary a renegotiation of his *modus operandi*—his institutional logic—vis-à-vis the newly encountered materiality and institutional reality of the foreign world being traveled. Traveling brings about a crisis in the subject's self-understanding by removing him from the accustomed uses and routines that tied him to a particular common-sense and repertoire of cultural utensils that until then enabled his manipulation of his world. The space traveled crystallizes as an Other world, "Other," because it confronts the subject as a world alien to his needs, as an uncanny immanence[7] that questions his control over the world. The irruption of an Other, massive, and omnipresent reality, governed by unknown or poorly guessed human and natural laws, cultural customs, and geo-graphical relationships, threaten to subject the traveler to a position of impotence—linguistic, material, and so on. The fear that results from the self's precarious position opens the way for the elaboration of symbolic mediations destined to render that radically Other reality into a discernible, pliable materiality.[8]

Thus, the destabilizing moment of travel calls for the elaboration of a discursive practice designed to explain the new experience. Recipe knowledge—the logic of the already known—as a practice derived from the discursive universe proper to the traveler's home culture and institutional experience, is quickly seen as a necessary but insufficient condition of understanding and survival. If the culturally and politically self-affirming character of his traveling necessitates the imposition of the home-made over the newly-discovered, the consciousness of the material character of that (not always symbolic) danger, the daily and empirical corroboration of that world's uncanniness, mobilizes the traveler to adopt a learning stance that will allow him to successfully deal with the new reality. As Eric Leed notes,

> travel retains its ancient significance and is given value by the fear that makes the individual "porous" and sensitive.... the fear of the wayfarer, the loss of security implicit in unaccommodated travel is a gain of accessibility and sensitivity to the world. Travel, from the moment of departure, removes those furnishings and mediations that come with a familiar residence. It thus substantiates individuality in its sense of "autonomy," for the self is now separated from a confirming and confining matrix. (1991, p. 10)

Travel, then, produces a radicalization of experience that forces the traveler into a double and contradictory gesture: an opening to the world—a learning destined to understand it—and a domination of both himself and that world—the imposition of an "autonomy" that constitutes his answer to that world, a strategy of (self)-

manipulation understood as survival and self-affirmation. As long as learning is inscribed in this politics of fear and survival, the auscultation of the new reality is an interested (instrumental) and reductive (allegorizing) act. The practice of metropolitan travel (its writing, its ethnographic impulse) is, therefore, the exertion of a violence that is not only descriptive but constitutive. It is, on the one hand, a material violence: a disciplining of the self and the Other (as well as the Other's usufruct); on the other, it is a representative violence: an aesthetic distortion exercised from a set of imperatives that are alien to the community it names without interpellating. [9]

Metropolitan travel is, in the last instance, a violence over the world. It presupposes two moments with an ensuing tension: an encounter of materiality (the Other beings that populate the world that is being traveled, that world, and its ecological structures) and a production of sameness and otherness. The first of these moments produces the *finding* (discovery's materiality), as well as the self's destabilization and fear in the face of the Other's irruption. The second moment is the result of the domesticating operations through which the traveler constructs his experience of that world: the semiotic conversion of that materiality into a datum and the elaboration of the hermeneutics of its discernment. Traveling produces otherness. The latter, from this perspective, is the fiction through which the experience of human coexistence is thematized, conjured, and exorcised from an imperative of survival and domination. This is why otherness—writing's and ethnography's creature—is more revealing of the order of the Same (of the self, the One, the 1) than of the Other. It is more a formalizing (an aesthetic rendering) of his fears, fantasies, and material interests, than a representation of the irreducible ecology it describes and reifies. In other words, the production of otherness presupposes both a perceptive sensibility (a reading) and a productive one (a writing) that function as a matrix of sameness, as an egology. [10]

The double character of otherness, a result of the tension between an opening to the world and the self's will to survival and domination, characterizes traveling as a crisis-ridden practice. But the traveler's discovery of a foreign world should not be understood simply as a production of knowledge (the writing moment). It is also the lived experience of a dramatic irruption of an Other into the order of the Same: the irruption of the Other carries with it the necessity of a reconfiguration of sameness, which has been thrown into a crisis as a result of that contact. What opens the gates to the dramatic irruption of the Other into the order of the Same is the face-to-face character of the encounter that traveling makes possible. Face-to-face communication[11] erodes the Other's anomie[12]—that render the Other into an other—through the production of:

1   a shared present that affirms the Other's coevalness;[13]
2   a continuous expressive exchange that makes visible the presence of the Other's subjectivity;
3   an orientation of expressivity towards the Other that allows the Other to become an interlocutor;

4   an intersubjectivity that is constructed from an abundance of symptomatic information, debunking the tendency to freeze communication in any one of its particular moments;

5   a massive presence of the Other, that militates against the Other's allegorical reduction;

6   a mutual proximity, an existential co-presence that produces the direct evidence of the Other and the self's consciousness of his own presence *to* the Other, the consciousness, therefore, of his own vulnerability.

The face-to-face encounter makes this irruption of the Other possible, bringing about the crisis necessary for the production of an otherness that subverts the order of the Same. As Peperzak explains,

> Another comes to the fore as other if and only if his or her "appearance" breaks, pierces, destroys the horizon of my egocentric monism, that is, when the other's invasion of my world destroys the empire in which all phenomena are, from the outset, a priori, condemned to function as moments of my universe. The other's face (i.e., any other's facing me) or the other's speech (i.e., any other's speaking to me) interrupts and disturbs the order of my, ego's, world; it makes a hole in it by disarraying my arrangements without ever permitting me to restore the previous order. For even if I kill the other or chase the other away, in order to be safe from the intrusion, nothing will ever be the same as before. (1992, pp. 19–20)

The presence of the Other as a being-for-herself provokes a cataclysm in the traveler's experience. And yet, and this is a most important proviso, that perforation of the order of the Same will not effectively bring the Other into it. No negotiation with the Other is here enacted. The perforation of the order of the Same will be re-elaborated, but from the ruins of his order. This is why in the discourse produced by that encounter, in literature as well as in ethnography, one does not find the native but the other: the phantasm, the relic, the remains of the cannibalized Other.[14] This double-edged mechanism of conjuration and exorcism establishes travel writing, insofar as an instance of historical writing, as a form of psychoanalysis, re-establishing sameness into the Other's historical remnant.[15] Here lies the irony of this practice of empire. While its newly constituted order rests upon the erasure and (not always merely symbolic) elimination of the Other, its very structure (its form and texture) remains captive to what it has eliminated:

> There is an "uncanniness" about this past that a present occupant has expelled (or thinks it has) in a effort to take its place. The dead haunt the living. The past: it "re-bites" [Il remord] (it is a secret and repeated biting). History is "cannibalistic," and memory becomes the closed arena of conflict between two contradictory operations: forgetting, which is not something passive, a loss, but an action directed against the past; and the mnemic trace, the return of what

was forgotten, in other words, an action by a past that is now forced to disguise itself. More generally speaking, any autonomous order is founded upon what it eliminates; it produces a "residue" condemned to be forgotten. But what was excluded re-infiltrates the place of its origin—now the present's "clean" [propre] place. It resurfaces, it troubles, it turns the present's feeling of being "at home" into an illusion, it lurks ... within the walls of the residence, and, behind the back of the owner (the ego), or over its objections, it inscribes the law of the other. (Certeau, 1993, pp. 3–4)

This phantasmal persistence of the Other in the order of the Same (Certeau's "law of the other") alerts us to the discursive character of that order. As discourse, then, otherness is able to articulate an imaginary where desire and experience are deployed experimentally:[16]

[L]iterature is the theoretic discourse of the historical process. It creates the non-topos where the effective operations of a society attain a formalization. Far from envisioning literature as the expression of a referential, it would be necessary to recognize here the analogue of that which for a long time mathematics has been for the exact sciences: a "logical" discourse of history, the "fiction" which allows it to be thought. (Certeau, p. 18)

As such, writing is an esemplastic playfulness, an essayistic, theorizing practice:

The literary text is like a game. With its sets of rules and surprises, a game is a somewhat theoretic space where the formalities of social strategies can be explained on a terrain protected from the pressure of action and from the opaque complexity of daily struggle. In the same way, the literary text, which is also a game, delineates an equally theoretic space, protected as is a laboratory, where the artful practices of social interaction are formulated, separated, combined, and tested. It is the field where a logic of the other is exercised, the same logic that the sciences rejected to the extent to which they practiced a logic of the same. (Certeau, p. 23)

Writing functions as a fiction that allows for the reconfiguration of the world in its totality under new imaginary and institutional imperatives, restoring a sense upon the self while forcing it upon the Other and the ecological totality both self and Other inhabit and articulate (in this manner, for example, the voyage to the "New World," represented as a traveling-back-in-time, allowed for the resignification of the relations between European modernity and antiquity, placing the experience of mercantilism as a climactic moment of the civilizing process, denying the native's coevalness and legitimizing the exploitation of the Amerindian, the African slave, and their world, as an educational and tutelary practice).[17] For this reason, otherness, while itself historical, is neither fully nor exclusively about the history it narrates. It is a fiction that takes the place of an irrecoverable absence. This is why the "law of the other" (the law that emerges over the remains of the Other for Certeau and makes possible an unlimited opening-to-the-other for Levinas) is not the law of the Other.[18] The archaeological or psychoanalytical possibility of such an articulation is only to be found beyond all remnant, in an act of negotiation that European writing has left unfulfilled in all its travels: as the Other has been inscribed into the discourse of the Same as a mutilated remnant, the archeological reconstruction of the Other's totality (and, therefore, of the totality of the self) cannot be achieved through the rearticulation of the order of the Same under a purely textual paradigm. Even if the critical discourse were to identify the Other's materiality found under the phantasmatic form of its inscription in the order of the Same, it would find nothing more than the logic of that transformation. It is, therefore, not sufficient to deconstruct a narrative order from its own assumptions. To be able to leave the egologic episteme it will be necessary to bring, from outside the text, the remaining vestiges of the Other's materiality.[19] A purely deconstructivist logic or a psychoanalytical one will find the Same's lacunae and aporias. It will never be able to reconstruct the ecology of the encounter, its existential and material engagement.

In short, while metropolitan travel is about a confrontation with an Other, travel writing is about the domestication of this encounter through the production of otherness. While travel is a most dislocating phenomenon of the "contact zone," travel writing happens, mostly, in an "incantation zone"—not the place anthropologists would like to think of as an encounter, but that of its substitute, the zone where the production of simulacra takes place. Travel writing is not about a negotiation of the Other's appearance but an allegorical enterprise of symbolic restoration—where the conjuring of the Other results in an always-already exorcised appearance.

I therefore disagree with Mary Louise Pratt's construction of travel writing in *Imperial Eyes* as a contact zone. Pratt does not differentiate the contact zone of the frontier with that of its textual remnant. While the former is anchored in the ecology of the frontier, bringing to the fore a reciprocal confrontation of diverse communities, materially engaged in strategies of domination, resistance, cooperation, survival, and extermination, in the unstable and contested realm of the frontier's materiality, the latter is the *result* of such a confrontation within the theoretical and imaginative confines of the Same's narrative logic. There is a subsuming, in Pratt's notion of "literature as contact zone, of these two spheres".[20] On the one hand, there is an understanding of the contact zone as an ecological, material phenomenon:

> 'Contact zone' in my discussion is often synonymous with 'colonial frontier.' But while the latter term is grounded within a European expansionist perspective (the frontier is a frontier only with respect to Europe), 'contact zone' is an attempt to invoke the spatial and temporal copresence of subjects previously separated by geographic and historical disjunctures, and whose trajectories now intersect. (Pratt, 1992, p. 6)

On the other, textual production is posited, itself, as such a zone of contact. This lack of differentiation between the contact zone as a material territory and the discursive practices it generates is partly anchored in a linguistic understanding of literature coupled with a bourgeois, mercantile understanding of language:

> I borrow the term 'contact' here from its use in linguistics, where the term contact language refers to improvised languages that develop among speakers of different native languages who need to communicate with each other consistently, usually in the context of trade. (Pratt, 1992, p. 6)

But, it is evident that, while in travel there is a constantly negotiated and open dynamic, in travel writing the negotiation does not happen amongst communities—it being a solitary elaboration performed within the discretion of the Same. These two practices cannot be subsumed without textualizing and rendering travel a metaphor, one of the predilect gestures of cultural studies' scholarship.

It is problematic to reduce a social practice (the encounters of the frontier) to a series of cultural objects (the texts that stand in its place). To do this obscures the meaning of their ecology: the analysis of cultural phenomena cannot leave their institutional dimension without becoming an hermeneutic of signs, textualizing its object of study, and missing from its purview the material conditions where that social semiotic takes place. The frontier that lies behind Pratt's narrative "contact zone" is an institutional practice: it presupposes an economic production of life, a geopolitics, a materiality that overflows and overdetermines any cultural artifact and its circulation. Pratt's lettered understanding of the contact zone substitutes the text with the communities that text articulates narratively, where, as John Beverley puts it: [21]

> In Pratt's metaphor, literature … can serve as a kind of "contact zone" where previously disarticulated subject positions, social projects, and energies may come together. (1993, p. xiii)

It would be in this literature as "contact zone" where subject positions, social projects, and previously diffused energies coalesce. I wonder, though, what escapes this "contact," what is it that is brought together, and where does this coalescing take place.

As a practice of empire in its confrontations with its periphery, travel writing history attaches itself to that of the imperial frontier, from the imaging of the contours of the trade routes of early exploration, through the conquest of world territories and colonial settlement, to the appropriation of natural resources and expansion of capitalist technology and modes of production of the neo-colonialist—or, in today's jargon, the globalizing—configurations of late capitalism. Its outline has therefore followed a movement from the forms of exterior exploration, carried through the fourteenth to the seventeenth centuries, to the interior exploration of the eighteenth century onward; from the logic of navigational charts to that of continental mapping; from the description of coastlines and landscapes to the systematic elaboration of ethnographic and natural histories. The narrative modes of travel writing have thus adopted their myriad forms as a literature of navigation, survival, monstrosities and marvels, civic description, textual mapping, and ethnographic manners-and-customs description—in all cases, pre- or post-Linnaean, coding its encounters through an allegorizing process that rendered the Other as an instance of the Same, whether in the form of the heroic, Christianizing crusader, the entrepreneurial capitalist avant-garde, or the "neutral" eye of the ethnographer.

As it has been previously argued, to place travel writing in the contact zone implies an inter-cultural encounter and negotiation. And yet, although placed in the context of the frontier, travel writing's relationship between the narrative self (the traveler) and its Others (its travelees) has been one of calculated non-reciprocity: the target of its defamiliarization processes—the aesthetic operations through which what and whom is traveled assume the character of an other—have coincided, for the most part, with the relations of economic and military power attendant to each historical period. This delimitation of the terms of the encounter has been produced by narrative assignation: the narrative traveler and travelee coincide, respectively, with the political Same and Other as defined by metropolitan hegemony. Travel writing therefore is at the same time a (one-sided) product (of the real-) and a (metropolitan) producer of the (narrative-) contact zone. It locates itself in the frontier *narratively*. The writing of this incantation zone erases the zone of contact that forms the materiality of its representation. Further, its production is monologically situated in the metropolis and is aimed at home consumption.

In contrast with travel, travel writing does not rehearse a (material) encounter (of the Other). In its stead, it performs an apparition (the other's). In this semiotics of empire, the act of thematizing the Other becomes both an erasure (of the Other as such) and an inscription (of the allegorized Other) by a seeing gaze that does not register its being seen. The conversion of the traveling eye to the writing gaze points to an inscription and erasure of materiality—rendered as "objectivity." The eye/I that travels is a most delicate and vulnerable organ. It can be seen, (and therefore) slashed, obscured, forever closed, obliterated. The gaze that writes is but its survived remnant, placidly and securely located outside the dangers of travel, out of bounds of the Other's grasp, (and therefore) indifferent to the Other's scrutiny. The gaze is but the eye's postscript, its safely-arrived souvenir. The symbolic economy of this leap from travel to travel-writing, from travel to ethnography, implicit in the displacement from the eye to the gaze, forms the conditions of possibility of a movement from a body-bound to an embodied experience, allowing for the transformation of the contact zone into its incantational mutant. The very fact that in the experience of traveling this being seen, spoken to, challenged, and denied by the Other's very existence is inescapable, serves to highlight the allegorical operations that code that encounter as a self-affirming event. Travel writing, thus, is not about the apparition of the Other but about its domestication. It is not travel—its destabilizing, dis-centering experience—but its exorcism. It is just as much about the production of others as it is a production of the Same. It is produced from and for home and, as such, in its myriad forms, travel writing has produced the domestic subject of empire.

Beyond the remnants

Literature and anthropology, thus seen as forms of travel writing, confront us with the question of their political situatedness: the ecological effects of their being in the world, the cost of their performances upon the materiality they reduce, thematize, and circulate within their symbolic economies. Are their fates necessarily connected to an (un)intended affirmation of Empire? The question can be formulated historically—in which case the answer does not seem very encouraging—or theoretically. The latter path allows us to reformulate the question in a more hopeful vein: what are the conditions of possibility of a writing that constitutes itself as an open conversation among equals, without others and Others? Can literature, anthropology, and, more generally, writing, become detached from the forms of state power and hegemonic discourse that have, so far, constituted their very conditions of possibility?[22] Is such a move a necessary one to guarantee a democratization of voice, social practice, and the institutional order? Perhaps the question has to be still reformulated in a way that avoids getting caught up within the very discursive structures that constitute its order as a closed, predetermined field. Perhaps this can be achieved by moving away from cultural studies' incestuous politics of textual desire to one of loving intercourse among bodies: that is, perhaps it is necessary to reposition the argument outside the confines of interdisciplinarity and restore writing to its political and existential overdeterminations: not whether the text and its writing can perform such tasks but whether they can help in rendering it performable.[23] The pertinence of these questions at the moment of global aporia presently confronting us, with its material and representational crisis, make the ongoing discussion regarding writing, knowledge, and the de /re/ territorialization they imply, a timely and important one worth meditating upon.

Notes

1   Janet Heller's problematic notion of "new rituals" constitutes a good example of the case in point (see her essay in the present volume).
2   I am thinking of texts such as Benedict Anderson's *Imagined Communities*, where the range of materiality that constitute nations as overdetermined ecologies is replaced by a textual analysis of very few works of literature, and where "nation" is reduced to "nationalism."
3   For a discussion of the place of materiality in the constitution of a semiotic of signs, see my Ideología y espectacularidad en la Comedia de Santos.
4   That the "encounter" be rendered as that of disciplines, in the realm of the university, is a tell-tale sign of the ongoing operations of metropolitan appropriation, where the university becomes the privileged place where the "new" travelers of the old capitalist vanguard, reappeared under the garments of "nomad" intellectuals, reside and bring into intelligibility the noise of the surrounding world. The substitution of the anthropologist and his "artifacts" by the cultural critic and his "texts" is, in this sense, illustrative of such a move.
5   Let me, at this point suggest the ways in which I utilize the notions of literature, anthropology, and ethnography. I understand literature as the writing practices that constituted the lettered arm of European states and their colonies—overlooking the nineteenth-century differentiation between a fictional and a non-fictional literature. Criticism, here, as well as the literary field of the Humanities, is but a very small parcel of the writing practices that permeate most contemporary societies. I differentiate between anthropology and ethnography in the following heuristic manner. While ethnography deals with the study of specific communities, anthropology's main function is to theorize

and bring about the systematization of ethnographic work—the organic development and bringing together of analytical tools, the construction and examination of a comparatist and integrated corpus—from which to extract general principles that guide the self-development of the discipline.

6   When the Subaltern Travels: Slave Narrative and Travel Writing in the Nineteenth-Century Caribbean.

7   I follow Levinas' understanding of this non-mediated confrontation. As Adriaan Peperzak notes,

> Levinas understands Heidegger's attempt to think Being in the light of the expression *es gibt* (the normal German equivalent of the English *there is* and the French *il y a*) as the celebration of a profound generosity by which Being would bestow light, freedom, truth, and splendor to all beings. The *il y a* does not, however, strike Levinas as particularly generous but rather as an indeterminate, shapeless, colorless, chaotic, and dangerous "rumbling and rustling." The confrontation with its anonymous forces generates neither light nor freedom but rather terror as a loss of selfhood. Immersion in the lawless chaos of "there is" would be equivalent to the absorption by a depersonalizing realm of pure materiality. (p. 18)

8   As Sander L. Gilman suggests,

> The infant's movement from a state of being in which everything is perceived as an extension of the self to a growing sense of a separate identity takes place between the ages of a few weeks and about five months. During that stage, the new sense of "difference" is directly acquired by the denial of the child's demand on the world. We all begin not only demanding food, warmth, and comfort, but by assuming that those demands will be met. The world is felt to be a mere extension of the self. It is that part of the self which provides food, warmth, and comfort. As the child comes to distinguish more and more between the world and self, anxiety arises from a perceived loss of control over the world. But very soon the child begins to combat anxieties associated with the failure to control the world by adjusting his mental picture of people and objects so that they can appear "good" even when their behavior is perceived as "bad."
>
> With the split of both the self and the world into "good" and "bad" objects, the "bad" self is distanced and identified with the mental representation of the "bad" object. This act of projection saves the self from any confrontation with the contradictions present in the necessary integration of "bad" and "good" aspects of the self. The deep structure of our own sense of self and the world is built upon the illusionary image of the world divided into two camps, "us" and "them." "They" are either "good" or "bad." Yet it is clear that this is a very primitive distinction which, in most individuals, is replaced early in development by the illusion of integration.
>
> Stereotypes are crude sets of mental representations of the world. They are palimpsests on which the initial bipolar representations are still vaguely legible. They perpetuate a needed sense of difference between the "self" and the "object," which becomes the "Other." Because there is no real line between self and Other, an imaginary line must be drawn; and so that the illusion of an absolute difference between self and Other is never troubled, this line is as dynamic in its ability to alter itself as is the self. This can be observed in the shifting relationship of antithetical stereotypes that parallel the existence of "bad" and "good" representations of self and Other. (1985, pp. 17–18)

9   I have arbitrarily chosen to use the masculine form to describe the Same and the feminine to refer to the Other. I do not intend this use to be thought of as an essentializing gesture but one that metaphorically points to a historically located patriarchal system of

domination and representation. Its purpose is intended as purely dramatic, performative, as well as stylistic (avoiding the profusion of masculine and feminine pronouns).

10   In Adriaan Peperzak's explanation of Levinas' notion of the face,

> The otherness of the Other is concretized in the face of another human.... . I can see another as someone I need in order to realize certain wants of mine. She or he is then a useful or enjoyable part of my world, with a specific role and function. We all belong to different communities, in which we function more or less well on the basis of reciprocal needs. I can also observe another from an aesthetic perspective, for example, by looking at the color of her eyes, the proportions of his face, and so on. But none of these ways of perception allows the otherness of the other to reveal itself. All aspects manifested by a phenomenological description that starts from these perspectives are immediately integrated by my self-centered, interested, and dominating consciousness. These ways of looking at them transform the phenomena into moments of my material or spiritual property. The sort of phenomenology based on these and similar observations is a form of egology. (p. 19)

11   For a discussion of the face-to-face, see Peter L. Berger and Thomas Luckman's *The Social Construction of Reality*, 1967, pp. 28–34.

12   Anomie, in counter-distinction to the face-to-face, produces: 1) a spatial and temporal discontinuity (where the Other is seen as belonging to a different historical time or another stage of civilization); 2) the Other's intermittence or lack of expressivity (which allows the Other's objectification); 3) an orientation of expressivity toward a third party that is not the Other (transforming communication into an spectacle); 4) a maximizing of discursive typification and a minimizing of the Other's existential presence (allowing for the reduction of the Other to a role, an institutional performativity, or a thing.

13   Johannes Fabian has formulated an incisive critique of anthropology's denial of coevalness in his *Time and the Other: How Anthropology Makes Its Object.*

14   Michel de Certeau makes a very interesting analysis of this cannibalistic dynamic of Sameness over the Other in Montaigne's 'Of Cannibals': The Savage 'I', in *Heterologies*, 1993, pp. 67–80.

15   Certeau makes the following distinction:

> Psychoanalysis and historiography ... have two different ways of distributing the *space of memory*. They conceive of the relation between the past and present differently. Psychoanalysis recognizes the past *in* the present; historiography places them one beside the other. Psychoanalysis treats the relation as one of imbrication (one in the place of the other), or repetition (one reproduces the other in another form), of the equivocal and of the *quidproquo* (What "takes the place" of what? Everywhere, there are games of masking, reversal, and ambiguity). Historiography conceives the relation as one of succession (one after the other), correlation (greater or lesser proximities), cause and effect (one follows from the other), and disjunction (either one or the other, but not both at the same time). (p. 4)

16   It is important to see the complex character of discursivity in its relation to otherness. As Certeau explains,

> discourses constitute forms of actual social interaction and practice. As such, they are not irrational, but they are subject to the pulls and pressures of the situations in which they are used as well as to the weights of their own tradition. They must always handle the complex interplay of that which is of the order of representation and the nonrepresentable part which is just as much constitutive of them, their own other ... . This other, which forces discourses to take the meandering appearance that they have, is not a magical or a transcendental entity; it is the discourse's mode of relation to its own historicity in the moment of its utterance. (p. xx)

17 For a discussion of this missionary aesthetic in connection to modes of institutional life see my *Cruzados, mártires y beatos: emplazamientos del cuerpo colonial* (1995).
18 Neither Certeau nor Levinas differentiate between Other and other, that is, between the real Other and her phantasm made to circulate the symbolic economy of the Same. Although one can not determine that this absence points to their identification, the void generated by the Other's disappearance renders Certeau's and Levina's conclusions problematic.
19 For a discussion of this type of hermeneutic and the need to bring about a pluritopic reading of texts, histories, and materiality, see Walter Mignolo's *The Darker Side of the Renaissance* (1985).
20 See her Arts of the Contact Zone.
21 See John Beverley's *Against Literature*. For a self-critique of his previous unproblematic acceptance of the notion of literature-as-contact zone, consult Beverley's (1996, January–March). Respuesta a Mario Cesareo, in *Revista Iberoamericana*, pp. 225–33.
22 For a discussion of such a possibility, see John Beverley's *Against Literature* and the debate that followed its publication in my Hermenéuticas del naufragio y naufragio de la hermenéutica: comentarios en torno a *Against Literature*, and Beverley's Respuesta a Mario Cesareo, both in *Revista Iberoamericana*.
23 Although articulating an answer to this question is well beyond the scope of the present article, I would suggest that such an alternative is indeed possible. I carry on a discussion of this problematic in Sur: problemas hermenéuticos de la territorialidad periférica (forthcoming).

References

Anderson, B. 1983. *Imagined Communities: Reflections on the Origin and Spread of Nationalism*. London, New York: Verso.

Berger, P. L. and Luckman, T. (1967). *The Social Construction of Reality: A Treatise in the Sociology of Knowledge*. New York: Anchor.

Beverley, J. (1983). *Against Literature*. Minneapolis: University of Minnesota Press.

—— (1996, January–March). Respuesta a Mario Cesareo. *Revista Iberoamericana*, pp. 225–33.

Certeau, M. de. (1993). *Heterologies: Discourse on the Other*. Minnesota: University of Minnesota Press.

Cesareo, M. (1987). Ideología/Espectacularidad en la Comedia de Santos. *Gestos*, 2.4, 62–87.

—— (1995). *Cruzados, mártires y beatos: emplazamientos del cuerpo colonial*. West Lafayette, IN: Purdue University Press.

—— (1996, January–March). Hermenéuticas del naufragio y naufragios de la hermenéutica: comentarios en torno a *Against Literature*. *Revista Iberoamericana*, pp. 211–24.

—— (1999). When the Subaltern Travels: Slave Narrative and Travel Writing in the Nineteenth-Century Caribbean. In L. Paravisini-Gebert, and I. Romero-Cesareo (Eds), *Women at Sea: Writing and the Margins of Caribbean Discourse* (pp. 99–134). New York: Palgrave.

—— (forthcoming). Sur: problemas hermenéuticos de la territorialidad periférica.

Fabian, J. (1983). *Time and the Other: How Anthropology Makes Its Object*. New York: Columbia University Press.

Gilman, S.E. (1985). *Difference and Pathology: Stereotypes of Sexuality, Race, and Madness*. Ithaca: Cornell University Press.

Leed, E.J. (1991). *The Mind of the Traveler: From Gilgamesh to Global Tourism*. New York: Basic.

Mignolo, W. (1995). *The Darker Side of the Renaissance: Literacy, Territoriality, and Colonization*. Ann Arbor: University of Michigan Press.

Peperzak, A. (1992). *To the Other: An Introduction to the Philosophy of Emmanuel Levinas*. West Lafayette, IN: Purdue University Press.
Pratt, M.L. (1991). Arts of the Contact Zone. *Profession*, pp. 33–40.
—— (1992). *Imperial Eyes: Travel Writing and Transculturation*. New York: Routledge.

Index